Supreme Attachments

Supreme Attachments

Studies in Victorian Love Poetry

KERRY McSWEENEY

Ashgate

Aldershot • Brookfield USA • Singapore • Sydney

Published by
Ashgate Publishing Limited
Gower House
Croft Road
Aldershot
Hants
GU11 3HR
England

Ashgate Publishing Company
Old Post Road
Brookfield
Vermont 05036–9704
USA

The author has asserted his moral right under the Copyright, Designs and Patents Act, 1988, to be identified as the author of this work.

British Library Cataloguing in Publication Data

McSweeney, Kerry, 1941–
    Supreme Attachments: Studies in Victorian Love Poetry.
    (The Nineteenth Century series)
    1. Love poetry, English—History and criticism.   2. English
    poetry—19th century—History and criticism.
    I. Title.
    821.8'09'3543

    ISBN 1–84014–202–2

Library of Congress Cataloging-in-Publication Data

McSweeney, Kerry, 1941–
    Supreme attachments: studies in Victorian love poetry/Kerry
McSweeney.
        p.   cm. (Nineteenth Century series)
    ISBN 1–84014–202–2 (hardcover)
    1. Love poetry, English—History and criticism.   2. English
    poetry—19th century—History and criticism.   3. Great Britain—
    History—Victoria, 1837–1901.   I. Title.   II. Series: Nineteenth
    Century (Aldershot, England).
    PR595.L7M38   1998
    821'.80803543—dc21   98–12823
                                                                 CIP

ISBN 1 84014 202 2

This book is printed on acid free paper

Typeset in Sabon by Manton Typesetters, 5–7 Eastfield Road, Louth, Lincolnshire, LN11 7AJ and printed in Great Britain by University Press, Cambridge

Contents

The Nineteenth Century
General Editors' Preface

The aim of this series is to reflect, develop and extend the great burgeoning of interest in the nineteenth century that has been an inevitable
feature of recent decades, as that former epoch has come more sharply
into focus as a locus for our understanding not only of the past but of
the contours of our modernity. Though it is dedicated principally to the
publication of original monographs and symposia in literature, history,
cultural analysis, and associated fields, there will be a salient role for
reprints of significant texts from, or about, the period. Our overarching
policy is to address the spectrum of nineteenth-century studies without
exception, achieving the widest scope in chronology, approach and
range of concern. This, we believe, distinguishes our project from comparable ones, and means, for example, that in the relevant areas of
scholarship we both recognize and cut innovatively across such parameters as those suggested by the designations 'Romantic' and Victorian'.
We welcome new ideas, while valuing tradition. It is hoped that the
world which predates yet so forcibly predicts and engages our own will
emerge in parts, as a whole, and in the lively currents of debate and
change that are so manifest an aspect of its intellectual, artistic and
social landscape.

Vincent Newey
Joanne Shattock

University of Leicester

Preface

The Victorian poetry of sexual love between men and women has not been as fully studied as other components of the literary achievement of the period, and some of the attention it has received has been more concerned with the Victorian (the society and ideology of the age) than with the poetry or the love. In choosing my subjects, I have preferred quality to representativeness, and poems that express or represent aspects of the experience of loving to those that simply articulate ideas about love. And my title alludes to a passage in a homily delivered by Newman in 1852: 'It is by the law of our nature, the happiness of everyone, man and woman, to have one central and supreme attachment, to which none other can be compared' (275).

I am not suggesting that Victorian love poetry can be treated apart from its social and cultural context, nor have I attempted to do so. In the introduction to her *Victorian Women Poets: Writing Against the Heart*, Angela Leighton observed that in both the texts she discussed and her treatment of them there was a tension between the historical context on the one hand and formalist and aesthetic considerations on the other. In working on this study I sometimes experienced a similiar tension. It could hardly have been otherwise given my method of combining biographical, social and/or literary historical contextualization with detailed readings of poems. When there were competing interests, I tried to be guided by Theodor Adorno's dictum in 'On Lyric Poetry and Society':

> nothing that is not in the works, not part of their own form, can legitimate a determination of what their substance ... represents in social terms. To determine that, of course, requires both knowledge of the interior of the works of art and knowledge of the society outside. But this knowledge is binding only if it is rediscovered through complete submission to the matter at hand. (i, 39)

An earlier version of my discussion of Hardy's *Poems of 1912–13* appeared in *Victorian Poetry*.

Acknowledgements

Poetry by Emily Dickinson is reprinted by permission of the publishers and the Trustees of Amherst College from *The Poems of Emily Dickinson*, Thomas H. Johnson, ed., Cambridge, Mass.: The Belknap Press of Harvard University Press; copyright © 1951, 1955, 1979, 1983 by the President and Fellows of Harvard College and from *The Complete Poems of Emily Dickinson*, Thomas H. Johnson, ed.; copyright 1929, 1935 by Martha Dickinson Bianchi; copyright © renewed 1957, 1963 by Mary L. Hampson: Little, Brown and Company, Boston.

Note on Texts and Citations

Unless otherwise noted, the following editions are used for quotations from the poems of the principal subjects of this study. For full bibliographical details, see List of Works Cited. Part and section numbers, line numbers or page numbers are given only when a passage would otherwise be difficult to locate.

Barrett Browning   The text for quotations from *Aurora Leigh* is my Oxford World's Classics edition (1993). For all other poems, Charlotte Porter and Helen A. Clarke's edition of the *Complete Works* (1900) is the text cited.

Browning   *Poems*, ed. John Pettigrew (1981).

Clough   The text for quotations from *The Bothie* is Patrick Scott's facsimile edition (1976) of the first (1848) edition. For all other poems, J. B. Phelan's *Selected Poems* (1995) is the text cited.

Dickinson   Thomas H. Johnson's three-volume edition (1955). In quoting from the poems, I have incorporated the presentational emendations Johnson made for his one-volume edition (e.g., *ecstatic* for *extatic*).

Hardy   *Complete Poetical Works*, ed. Samuel Hynes (1982–85).

Lawrence   The texts for quotations from *Love Poems and Others* and *Amores* are the first British editions. For quotations from *Look! We Have Come Through!* I have used the *Complete Poems*, eds Vivian de Sola Pinto and Warren Roberts (1964).

Meredith   *Poems*, ed. Phyllis B. Bartlett (1978).

Morris   *Collected Works*, ed. May Morris (repr. 1966).

Patmore   *Poems*, ed. Frederick Page (1949).

Rossetti, C.   *Complete Poems*, ed. R. W. Crump (1979–90).

Rossetti, D.   *Poems*, ed. Oswald Doughty (1961).

Tennyson   *Poems*, ed. Christopher Ricks (1987). Quotations from *The Princess* are identified by volume and page number; those from *Maud* by part and section numbers.

For Susanne with love

CHAPTER ONE

Introduction

A poet should express the emotion of all the ages and the thought
of his own.

Thomas Hardy

1

In his 'General Introduction for My Work', William Butler Yeats insisted
on the importance of traditional formal and metrical elements in lyric
poetry:

> all that is personal soon rots; it must be packed in ice or salt ... If I
> wrote of personal love or sorrow in free verse, or in any rhythm
> that left it unchanged, amid all its accidence, I would be full of self-
> contempt because of my egotism and indiscretion, and foresee the
> boredom of my reader. I must choose a traditional stanza, even
> what I alter must seem traditional ... Ancient salt is best packing.
>
> (522)

What Yeats found it necessary to affirm in 1937, most of the Victorian
love poets took for granted. The many examples of their use of ancient
salt include the trio of superlative love lyrics from Tennyson's *Princess*,
each of which has a different model: 'Come down, O maid' derives
from Theocritian pastoral; 'Now sleeps the crimson petal' is an adaptation of the Persian *ghazal*; and the exquisite poem of yielding, 'Ask me
no more', is a *responsio* to a love invitation in the manner of a number
of Elizabethan and seventeenth-century lyrics. Other examples are the
love sonnets of Dante Rossetti, the models for which are found in the
poems he translated in *The Early Italian Poets: From Ciullo D'Alcamo
to Dante Alighieri (1100–1200–1300) in the Original Metres together
with Dante's Vita Nuovo* (1861), and William Morris's 'Summer Dawn',
an adaptation of the Provençal aubade (not in what has come to be the
usual sense of this term, but aubade as a particular kind of nocturne,
the serenade or evening song being another); as the summer night
wanes, Morris's speaker yearns for the answering voice of the beloved
as expectantly as the natural world waits for dawn:

> Far out in the meadows, above the young corn,
>   The heavy elms wait, and restless and cold
> The uneasy wind rises; the roses are dun;

> Through the long twilight they pray for the dawn,
> Round the lone house in the midst of the corn.
>   Speak but one word to me over the corn,
>   Over the tender, bow'd locks of the corn.

'It is', said Walter Pater, 'the very soul of the bridegroom which goes forth to the bride: inanimate things are longing with him: all the sweetness of the imaginative loves of the Middle Age, with a superadded spirituality of touch all its own, is in that' (749).

These adaptations of traditional forms are a reminder that the principal phases of the experience of sexual love are no more changed by the particular constructions of a given cultural period than are the essential characteristics of the experience of bereavement that find expression in elegies. In his analysis of love in the later twentieth century, Michael Ignatieff used an excellent analogy:

> We want to write our own script and our own plot. And we cannot
> ... because love is itself discursive: we are the heirs of romantic
> traditions which move us, despite ourselves. It hurts our narcis-
> sism, our conviction that we should be the artists of our own lives,
> to discover that most of us are not the playwrights of our scripts
> but only adequate players of old parts. If the parts are good ...
> then we should behave towards the discursive past of love as a
> good director behaves towards a good play: updating it so that
> modern audiences are not alienated by anachronism but keeping
> faithful to the spirit of the text. Indeed ... it becomes an essential
> activity of the intelligence to safeguard the meaning of the roman-
> tic tradition (the integrity of love poetry for example) ... .
>
> (413)

This analogy can be usefully applied to the Victorian poets' re-enactments and reinterpretations of the parts in the drama of romantic love between men and women. Consider, for example, the lyric expressions by the principal love poets of three phases of love relationships.

Later love

These lyrics are not simply expressions of abiding love like Tennyson's lovely 'June Bracken and Heather', which was written for his wife on her seventy-seventh birthday; and not simply poems of second love, like Seamus Heaney's 'Twice Shy'. In a later-love poem, the love is informed and enriched by earlier loves, as in Shakespeare's sonnet 31 ('Thy bosom is endearèd with all hearts'). In her later-love sequence, *Sonnets from the Portuguese*, Elizabeth Barrett Browning speaks of gathering 'the north flowers to complete the south,/And catch[ing] the early love up in the late' (sonnet 33). And Philip Larkin's 'When first we faced' notes that behind 'The excitement and the gratitude' there is a sense of

'how much our meeting owed/To other meetings, other loves'. It does
not matter if the later love is in fact a first love, as in Barrett Browning's
case, where 'the early love' is familial, not sexual. Nor that the later
beloved is the same person as the early, as would seem to be the case in
Wallace Stevens's 'Re-statement of Romance'. Victorian examples include Dante Rossetti's Willowwood sonnets from *The House of Life*,
and 'Life-in-Love' (sonnet 36) and 'The Love-Moon' (sonnet 37) from
the same work. In Christina Rossetti's 'Autumn Violets', a 'later sadder
love' is figured as 'A grateful Ruth tho' gleaning scanty corn'. Browning's dramatic lyric, 'St Martin's Summer', is a cynical variation on the
type. And perhaps the most striking single Victorian lyric of later love is
Patmore's bereavement ode, 'Tired Memory', which adumbrates the
process by which he became drawn to the woman who became his
second wife.

Anticipation as virtual fulfilment

The subject of these lyrics is not first love, which is prothalamic rather
than epithalamic; nor do they involve petition or persuasion (as a rule
the beloved is not directly addressed). It is rather an idealization of
desire in the manner of the 'Pervigilium Veneris' or numerous Trouba-
dour lyrics. What is represented is 'a brief and ecstatic moment of
transition, epitomizing the very essence and centre of romantic love
when consummation is anticipated but not yet achieved and the inevitable difference it creates not yet experienced' (Shaw, 137). There are a
number of outstanding Victorian examples. The finest include Morris's
'Thunder in the Garden'; Patmore's 'The Day after To-morrow', and
Browning's masterly 12-line 'Meeting at Night', of which Isobel
Armstrong noted: 'It is a poem about living in sexual time, timelessly
long *and* momentary. The pressure of the poem is all to the final
intensity of its ending, and yet it does not hurry to its end. Included in
the ending is the whole experience of the poem' (268–9). And there is
Tennyson's magnificent lyric from *Maud*, 'I have led her home'. Given
the subtlety of the phase of love experience that is its subject, and its
success in creating the mood of virtual fulfilment, it is understandable
that two professional critics could come to believe that the subject of
Tennyson's poem is sexual consummation (Buckler, 219; Culler, 209).
But it is not so: only a 'long loving kiss' has sealed the love of the
speaker and Maud, nothing more. Maud retains her 'maiden grace' and
is still a 'bride to be'.

Invitation to love

This being perhaps the commonest subject of love poetry, it is notewor-thy that there are comparatively few Victorian examples. Two reasons for the paucity are suggested by what are perhaps the period's finest specimens: Tennyson's 'Now sleeps the crimson petal' and Browning's 'Two in the Campagna'. These variations on the *carpe diem* topos show that while there are continuities between Victorian love poems and those of earlier periods, there are differences as well. Tennyson's lyric is from *The Princess*, in which the title character denounces the tradi-tional male love lyric, and is unlike earlier poems of erotic invitation in intimating female as well as male sexual pleasure. Browning's poem is also revisionary. As in the eighth song in Sidney's *Astrophil and Stella*, the setting of the male lover's address to his beloved is a suggestive natural landscape – 'primal naked forms of flowers' and earth lying 'bare to heaven above' (like Danaë beneath starry Zeus). And as in Donne's 'The Ecstasy', the lover is concerned with the relationship of soul to body. But whereas in these Renaissance poems the invitation is to enjoy the pleasures of physical love, in 'Two in the Campagna' the invitation is to open oneself to spiritual love. 'Let us, O my dove', the speaker entreats his beloved in a startling reversal of conventional expectation, 'Let us be unashamed of soul'.

2

What is 'Victorian' about the love poetry of the post-Romantic decades of the nineteenth century? One part of the answer is the enormous seriousness and importance attached to love relationships. Of course, seriousness in the literary treatment of love is nothing new. There is, for example, the bogus intensity of 'the old stock love of playwrights and romancers' that Walt Whitman derided: 'unnatural and shocking pas-sion for some girl or woman, that wrenches [the lover from his] man-hood ... It seeks nature for sickly uses. It goes screaming and weeping after the facts of the universe' (Hindus, 43). A certain amount of this debased romantic love is found in Victorian poetry – in Tennyson's, for example, which was the subject of Whitman's animadversions, and *mutatis mutandis* in some women poets, like those whose verses are dismissed by the title character of Barrett Browning's *Aurora Leigh*: 'The heart in them was just an embryo's heart/Which never yet had beat ... Just gasps of make-believe galvanic life' (iii, 247–9).

The particular seriousness of Victorian love poetry is related to the religious and intellectual climate of the period. As is well known, the subsidence of traditional foundations of Christian belief in God and the immortality of the soul created great anxiety during the period. Many, like Tennyson in *In Memoriam*, were led to seek the grounds for super-natural belief in personal experience rather than in the Bible, dogma or the reasoning faculties. For Tennyson, as for many others, the experience of human love provided the strongest evidence. Consider Coventry Patmore's views on first love as poetical subject matter. Earlier in the nineteenth century the subject was treated wittily by Byron in *Don Juan*: 'first love, – that all/Which Eve has left her daughters since her fall' (I, clxxxix) – 'all' being a double entendre meaning both 'the only thing' and 'the All feeling', that is, an expansion of consciousness experience. And it was treated sentimentally by Tom Moore in 'Our First Young Love', which affirms that no illumination in later life will ever 'shed lustre o'er us/Like that first youthful ray' (311). In contrast, Patmore declared that the 'life's transient transfiguration in youth by love' was the key moment in an individual's existence; the 'whole of after-life' depended on how this moment was subsequently regarded. Since love had come to be 'much more respected and religion much less than of old', the 'greatest of all the functions of the poet' was to help ensure that this 'transfiguration of the senses' and its 'sacramental character' was not forgotten or profaned in later life (1913, 337–9).

Patmore was not alone in looking to intense love relationships for intimations of a higher supernatural love – for the felt assurance that, as Browning puts it in one of his poems, earth's gain is heaven's gain too. Consider Dante Rossetti's three-stanza lyric 'Sudden Light':

> I have been here before,
> But when or how I cannot tell:
> I know the grass beyond the door,
> The sweet keen smell,
> The sighing sound, the lights around the shore.
>
> You have been mine before, –
> How long ago I may not know:
> But just when at that swallow's soar
> Your neck turned so,
> Some veil did fall, – I knew it all of yore.

In these two stanzas, an intimate moment between lovers suddenly evokes the uncanny sense of *déjà vu*. This is a version of the expansion of consciousness that is a common feature of the intensities of romantic love, the ecstatic sense of not being 'entirely contained here', of there being 'an existence of yours beyond you', as Catherine puts it in *Wuthering Heights* in trying to explain her bond with Heathcliff (ch. 9). The third stanza of Rossetti's poem, however, adds a new, distinctly Victorian, note:

> Has this been thus before?
>   And shall not thus time's eddying flight
> Still with our lives our love restore
>   In death's despite,
> And day and night yield one delight the more?

What is felt and experienced in the present prompts a wish for the future: that this ecstatic moment may be a token or prefiguration of a life after death.

Love relationships had a comparably important value for Victorians who had accepted that there was no beyond, no providential order, no transcendent dimension to human existence. This recognition is at the centre of one the period's best-known love poems, Matthew Arnold's 'Dover Beach'. 'Ah, love, let us be true/To one another', implores the poem's speaker, the reason being that there is nothing else left to which to be true, nothing else to give comfort and support. In Arnold's figure, the 'Sea of Faith' – both traditional Christian beliefs and the Romantic faith in a beneficent Nature – that had been once 'at the full', that had invested the visible world with the illusion of plenitude, was now in permanent withdrawal. As a result,

> the world, which seems
> To lie before us like a land of dreams,
> So various, so beautiful, so new,
> Hath really neither joy, nor love, nor light,
> Nor certitude, nor peace, nor help for pain;
> And we are here as on a darkling plain
> Swept with confused alarms of struggle and flight,
> Where ignorant armies clash by night.

One reason religious belief had come to seem an illusion, as Arnold powerfully declaimed, was the rise of the geological and biological sciences, the impact of which was registered in the love poetry of the Victorians. In 'Natura Naturans', his celebration of the 'genial heat' of sexual attraction as the antecedent *sine qua non* of human love, Arthur Hugh Clough flamboyantly blended Lucretian conceptions of nature as maternal nurturer with evolutionary thinking concerning the development of species. But a number of other Victorian poems recognize that the processes of nature discovered by modern science have negative implications for the status of romantic love. For the speaker of Tennyson's *Maud*, for example, the beloved might come to seem 'the countercharm of space and hollow sky' and create the illusion that the 'happy stars' beat in time 'with things below'. But the 'sad Astrology' of modern science had shown the stars to be 'innumerable, pitiless, passionate eyes,/Cold fires, yet with power to burn and brand/His nothingness into man' (I, xviii).

A similar recognition is differently conveyed in Louisa Bevington's 'Egoisme à deux':

> When the great universe hung nebulous
>   Betwixt the unprevented and the need,
> Was it foreseen that you and I should be? –
>   Was it decreed?
>
> While time leaned onward through eternities,
>   Unrippled by a breath and undistraught,
> Lay there at leisure Will that we should breathe? –
>   Waited a Thought?
>
> When the warm swirl of chaos-elements
>   Fashioned the chance that woke to sentient strife,
> Did there a Longing seek, and hasten on
>   Our mutual life?
>
> That flux of many accidents but now
>   That brought you near and linked your hand in mine, –
> That fused our souls in love's most final faith, –
>   Was it divine?

The first two lines of each stanza are scientific-sounding references to the origin of the universe, cosmic temporality, the origin of the species, and the forces that have brought the two lovers together. The third and fourth lines raise the familiar Victorian question: does human love have a transcendent, supernatural dimension – is there a providence, a will, a thought, a longing, or a 'divine' something that underwrites the fusion of our souls in a love relationship? As the tone of rueful wonderment intimates, the questions posed in Bevington's poem are rhetorical. This implicit or implied answer to them is 'agnostic at best' (Hickok, 20). The speaker's wonder is double-sided – wonder both at the temporal and spatial vastness of the cosmos, and at the disproportion between it and the egotism of the terrestrial lovers who have presumed to posit the possibility of a gratifying connection between human and putatively 'divine'.

But the discontinuity between cosmic scale and human longing does not undercut the reality and value of human love. The lovers are linked, their souls fused, in love's self-authenticating faith. What the poem implicitly and ruefully recognizes is that this love is contingent, finite and mortal. Bevington made the same point more directly in another lyric, 'Measurements'. The love within her heart is subjectively great:

> It sees in two dear eyes, infinity,
> It finds in one sweet hour, eternity,
> It has one measure: – nearness, or apart.

But while from this egocentric point of view the world is little and love great, the person who would 'rise triumphant over fate' must learn to see more objectively – must learn to see 'Earth's breadth, love's narrowness' (123).

What these and other Victorian love poems record is the painful passage from sacred to profane conceptions of love – or, to use Georg Simmel's terms, from Platonic to modern conceptions. The 'point of departure', says Simmel, 'the immediate subjective fact of the feeling of love', as well as 'the feeling that in love there lives something mysterious, beyond the contingent individual existence and meeting, beyond the momentary sensual desire, and beyond the mere relations between personalities', have been essential aspects of the experience of loving since the Greeks. What has changed is the point of arrival. The 'great problem of the modern spirit [is] to find a place for everything which transcends the givenness of vital phenomena within those phenomena themselves, instead of transposing it to a spatial beyond' (236, 242–3).

3

'Ah love, let us be true to one another.' For Patricia Ball in *The Heart's Events*, her excellent study of Victorian love poetry, its distinctive feature was less the intellectual content than that it was 'a poetry of relationships' that tended to centre on 'the history, the crises or the key moments of a relationship' – unlike Romantic poetry which was 'inspired by the idea of the autonomous self, an independent adventure not a shared expedition'. In Victorian poetry, love is known not as it appears in a vision, but in 'the dramatic actuality of a relationship' (1). Isobel Armstrong (1993) uses a different discourse to make the same point: '*relationships* and their representation become the contested area ... above all between self and the lover. Gender becomes a primary focus of anxiety and investigation in Victorian poetry which is unparalleled in its preoccupation with sexuality and what it is to love' (7).[1]

Two other distinguishing features of Victorian love poetry follow from the emphasis on relationships: the principal site – present or prospective – of love relationships is marriage; and there is an increased emphasis on the female point of view in love relationships. In *Don Juan*, Byron opined that 'Love and Marriage rarely can combine':

> There's doubtless something in domestic doings
>   Which forms, in fact, true Love's antithesis;
> Romances paint at full length people's wooings,
>   But only give a bust to marriages;
> For no one cares for matrimonial cooings,

> There's nothing wrong in a connubial kiss:
> Think you, if Laura had been Petrarch's wife,
> He would have written sonnets all his life?
>
> (III, v, viii)

This is true enough in the sense that traditional love poetry had little to do with marriage. A socio-cultural explanation of why the case is different with Victorian poetry is suggested by a passage in John Stuart Mill's *The Subjection of Women*:

> The association of men and women in daily life is much closer and more complete than it ever was before. Men's life is more domestic. Formerly, their pleasures and chosen occupations were among men, and in men's company: their wives had but a fragment of their lives. At the present time, the progress of civilization, and the turn of opinion against the rough amusements and convivial excesses which formerly occupied most men in their hours of relaxation – together with (it must be said) the improved tone of modern feeling as to the reciprocity of duty which binds the husband towards the wife – have thrown the man very much more upon home and its inmates, for his personal and social pleasures.
>
> (394)

During the Victorian period, marriage, the institution that Mill describes as 'the most fundamental of the social relations' (395), underwent a redefinition and a valorization. The traditional contextualization (stemming from Walter E. Houghton's *Victorian Frame of Mind*) is summarized by Stephen Mintz. For the Victorians, married love was the solution to 'some of the deepest needs and problems of the age'. It was the 'antidote to positivistic and materialistic conceptions of man'; 'a resolution to religious anxiety and confusion'; and a moral locus offering an alternative to 'competitive and impersonal market values' (198). A revisionist explanation is offered by Mary Poovey in her *Uneven Developments: The Ideological Work of Gender in Mid-Victorian Britain*. During the period, the 'model of a binary oppostion between the sexes ... was socially realized in separate but supposedly equal "spheres"'; the 'domestic ideal' became the anchor of social relations and was 'a crucial component in a series of representations that supported both the middle class's economic power and its legitimation of this position' (8–10).

As Poovey emphasizes, the domestic ideal 'was also a site of cultural contestation during the middle of the nineteenth century' (9). A number of the poets responded to the demand that poets directly engage with the issues of the age and made energetic and innovative attempts to explore love relationships in generically hybrid long poems. These poems show the influence of the dominant literary form of the period – the realist novel – and lend support to Bakhtin's hypothesis that, as the novel becomes the dominant form, other genres undergo a 'novelization' (6–7). Clough, for example, recognized that the mid-century reading public much preferred novels to poetry. For the latter 'to be widely popular', he believed it would have to deal 'more than at present it usually does, with general wants, ordinary feelings, the obvious rather than the rare facts of human nature ... the actual, palpable things with which our every-day life is concerned' (Armstrong, 1972, 155). Clough's solution is found in three remarkable long poems that explore love, sexuality and marriage, the first of which, *The Bothie of Tober-na-Fuosich*, is a *mélange* of mock-epic, pastoral and common features of nineteenth-century realist fiction – individualized and psychologically realized characters, dialogue, and concern with social questions and the relation of the individual to society.

Tennyson's principal contribution to the woman question was his 'medley', *The Princess*. Barrett Browning's was her *magnum opus*, the verse novel *Aurora Leigh*, a farrago of *Künstlerroman*, social satire, tract for the times, treatise on poetics, cultural prophecy, theodicy – and love story. As analysed by Coventry Patmore, the problem for the mid-nineteenth-century love poet was twofold: on the one hand, 'the age of narrative poetry [had] passed for ever'; on the other, while contemporary poets were 'highly "self-conscious" in comparison with their predecessors', they were as yet 'not sufficiently so for the only system now possible, – the psychological' (Fredeman, 1975, 27). His solution was the mixture of lyrical and narrative modes used in *The Angel in the House*, his enormously popular 'attempt to invest an ordinary Victorian courtship and marriage in the prosperous middle classes with as deep a spiritual and psychological significance as was felt to attach to the great poetic loves of the past' (House, 129).

Most of these poems addressed the problem of women's inferior education and social position that was succinctly formulated by Mill:

> All women are brought up from the very earliest years in the belief that their ideal of character is the very opposite to that of men; not self-will, and government by self-control, but submission, and yielding to the control of others. All the moralities tell them that it is the duty of women, and all the current sentimentalities that it is their nature, to live for others; to make complete abnegation of themselves, and to have no life but in their affections ... When we put together three things – first, the natural attraction between opposite sexes; secondly, the wife's entire dependence on the husband ... and lastly, that the principal object of human pursuit, consideration, and all objects of social ambition, can in general be sought or obtained by her only through him, it would be a miracle if the object of being attractive to men had not become the polar star of feminine education and formation of character.
>
> (318–19)

At the end of Clough's *Bothie* and Tennyson's *Princess*, a companionate marriage of complementary individuals based on sexual attraction is celebrated as the answer to the woman question: 'The woman's cause is man's', we read at the end Tennyson's poem, 'they rise or sink/Together, dwarfed or godlike, bond or free':

> If she be small, slight-natured, miserable,
> How shall men grow? ...
>   in true marriage lies
> Nor equal, nor unequal: each fulfils
> Defect in each, and always thought in thought,
> Purpose in purpose, will in will, they grow.
>
> (ii, 289–91)

When Barrett Browning read *The Princess*, she professed herself 'to be a good deal disappointed' (i, 1898, 367). But while she felt let down by Tennyson's fairy-tale fantastications, she could hardly have failed to notice that *The Princess* explores the relation of sexual love, marriage and the nurturing of children to the intellectual and vocational aspirations of nineteenth-century women, and that Tennyson's views on the subject were in essential agreement with her own. What is thematically different in *Aurora Leigh* is that her valorization of marriage is cast in religious terms. Love is a 'sacramental gift/With eucharistic meanings' (i, 90–91). Its highest expression is 'God's love'; next highest is 'the love of wedded souls' (ix, 881–2), the terrestrial analogue of the love of God on which it depends.

But marriage was also critically examined by the Victorian love poets. It is notable that in the later long poems of both Clough (*Amours de Voyage* and *Dipsychus*) and Tennyson (*Maud* and *Idylls of the King*) romantic love culminating in marriage is shown to be a highly problematic proposition. Meredith's *Modern Love*, his extraordinary conflation of sonnet sequence, melodrama and psychological novel, anatomizes the deterioration of a marriage based on romantic love. Morris' personal poems of 1865-75 and Hardy's *Poems of 1912-13* both show how much in later years can go wrong with romantic love culminating in marriage. And so do an appreciable number of Browning's poems, including 'James Lee's Wife', a lyric sequence that analyses a failed romantic marriage from the wife's point of view. As Browning explained in a letter:

> I meant them [the couple] for just the opposite [of 'proletaire'] – people newly-married, trying to realize a dream of being sufficient to each other, in a foreign land (where you can try such an experiment) and finding it break up, – the man being *tired* first, – and tired precisely of the love.
>
> (Curle, 109)

4

Browning's poem is also an example of the Victorian poets' increased interest in the female point of view in love relationships. In the love poetry of the Italian *stilnovisti* – the school of which Dante was the master – the lady 'exists chiefly in the lover's heart … The poet describes himself first and always. Ultimately, this poetry has little to do with women' (Valency, 210). The love poetry of Philip Sidney and John Donne, to take two Elizabethan examples, is composed exclusively from the view point of the man. And, as Anne Mellor has observed, 'when we look closely at the gender implications of romantic love' in the principal male poets of the Romantic period, 'we discover that rather than embracing the female as a valued other, the male lover usually effaces her into a narcissistic projection of his own self' (25).

A close look at the central male love poets of the Victorian period reveals something different. There are exceptions of course. In Arnold's lyric poetry, for example, the female other exists only as 'a sort of mournful cosmic last resort' (to cite Anthony Hecht's parody of 'Dover Beach', 17). And Dante Rossetti's love poems are like the portraits of the painter in his sister Christina's sonnet 'In an Artist's Studio': the face in all of them is the same face with the same meaning, 'Not as she is, but as she fills his dream'.

Examples of the male love poet's concern with the female point of view include the numerous poems by Browning and Hardy with female speakers. Morris's 'Why Dost Thou Struggle' is the attempt of a husband to see his failed marriage from his wife's point of view. In other works women are shown to be sexual beings – to be love subjects and not simply love objects. Elspie Mackaye in Clough's *Bothie* is given two superb speeches concerning the sexual force that she feels working within her. In Meredith's *Modern Love* a number of the conventions of Petrarchan love poetry are ironically evoked. The most striking, 'Lady, this is my sonnet to your eyes' (section 30), recalls the convention of indicating the beloved's exalted spiritual nature through descriptions of the windows of her soul. 'My lady carries love within her eyes', begins a sonnet from Dante's *Vita Nuovo* (in Dante Rossetti's translation):

> All that she looks on is made pleasanter;
> Upon her path men turn to gaze at her;
> He whom she greeteth feels his heart to rise,
> And droops his troubled visage, full of sighs,
> And of his evil heart is then aware:
> Hate loves, and pride becomes a worshipper.

> (1959, 351)

But the eyes of the wife in Meredith's poem have an altogether different aspect and effect. They belong to a self-conscious, sexual being and are usually 'glazed/And inaccessible'. They have 'soft fires,/Wide gates, at love-time, only', and at other times can seem 'guilty gates' that indicate infidelity by 'shutting all too zealous for their sin' (sections 36, 2).

The most important point concerning the female perspective in the love poetry of the Victorians is that during the period a tradition of love poetry by female poets was established. When she searched English poetic history for female antecedents, Barrett Browning was forced to lament: 'I look everywhere for grandmothers and see none.' In her view, Joanna Baillie (1762–1851) was 'the first female poet in all senses in England' (1898, i, 232, 230). But Barrett Browning was a sensitive and discriminating reader of the two principal female poets of the next generation, Felicia Hemans (1793–1835) and Letitia Elizabeth Landon (1802–38), the originators of a line of Victorian love poetry by women. Given the domestic ideology of separate spheres, love and intimate personal relationships were the natural subject for female poets. As Mary Ann Stodart (1842) insisted in the 'Poetry and Poetesses' chapter of her *Female Writers: Thoughts on their Proper Sphere and on their Powers of Usefulness*, 'the point where lies the true poetic power of woman ... is in the heart – over the head – and especially in the peculiarities of her own heart' (quoted in Leighton and Reynolds, xxix). In Christina Rossetti's pithier formulation, 'Men work and think, but women feel' ('An "Immurata" Sister').

In the past two decades there has been increasing interest in identifying and exploring the tradition of nineteenth-century female poets.[2] The emphasis on a distinctive female poetic tradition has been eye-opening concerning the emotional experience of women in the nineteenth century, and has provided an essential context for sympathetic and informed reading of the love poetry of Victorian women. But there are trade-offs and dangers involved. One is that aesthetic considerations will be marginalized. The point was succinctly made by Elizabeth Bishop in objecting in principle to the inclusion of her poems in anthologies of women's writing: 'Undoubtedly gender does play an important part in the making of any art, but art is art and to separate writings, paintings, musical compositions, etc., into two sexes is to emphasize values in them that are not art' (Adcock, 97). In their work on Victorian women poets, Angela Leighton and Isobel Armstrong both recognized the need for a balance between the cultural and ideological concerns of feminist critics and aesthetic concerns. But after a point, this balance is difficult to maintain because once aesthetic considerations are foregrounded, qualitative discriminations inevitably follow.[3]

Take, for example, Barrett Browning's 'Lady Geraldine's Courtship', a ballad narrative of 412 lines, using the eight-stress trochaic line of 'Locksley Hall' in *abab* quatrains instead of Tennyson's couplets. In Dorothy Mermin's (1989) critical study, *Elizabeth Barrett Browning: The Origins of a New Poetry* (the 'new' means poetry by women), the poem is highly rated: 'This was Elizabeth Barrett's first experiment in bringing together poetry and the novel, visionary imagination and the modern world ... With it she triumphantly – like Geraldine – takes imaginative possession of a new poetic territory' (111–12). A very different impression of poem, 140 lines of which were composed in a single day (Barrett Browning, 1898, i, 177), is found in George Saintsbury's *History of English Prosody*, where it is used to exemplify the faults of Barrett Browning's lyric verse: her 'fatal want of form', 'faults in diction' and 'ear for rhyme [that] was probably the worst on record in the case of a person having any poetic power whatever'. For Saintsbury, the 'strange welter of preposterous and genuine feeling – ridiculous bombast and true poetic expression' made the process of reading a poem like 'Lady Geraldine's Courtship' 'something like that of eating with a raging tooth – a process of alternate expectation and agony' (iii, 242–4).

The other principal danger is that considering Victorian women's poetry in a gender-specific rather than an intergendered context can lead to serious literary-historical distortions. Consider, for example, the influence of Sappho on nineteenth-century love poets. Poems with 'Sappho' in the title are a staple of female love laments: there is Hemans's 'The Last Song of Sappho'; Landon's 'Sappho's Song' from *The Improvisatrice*; Caroline Norton's 'The Picture of Sappho'; and two poems by Christina Rossetti, 'Sappho' and 'What Sappho would have said had her leap cured instead of killing her'. Moreover, except for the last, these titles could with equal appositeness have been used for many of the female laments by these and other Victorian women poets.

The most striking Victorian appropriation of Sappho, however, was not by a female poet; it was by Tennyson. In her 'Sappho and the Making of Tennysonian Lyric', Linda H. Peterson (1994) has showed how 'Sappho helped Tennyson comprehend his lyric sensibility and his place in poetic history' (127). In a letter of 1830, Arthur Hallam compared his friend's poetry to 'the fragments of Sappho, in which I see much congeniality to Alfred's peculiar power'. The power was that of 'sensuous perception', especially as it related to the relation between inner feeling and outer phenomena, between consciousness and perception (1981, 401–2). Peterson calls attention to 'the density of the allusions to Sappho' in the poems Tennyson wrote in the early 1830s, which 'mark her profound influence and presence'. Before Tennyson, female poets, 'as part of a self-consciously feminine literary agenda', had 'assumed Sappho's persona or used her words'. Tennyson entered their domain and 'assumed their poetic voices', a 'takeover [that] launched him to preeminence as a lyrist, allowing him to create poetry that consciously developed and counterpointed feminine and masculine strains' (121–33).

On a smaller scale, the same counterpointing can be seen in the poetry of Browning. In 'A Woman's Last Word', 'In a Year' and the opening lyrics of 'James Lee's Wife', for example, Browning used the topos of female lament to express a more emotional and less cerebral, more passive and less robust, side of his poetic sensibility. One can hardly say of these excellent poems what Randall Jarrell said of the female speaker of Robert Lowell's 'The Mills of the Kavanaughs': 'You feel, "Yes, Robert Lowell would act like this if he were a girl"; but whoever saw a girl like Robert Lowell' (234–5). One must rather say, as one must of Tennyson's Mariana poems, that one of the two most gifted poets of the period exploited the 'natural' subject matter of female poets with finer results than most of the comparable distaff performances.

For Swinburne, the author of 'Anactoria', the most spectacular Sappho poem of the Victorian period, there is a single non-gendered tradition to which all suffering love poets belong – the tradition that begins with 'the supreme head of song', as Swinburne calls Sappho in 'Ave atque Vale', his elegy on Baudelaire. Thomas Hardy felt the same; in his elegy on Swinburne, 'A Singer Asleep', Sappho is called 'the music-mother/Of all the tribe that feel in melodies'. This link is the basis of the visionary consolation at the elegy's climax:

> And one can hold in thought that nightly here
> His phantom may draw down to the water's brim,
> And hers [Sappho's] come up to meet it, as a dim
> Lone shine upon the heaving hydrosphere ...
>
> One dreams him sighing to her spectral form:
> 'O teacher, where lies hid thy burning line;
> Where are thy songs, O poetess divine
> Whose very orts are love incarnadine?'
> And her smile back: 'Disciple true and warm,
>   Sufficient now are thine'.

Here is the imaginative adumbration of a non-gendered lyric tradition that recognizes Sappho's immortal daughters (as Dioscorides called her poems in the third century BC) as the beginning of a tradition that embraces both male and female poets. This tradition suggests that the model Anne Mellor has proposed for the literature of the Romantic period is equally appropriate for the subjects of this study – 'masculine' and 'feminine' not as 'binary opposites' but rather as the endpoints on 'a fluid continuum' ranging not only through the entire corpus of Victorian love poetry 'but also through the corpus of individual writers' (11).[4]

5

In his English idyll, 'Edwin Morris', Tennyson satirizes two older ways of love – the traditional conservatism of the curate ('God made the woman for the man,/And for the good and increase of the world') and the conventionally romantic idealizations of the title character, a 'full-celled honeycomb of eloquence/Stored from all flowers' who speaks in fatuous hyperboles. Both these attitudes are contrasted with those of the poem's speaker who could, he thinks, love wholeheartedly 'but for a thought or two':

> 'tis from no want in her:
> It is my shyness or my self-distrust,
> Or something of a wayward modern mind
> Dissecting passion.

Tennyson's poem exemplifies a final distinctive feature of the love poetry of the Victorians: a self-consciousness about the experience of loving that leads to introspection and analysis. Several of the major love poems of the period – Meredith's *Modern Love* and Clough's *Amours de Voyage* and *Dipsychus*, for example – show the corrosive effects on love relationships of intense self-consciousness and 'Deep questioning', 'that fatal knife ... which probes to endless dole', as Meredith's narrator calls it (section 50). And in several of Arnold's love poems introspective analysis leads to the recognition of what Georg Simmel identified as another distinguishing characteristic of 'modern' love: 'that there is something unattainable in the other; that the absoluteness of the individual self erects a wall between two human beings which even the most passionate willing of both cannot remove' (246). 'The Buried Life', for example, has no positive answer to the questions it poses:

> is even love too weak
> To unlock the heart, and let it speak?
> Are even lovers powerless to reveal
> To one another what indeed they feel?

And 'To Marguerite – Continued' ends with the recognition that the 'deep desire' for union of lovers on their separate islands can never be realized; between them will always be 'The umplumbed, salt, estranging sea'.

In some Victorian poets, self-consciousness concerning the experience of loving is manifested in self-consciousness concerning the writing of love poetry – in particular the reflexive concern with the relation of their creative activity to the forms, conventions and discourses of earlier love poetry. The Spirit in Clough's *Dipsychus*, for example, speaks for the poet when he remarks that 'With the high amatory-poetic/My temper's no way sympathetic' (I, iii). And the subject of Hardy's 'I Said to Love' is the inadequacy of traditional amatory figuration:

> 'It is not now as in old days,
> When men adored thee and thy ways
>   All else above;
> …
> 'Thou art not young, thou art not fair,
> No elfin darts, no cherub air,
>   No swan, nor dove
> Are thine; but features pitiless,
> And iron daggers of distress,'
>   I said to Love.

A final example is Browning's brilliant dramatic lyric, 'A Serenade at the Villa'. Saintsbury called the poem 'that most really puzzling piece in all Browning' (iii, 229), but it becomes comprehensible once it is recognized as a poem about love poetry. In its opening stanzas, the speaker describes the natural setting in which he had serenaded his beloved the previous night:

> Not a twinkle from the fly,
>   Not a glimmer from the worm;
> When the crickets stopped their cry,
>   When the owls forbore a term,
> You heard music; that was I.
>
> Earth turned in her sleep with pain,
>   Sultrily suspired for proof:
> In at heaven and out again,
>   Lightning! – where it broke the roof,
> Bloodlike, some few drops of rain.

On this most inappropriate of nights, when 'Life was dead and so was light', the serenader does the best he can:

> What they could my words expressed,
>   O my love, my all, my one!
> Singing helped the verses best,
>   And when singing's best was done,
> To my lute I left the rest.

He leaves at dawn and afterwards wonders about the reception of his performance: 'What became of all the hopes,/Words and song and lute as well?'

He imagines and describes two contrasting reactions. There is a certain degree of congruence between them in that both assume a beloved preoccupied with thoughts of mortality and the possible compensations of the serenader's love. This has led some commentators to assume that the beloved is ageing and even near death. But there is no reason to think that the lady is near or at the end of her life any more than was Barrett Browning, when in the fourth of her *Sonnets from the Portuguese* she employed the serenade motif in considering herself as a desolate house in contrast to the golden fullness of Browning's song ('My cricket chirps against thy mandolin'). It is better to say that the concern with mortality and its relation to love has its source in the speaker's awareness of the atmospheric conditions described in the poem – for example, the female earth turning in her sleep in pain – and their contextual implications.

The first reception of his song imagined by the speaker is wishful and idealizing:

> Say, this struck you – 'When life gropes
>   Feebly for the path where fell
> Light last on the evening slopes,
>
> One friend in that path shall be,
>   To secure my step from wrong;
> One to count night day for me.'

The second considers the song in its phenomenological context. The woman's response to the serenade is imagined to be conditioned by her response to a more powerful text – the book of nature, that on this minatory night contains a proleptic image of mortality – of 'the final storm':

> 'When no moon succeeds the sun,
>   Nor can pierce the midnight's tent,
> ...
> When the fire-fly hides his spot,
>   When the garden-voices fail
> In the darkness thick and hot, –
>   Shall another voice avail,
> That shape be where these are not?
>
> Has some plague a longer lease,
>   Proffering its help uncouth?
> Can't one even die in peace?
>   As one shuts one's eyes on youth,
> Is that face the last one sees?'

The task of determining which is the more adequate response is not difficult. There can be no question that the second response is not only much more powerfully and fully articulated but also aesthetically preferable in that it integrates and interrelates the principal features of the poem. Moreover, this reading is endorsed in the poem's last stanza, which expresses the speaker's sense of the response of the setting itself to his serenade:

> Oh how dark your villa was,
>   Windows fast and obdurate!
> How the garden grudged me grass
>   Where I stood – the iron gate
> Ground its teeth to let me pass!

This determination, however, is not the only food for thought that 'A Serenade at the Villa' offers. As soon as the reader begins to assess the two receptions of the speaker's love song, Browning's poem becomes a meta-poem – a poem about poetry. John Maynard (1976) has argued that the speaker's voice is primarily that of 'the Romantic tradition of perception and feeling out of which Browning grew', and that the serenade 'also stands for poetry; the serenader's occupation is that of the poet in the post-Romantic world' (4–6). This is suggestive but too broad brush; I would emend Maynard's formulation to say that the serenade specifically stands for love poetry.

In the fourth book of *Paradise Lost*, Milton used the serenade, 'which the starv'd Lover sings/To his proud fair' as a synecdoche for the traditional content and forms of love poetry that would be 'best quitted with disdain'. Browning makes a similar use of the form. In particular, as Maynard recognized, it is the Romantic poetry of Shelley, author of 'The Indian Serenade', against which 'A Serenade at the Villa' needs to be read. The crucial intertextual relationship is with 'The Two Spirits: An Allegory', to which there is an overt allusion ('count night day for me') in stanza vii. In Shelley's poem, a spirit, 'plumed with strong desire', wishes to 'cross the shade of night' and reach the deathless stars. Within his heart is the illumination of love which, he asserts, will 'make night day'. Another spirit prudentially warns that 'a Shadow tracks thy flight of fire', that storms threaten and that 'Night is coming'. The contrasting receptions of the lover's serenade in Browning's poem are rescorings of the debate of the two spirits in Shelley's poem – but in the Victorian poem it is the un-Romantic spirit that has the last and strongest word.

Thus, 'A Serenade at the Villa' adumbrates all of the distinctive features of Victorian love poetry identified in this chapter: a concern with the relationship of love to mortality; a preoccupation not with the Romantic high – the 'all' feeling in the present – but with the possibility of future transcendence; a concern with the point of view of both parties in the love relationship, more particularly with the woman as (in George Eliot's phrase) an equivalent centre of self; a recognition of the importance of context – not absolute Romantic love but love as sub-dued to what it works in (the natural world in this poem, in other poems the social, ideological or institutional setting); and finally, a self-consciousness about romantic love and its poetic expression in relation to earlier experience and expression.

Notes

1. In addition to Ball, general studies of Victorian love poetry include Isobel Armstrong's 'Browning and the Victorian Poetry of Sexual Love' (1974); W. S. Johnson's *Sex and Marriage in Victorian Poetry* (1975); the 'Love Poetry' chapter in Bernard Richards' *English Poetry of the Victorian Period 1830-1890* (1988); Rod Edmond's *Affairs of the Hearth: Victorian Poetry and Domestic Narrative* (1988); and Eric Griffiths' 'Companionable Forms' in his *The Printed Voice in Victorian Poetry* (1989).
2. Recent anthologies of poems by Victorian women include Angela Leighton and Margaret Reynolds's *Victorian Women Poets* (1995); and Isobel Armstrong et al.'s *Nineteenth-Century Women Poets* (1996). General critical studies include Sandra M. Gilbert and Susan Gubar, 'Strength in Agony: Nineteenth-Century Poetry by Women', the final part of their *The Madwoman in the Attic: The Woman Writer and the Nineteenth-Century Literary Imagination* (1980); Dorothy Mermin's 'The Damsel, the Knight, and the Victorian Female Poet', *Critical Inquiry* 13 (1987): 64–80; Angela Leighton's *Victorian Women Poets: Writing Against the Heart* (1992); and Isobel Armstrong's 'A Music of Thine Own', ch. 12 of her *Victorian Poetry: Poetry, Poetics and Politics* (1993).
3. In a review of Leighton and Reynolds's anthology of *Victorian Women Poets*, Peter Keating observed: 'if a discussion of Victorian poetry is to focus exclusively on women, "the Best in art now" [a phrase from *Aurora Leigh*] has to be discarded ... The issue never arises with Victorian fiction where qualitative distinctions have no need to involve gender at all'. But to 'talk of Victorian women poets in isolation from the men is to concern oneself with an alternative tradition that may well be distinctive and in need of careful definition, but cannot be representative of "the Best", except within its own restricted terms of reference' (27).
4. Another line of argument concerning the distortions caused by a gender-specific reading of Victorian poetry could be developed from an observation of Mill's in *The Subjection of Women*:

> All women who write are pupils of the great male writers. A painter's early pictures, even if he be a Raphaelle, are indistinguishable in style from those of his master. Even a Mozart does not display his powerful originality in his earliest pieces. What years are to a gifted individual, generations are to a mass. If women's literature is destined to have a different

collective character from that of men, depending on any difference of natural tendencies, much longer time is necessary than has yet elapsed, before it can emancipate itself from the influence of accepted models, and guide itself by its own impulses. But if, as I believe, there will not prove to be any natural tendencies common to women, and distinguishing their genius from that of men, yet every individual writer among them has her individual tendencies, which at present are still subdued by the influence of precedent and example: and it will require generations more, before their individuality is sufficiently developed to make head against that influence.

(372)

CHAPTER TWO

Browning's Lessons in Love

... in these love-poems [from Browning's *Men and Women*] there is one thing that struck me particularly; that is their intense unmixed love; love for the sake of love, and if that is not obtained disappointment comes, falling-off, misery. I suppose the same kind of thing is to be found in all very earnest love-poetry, but I think more in him than in almost anybody else.

William Morris

1

The earnestness of Browning's love poetry is instanced not only in *Men and Women* (1855) but throughout his poetical works – from the febrile intensities of the speaker of *Pauline* (1833), his first published poem, to the *carpe diem* urgings of the speaker of 'Now' (1889), one of the very few sonnets Browning wrote over the six decades of his career:

> Out of your whole life give but a moment!
> All of your life that has gone before,
> All to come after it, – so you ignore
> So you make perfect the present, – condense,
> In a rapture of rage, for perfection's endowment,
> Thought and feeling and soul and sense –
> Merged in a moment which gives me at last
> You around me for once, you beneath me, above me –
> Me – sure that despite of time future, time past, –
> This tick of our life-time's one moment you love me!
> How long such suspension may linger? Ah, Sweet –
> The moment eternal – just that and no more –
> When ecstasy's utmost we clutch at the core
> While cheeks burn, arms open, eyes shut and lips meet!

A variation on the invitation-to-love lyric, 'Now' is more celebration/ exhortation than seductive argument. The two strains are reconciled in the sonnet's formally unusual ending, which is neither a sestet nor a couplet but a self-contained *fggf* quatrain.

This closure is a small-scale example of the boldness and freedom with which Browning treated traditional poetic forms and conventions in his explorations and dramatizations of the experience of loving. As the Victorian critic David Masson noted, Browning did not 'seem at home in ... brief and purely lyrical effusions ... In his case, the head is constantly intruding its suggestions where the heart alone should be speaking'. He needed a 'larger space' for the representation of 'feeling or passion expanded and complicated into character and mode of existence' (Litzinger and Smalley, 180). Most of Browning's love poems are not exercises in traditional lyric forms, but rather what he called dramatic lyrics. They are lyric in that they are written in the first person in rhymed stanzas and express the speaker's thoughts and feelings. Unlike dramatic monologues, they do not require a specific occasion and setting, or a specific auditor (though, being love poems, they are often addressed to a beloved); nor is there interplay between speaker and *muta persona*. They are dramatic in the sense that each speaker's distinctive character and preoccupations are revealed through his/her utterance.

Browning's dramatic lyrics also tend to be longer than traditional love lyrics – but they need not be so in order to qualify as dramatic. Masson is misleading in associating the 'larger spaces' of Browning's dramatic lyrics with the length of a poem rather than with the amount of psychological space. 'Love in a Life' (1855), for example, is not the 'sentimental piece' or 'purely lyrical effusion' he describes it as being (Litzinger and Smalley, 180). I quote the poem *in toto*:

I

Room after room,
I hunt the house through
We inhabit together.
Heart, fear nothing, for, heart, thou shalt find her –
Next time, herself! – not the trouble behind her
Left in the curtain, the couch's perfume!
As she brushed it, the cornice-wreath blossomed anew:
Yon looking-glass gleamed at the wave of her feather.

II

Yet the day wears,
And door succeeds door;
I try the fresh fortune –
Range the wide house from the wing to the centre.
Still the same chance! she goes out as I enter.
Spend my whole day in the quest, – who cares?
But 'tis twilight, you see, – with such suites to explore,
Such closets to search, such alcoves to importune!

This variation on the expectation-as-virtual-fulfilment lyric is given an allegorical overlay by its title. One could say that the house is life; that to love is to seek and not give up the quest, to have a reach exceeding one's grasp; and that the journey not the arrival is what matters. One could – but such uplifting commentary does not sound right for this poem and would in fact serve better as a gloss for 'Life in a Love', its less interesting companion poem.

'Love in a Life' is about the sexual life, not the life of the spirit. The quest or 'hunt' brings *frissons* that depend on the speaker's heightened expectation, which eroticizes the furnishings of the house – the couch, the cornice-wreath, the looking-glass. The speaker does not seem to want 'herself' as much as the delicious 'trouble' of pursuing her. Note the 'But' at the beginning of the penultimate line: one expects that a qualification of the preceding 'who cares?' will follow (for example: 'I care because the night is coming in which no man can hunt'). But what follows is a reaffirmation of the sweetness of exploring suites. In the poem's most conspicuous rhyme, the speaker's fortune is to importune.

Is this pursuit a wholesome exercise? Are not the speaker's tastes as peculiar as the stanzas that enumerate his titillations are lopsided? The word 'hunt', after all, has predatory overtones; and a primary meaning of 'importune' is to solicit for an immoral purpose. And perhaps there is no woman in the speaker's house or in his life (after all she never appears), in which case he might be thought to be engaging in mastur-batory foreplay. Thus, what might appear at first glance to be a pure effusion is in fact a sketch of an intriguing personality and a deconstruction of the expectation-as-virtual fulfilment lyric – just as 'A Serenade at the Villa' is of the traditional lyric of complaint.

One way of sorting out the various speakers of Browning's love poems is to realize that a number of the poems are connected to a kind of thematic grid – the concept of the 'infinite moment' (or 'moment eternal' as it is called in 'Now'). As the speaker of 'Cristina' (1842) explains, there are 'moments,/Sure though seldom ... When the spirit's true endowments/Stand out plainly from its false ones'. These moments reveal that 'the true end, sole and single' of human existence is 'With some other soul to mingle'. If the moment is unseized, 'the soul loses what it lived for,/And eternally must lose it'. If the moment is seized, if souls are mixed 'In spite of the mortal screen' – I am now quoting from 'By the Fire-Side' (1855) – then the basis for mutual happines has been established and 'the gain of earth must be heaven's gain too' – meaning that one has also gained the felt assurance of an infinite or immortal dimension to human love.

The infinite moment is the conceptual given of many of Browning's love poems; however, it is not of itself what makes these poems compel-ling. It is rather Browning's great lyric and dramatic powers of repre-senting different kinds of lovers and loving – from the idealizing to the pathological. To adapt the figure Browning used in distinguishing his wife's poetry from his own: it is not the pure white light of the infinite moment that one tends to find in his finest love poems, but its refractions in the broken prismatic hues of their speakers.

Take, for example, 'Porphyria's Lover' (1842) and 'Mesmerism' (1855), each of which is a *reductio ad absurdum* of the infinite moment. The

former is a dramatic lyric in five-line tetrameter stanzas rhyming *ababb*
– a fact as often unnoticed as the rhyming pentameter couplets of 'My
Last Duchess' because of the generic overlay of a Poe-like short story
about the sex-murder of a beautiful young woman told from the perpe-
trator's point of view. Despite Porphyria's apparent devotion, her lover
is vexed that she is

> Too weak, for all her heart's endeavour,
> To set its struggling passion free
>   From pride, and vainer ties dissever,
>   And give herself to me for ever.

A moment later he realizes he is mistaken: 'at last I knew/Porphyria
worshipped me ... That moment she was mine, mine'. To prolong this
moment, to realize the moment eternal, he strangles her.

'Mesmerism' is a more disturbing poem. Its run-on stanzas with their
repetitions of phrase and strong intra-sentence rhymes at short intervals
suggest the obsessive energy and manic desire of the speaker, who
describes 'a method as strange as new' that will enable him to get 'All I
want' from the absent woman on whom he brings his hypnotic thought
to bear

> Till I seemed to have and hold,
>   In the vacancy
>   'Twixt the wall and me,
> From the hair-plait's chestnut-gold
> To the foot in its muslim fold –
>
> Have and hold, then and there,
>   Her, from head to foot,
>   Breathing and mute,
> Passive and yet aware,
> In the grasp of my steady stare –
>
> Hold and have, there and then,
>   All her body and soul
>   That completes my whole,
> All that women add to men,
> In the clutch of my steady ken –

The phrase 'have and hold' is used in the Anglican marriage service, of
which the speaker's discourse is a parody – a pornographic rescoring of
the sacramental. The 'clutch of my steady ken' is the male gaze, about
which late twentieth-century feminist critics have nothing to tell Browning, whose speaker compares imprinting the woman on the void to a
'calotypist's skill', that is, to an early form of photography.

But this is not all that the speaker intends to do. The next step is to
command the woman's very soul to advance and 'inform the shape' he

has realized. This requires the mesmeric influence operating through the hands, which 'give vent/To my ardour and my aim/And break into very flame'. When this is accomplished, the woman becomes more actively compliant with his sultanic possession of her:

> Like the doors of a casket-shrine,
>   See, on either side,
>   Her two arms divide
> Till the heart betwixt makes sign,
> Take me, for I am thine!
>
> 'Now – now' – the door is heard!
>   Hark, the stairs! and near –
>   Nearer – and here –
> 'Now!' and at call the third
> She enters without a word.

At the end of the poem, the speaker's thoughts, like those of Porphyria's lover, turn weirdly to God, the supreme creator, who is beseeched to grant full temporary control of the soul that He ownest and to put off to the future the day of reckoning.

Other dramatic lyrics make different use of the infinite-moment topos, for example 'Youth and Art' (1864). The poem's opening line – 'It once might have been, once only' – reiterates a key aspect of the topos: that there is a one-time-only point in a relationship which if seized makes all the difference: 'Oh, the little more, and how much it is!/And the little less, and what worlds away', as the speaker of 'By the Fire-Side' puts it. In 'Youth and Art', a female speaker addresses a male. She recalls the early days when the two were poor aspiring artists – she a singer, he a sculptor – who 'lodged in a street together', and wonders why it was that they never became intimate. Their Bohemian, emancipated existence and youthful high spirits are wonderfully evoked by the poem's principal metrical device – the two-syllable trochaic *b* rhymes:

> We studied hard in our styles,
>   Chipped each at a crust like Hindoos,
> For air looked out at the tiles,
>   For fun watched each other's windows.
> ...
> And I – soon managed to find
>   Weak points in the flower-fence facing,
> Was forced to put up a blind
>   And be safe in my corset-lacing.
> ...
> Why did not you pinch a flower
>   In a pellet of clay and fling it?
> Why did not I put a power
>   Of thanks in a look, or sing it?

> I did look, sharp as a lynx,
>   (And yet the memory rankles)
> When models arrived, some minx
>   Tripped up-stairs, she and her ankles.

In essence, the situation of this female speaker is that of numerous poems by nineteenth-century female poets. As Letitia Elizabeth Landon put it in her 'Stanzas on the Death of Mrs. Hemans', 'dearly purchased is the gift,/The gift of song' (Leighton and Reynolds, 44). The climactic irony of 'Youth and Art' is that the speaker has been unsuccessful in *both* love and art. Unlike the man, who has been 'dubbed knight and an R.A.', she has not been professionally successful, merely socially so owing to her marriage to 'a rich old lord'. In the closing stanzas, exuberant reminiscence has turned into bitter mockery of present spiritual impoverishment:

> Each life unfulfilled, you see;
>   It hangs still, patchy and scrappy:
> We have not sighed deep, laughed free,
>   Starved, feasted, despaired, – been happy.
>
> And nobody calls you a dunce,
>   And people suppose me clever:
> This could but have happened once,
>   And we missed it, lost it for ever.

The ending of 'Youth and Art' might be said to point a moral; but I would much prefer to use a different term in referring to what one can learn about the experience of sexual love from Browning's dramatic poems. They are 'lessons in love' in the sense that D. H. Lawrence surely meant when he used the phrase in an inscription to a volume of Browning's love poems he gave as a present in 1912 (see Woudhuysen). They are lessons not in the sense of precepts or rules but in the sense of offering insight into the psychology of love experience through dramatizations of the emotions of lovers. That is to say, in his finest love poems, Browning is a psychologist rather than a moralist or metaphysician.

But what does it mean to say that a poet is a psychologist? In the opening paragraph of the first of his three 'Contributions to the Psychology of Love', Freud observed that creative writers had long depicted love relationships, making use of 'a sensitivity that enables [them] to perceive the hidden impulses in the minds of other people, and the courage to let [their] own unconscious speak'. But the writers were 'under the necessity to produce intellectual and aesthetic pleasure, as well as certain emotional effects'. This meant that they could not reproduce 'the stuff of reality unchanged'. Moreover, they could 'show only slight interest in the origin and development of the mental states which they portray in their completed form' (165). Browning's dramatic love poems are not case histories; they are stylizations of love experience that produce aesthetic pleasure in and of themselves and intellectual pleasure through the subtlety, suggestiveness and force with which they show the reader something important to know about sexual love. In the following section, I offer as examples of his achievement four poems from *Men and Women*, each of which centres on a different phase or kind of love experience: 'Love among the Ruins', 'A Lovers' Quarrel', and 'Two in the Campagna' are dramatic lyrics. 'Andrea del Sarto', a dramatic monologue, shows that Browning's lessons in love are not restricted to a particular poetic form.

2

'Love among the Ruins' is another expectation-as-virtual fulfilment lyric. The poem's most striking feature is the emphatic regularity of the metre and the alternation of long and very short rhyming lines. Together with the strong rhymes, which create a pause at the end of the first (longer) line even when it is not required by sense or syntax, the unvarying metrical regularity creates a loosening of the stays of quotidian consciousness. As day and night slowly merge on a summer evening, there is an internal mingling within the speaker of his perceptions of the outer scene, the anticipation of meeting his girl, and musings about an ancient city, ruins of which are still visible (a working title for the poem was 'Sicilian Pastoral').

Paul Fussell's trashing of 'the coarseness of the metric' of 'Love among the Ruins' in his *Poetic Meter and Poetic Form* (91) is a consequence of his failing to consider the poem as a dramatic lyric (as he does consider Poe's equally metronomic 'Annabel Lee'). In Browning's poem, the metrical and formal features mime the consciousness of the young bucolic speaker who is strolling through the countryside on his way to a rendezvous with his 'girl'. What Fussell regards as the banality of verbal texture in the poem's first stanza ('a city great and gay'; 'our country's very capital', 'So they say') is not an instance of authorial ineptitude but rather an indication that the unlettered speaker knows little or nothing of the historical past of the region in which he lives and that, consequently, everything he imagines concerning the ancient city and its inhabitants are figments of his fantasy.

As he walks alone musing to himself, present and past are alternately dominant in his consciousness. In all but one of the stanzas, half the lines describe the present scene and half what the speaker imagines of the past. In addition, present and past are interrelated and intermingled in his reverie through numerous echoes, displacements, and macro-micro transmogrifications: solitary pastures/a 'multitude of men'; carpet of grass/colonnades, causeys, bridges, aqueducts; armies going forth/sheep going homeward; fiery spires and brazen pillars/treeless monochrome slopes and rills melting away in the twilight; sublime tower/little turret; the king and his dames/the speaker and his girl; gold/yellow hair; burning ring traced by the racing chariots/blood that burns.

When present and past are assessed in the poem's final lines, the verdict is that 'Love is best'. This conclusion has irked numerous readers. Even those who would presumably agree with the sentiment have been reluctant to assent to the simplistic-sounding affirmation of a love-smitten shepherd. Compare, for example, the end of Hardy's short lyric 'In Time of "The Breaking of Nations"' which weighs the outbreak of war in 1914 against two rural lovers whispering together and asserts that 'War's annals will cloud into night/Ere their story die'. Hardy's affirmation is tough-minded – earlier stanzas, for example, had suggested that agricultural toil has a similar permanence. And, since his lovers are whispering, the reader does not have to assent to anything they might say. In contrast, 'Love among the Ruins' might well seem a tender-minded, pastoral oversimplification.

But is it? Browning's poem, after all, is a dramatic lyric, as Hardy's is not, and as such provides prima facie justification for asking whether the speaker has been presented critically or ironically by the poet. In the case of 'Love among the Ruins', the obvious way to address this question is to ask if there is a deeper-than-apparent connection between the two subject components of the poem – between love in the present and what the ruins evoke in the speaker's imagination. Isobel Armstrong, for example, has censured the speaker for feeling superior to the vanished culture on whose ruins he is meditating. In the climactic fifth stanza, Armstrong (1993) says, 'history converges on' the lovers who have hubristically regarded their 'passion as self-sufficing' and not realized that it is 'as aggressive and exclusive as the desires of the dead society for triumph and empire' (19). This, however, is late twentieth-century politically correct commentary that anachronistically assumes that Browning shared the critic's post-colonial sensibility.

A better reading is provided by a psychological rather than ideological perspective. One can consider the violence, aggression and lust ascribed to the male inhabitants of the ancient city as projected on to it by the lover as he walks towards the girl – and thus as revealing below-the-surface complexities in male sexual attraction to the female. Eleanor Cook makes the excellent point that as he nears his rendezvous, the speaker's thoughts come increasingly to be on the past rather than on the girl and that, 'oddly enough the closer he comes to his beloved, the greater his vehemence grows' (168). But Cook does not draw the conclusion that there is a degree of displacement involved – that sultanic and lustful energies are part of the speaker's amorous feelings.

The poem's fifth stanza is the only one in which past and present do not divide the lines between them. In this climactic stanza the two parts of the speaker's reverie – the anticipated *frissons* of young love and the darker energies of sexual desire – come together:

> And I know ...
> That a girl with eager eyes and yellow hair
> 　Waits me there
> In the turret whence the charioteers caught soul
> 　For the goal,
> When the king looked, where she looks now, breathless, dumb
> 　Till I come.

In the last two lines, the most extraordinary in the poem, king and girl, as Armstrong puts it, 'share the same syntax' (19). The king, epitome of those whose 'Lust of glory pricked their hearts up', is imagined to be made 'breathless, dumb' with excitement by watching the 'burning ring' made by the racing chariots, and the girl to be 'breathless, dumb' in anticipation of her lover's arrival ('Till I come'). But the collocation or overlay tinctures the imagined arrival, making the last line of the stanza a double entendre. On one level the girl is imagined to be eagerly awaiting the speaker; on the other to be compliantly submissive to his penetration.

In the next stanza, the balance between present and past is recovered and the mood of first fine careless rapture is again dominant in the speaker's consciousness:

> When I do come, she will speak not, she will stand,
> 　Either hand
> On my shoulder, give her eyes the first embrace
> 　Of my face,
> Ere we rush, ere we extinguish sight and speech
> 　Each on each.

The girl will 'speak not' when he arives at the turret because she wants fully to savour the initial delight of his presence. The extinguishing here does not have the same connotations of penetration as does that of the boat quenching its speed in the slushy sand in Browning's 'Meeting at Night'. It rather describes an amorous mutuality of embracing and kissing which literally puts out (precludes) sight and speech and may figuratively be said to quench the phallic fires of the speaker's fantasy.

But in the concluding stanza of 'Love among the Ruins', the disturbing undertow is again felt:

> Oh heart! oh blood that freezes, blood that burns!
> 　Earth's returns

For whole centuries of folly, noise and sin!
   Shut them in,
With their triumphs and their glories and the rest!
   Love is best.

The heart to which the speaker refers is his own, now recognized as having something in common with the lustfully tumescent hearts of the king and his minions, just as the blood that burns in his arteries is connected with the fiery spires, burning rings and brazen pillars of the aggressive, acquisitive city. That the speaker is disturbed by this realization is intimated by the muted imperative urgency in the overtly exclamatory 'Shut them in', which carries a suggestion of repression.

The sweet reciprocated love of the speaker and his girl is best, then, not in comparison with the mores and values of a vanished society about which the speaker knows only what he imagines, but in comparison with the aggressive sexual energies within himself that find expression in his reverie. The coexistence of the two forces in a young man's feelings of love – more particularly, the residual presence of the latter even in the flood tide of the former – is the lesson in love given by 'Love among the Ruins'.

3

'A Lovers' Quarrel', the poem that follows 'Love among the Ruins' in Men and Women, offers an immediate qualification or at least complication of the statement that 'Love is best'. The poem is a version of the end-of-love poem, which is usually addressed to the beloved, as is nominally the case here. During the preceding three months, 'the mesmerizer Snow' had kept the lovers isolated in a private domestic space warmed by a hearth-fire and the presence of the other and unconcerned with the outside world: 'Foul be the world or fair/More or less, how can I care?' It was 'a time when the heart could show/All'.

The scintillating stanzas iv to x detail what the 'All' comprised, an egoisme à deux of inventive antics and make-believe in which everything was eroticized. The couple traced each other's faces with caricatural distortions; the Pampas' sheen was imagined to be broken by the leaping of a wild horse, 'Black neck and eyeballs keen'; they pretended to be seamen pacing the quarterdeck arm in arm 'in woeful case' – 'if no help, we'll embrace'; a newspaper offered, not a window on the public world, but subject matter for a suggestive tableau – the bride of Napoleon III at 'his gruesome side/That's as fair as himself is bold'; there were titillating exchanges of gender roles; and there was play at spiritualism:

> Try, will our table turn?
> Lay your hands there light, and yearn
>   Till the yearing slips
>   Through the finger-tips
> In a fire which a few discern,
>   And a very few feel burn,
> And the rest, they may live and learn!

But this winter love-nest was destroyed by a 'hasty word' of the speaker's – 'a moment's spite' ended their affair. The expansive egotism of romantic love ('I was You all the happy past') has been utterly deflated by mere 'pin-prick' or scratch of straw. The speaker's incredulity has given commentators their cue. Armstrong, for example, glosses the love affair as 'a model of the continual, free, unabashed creating of one another that goes on between two people ... the love was a mutual act of liberated imaginative invention ... There is and can be no explanation for the failure' (1974, 290–91). Daniel Karlin (1989), on the other hand, does have an explanation: 'It is not the world which destroys the lover's relationship, but the relationship itself which breaks under the strain of its perfection ... Having invested everything in their love's perfection, the least flaw in that perfection ruins the whole and ruins it for ever' (58).

I cannot agree with either view. Both of these excellent readers of Browning are in this instance too uncritical and idealizing in their account of the lovers' relationship. For one thing, they might have been more attentive to the dynamics of the stanza form, especially the unusual *aabbaaa* rhyme scheme. Its most salient feature is that a stanza's last line, ending with the fifth *a* rhyme, often seems redundant. The ear is satisfied with six lines; the seventh is *de trop*. In stanzas iv to x this is excellent for conveying a sense of the exuberant improvisation of the lovers during the winter months and the effervescent excesses of their make-believe. But elsewhere the extra line tends to make the speaker sound light-hearted and insouciant even when he says he is not. 'Wrong in the one thing rare – /Oh, it is hard to bear', he exclaims. But it does not sound hard to bear. Similarly, in the poem's opening two stanzas, while the burgeoning of spring is zestfully described, the withering of the relationship is registered only in the detachable closing line of each stanza. The effect to suggest a thinness and inconsequentiality of both the speaker's love affair and his manner of being.

Other features of the speaker's utterance also make a negative impression – for example the opening lines of stanza xv:

> Love, if you knew the light
> That your soul casts in my sight,
>   How I look to you

>   For the pure and true
>   And the beauteous and the right ...

This can be read as a conventional gambit to win back the woman. But
the lines also provide the reader with a standard by which to assess the
quality of the couple's love. Has the account of their winter cohabitation shown one anything of the 'soul's light' of the beloved? Was it not
rather the erotic incandescence of her body that lit up the speaker?
Perhaps the lovers were 'pure and true'; but all one learned about them
was the varieties of their make believe. And what could be meant by
'the right'? How could moral and ethical questions have any meaning in
the lovers' winter wonderland? If it was 'a time when the heart could
show/All' and that was all their hearts had to show, no wonder the
bubble burst at the merest touch of a sharp object.

   A final example is found in the unsettling, even sinister overtones of
the last two stanzas, in which the speaker looks forward to the November of the life cycle. This might look like a version of the Marvellian
gambit (none embrace in the grave) designed to win the beloved back,
but the fires the speaker mentions are not those of their former hearth.
They are the fingertip flames 'which a few discern' of stanza vii – the
mesmeric influence said to be visible to some as an effluence of light.
Earlier it was 'the mesmerizer Snow [with his] mute hand's to-and-fro'
that created the conditions of the winter love-nest. Now, in the poem's
final lines the speaker imagines taking this power on himself and drawing the beloved to him:

>   So, she'd efface the score,
>   And forgive me as before.
>   It is twelve o'clock:
>   I shall hear her knock
>   In the worst of a storm's uproar,
>   I shall pull her through the door,
>   I shall have her for evermore!

This recalls both the climax of the pornographic fantasy of 'Mesmerism' and the wish of Porphyria's lover that she give herself to him 'for
ever' – a wish that could only be realized by her murder.

   There is a lesson in love to be found in 'A Lovers' Quarrel', but it is
not that proposed by Armstrong or Karlin. It is the same lesson that
was discursively formulated by Rilke:

>   To take love seriously and to bear and to learn it like a task, this it
>   is that young people need. – Like so much else, people have also
>   misunderstood the place of love in life ... for convention has tried
>   to make this most complicated and ultimate relationship into some-
>   thing easy and frivolous, has given it the appearance of everyone's
>   being able to do it. It is not so ... young people who love each other

fling themselves to each other in the impatience and haste of their
passion, and they don't notice at all what a lack of mutual esteem
lies in this disordered giving of themselves; they notice it with
astonishment and indignation only from the dissension that arises
between them out of all this disorder.

(29–30)

4

As we have seen, 'Two in the Campagna' is an invitation-to-love poem
that reverses conventional expectations. What is on the speaker's mind,
what has tantalized him 'many times', is the yearning for spiritual
rather than simply physical love – for union of souls rather than
bodies:

> I would that you were all to me,
>   You that are just so much, no more.
> Nor yours nor mine, nor slave nor free!
> ...
> I would I could adopt your will,
>   See with your eyes, and set my heart
> Beating by yours, and drink my fill
>   At your soul's springs, – your part my part
> In life, for good and ill.

At the poem's beginning, the speaker attempts to 'catch at' – to articulate – 'a thought'. As the poem progresses, it becomes clear that the
thought concerns the relationship of spiritual to physical love. The
thought proves hard to formulate, and by the end of the poem the
speaker is frustrated by his failure:

> Just when I seemed about to learn!
>   Where is the thread now? Off again!
> The old trick! Only I discern –
>   Infinite passion, and the pain
> Of finite hearts that yearn.

Since 'Two in the Campagna' is both the representation of a failed
attempt at thinking something through and a powerful expression of
the speaker's feelings and yearnings, it is not surprising that the speaker
does not seem fully in control of his discourse and the meanings it
generates. For example, in the stanza quoted above, 'Only I discern' can
mean both that 'the sole thing I have come to recognize is a discontinuity' and that 'I am the only one to recognize this discontinuity' – that is,
his addressee and presumably the reader cannot be expected to discern
what he thinks about the discontinuity because he has not succeeded in
formulating and communicating his 'thought'.

Or consider his statement and the end of stanza vii: 'How is it under our control/To love or not to love?' There are at least two possible construals: (a) on the analogy with the natural world, how can it possibly be under our control to love or not. That is, is there not a transpersonal force (a 'heaven' looking on) to which we should leave ourselves open? The 'fault' and the 'core [of] the wound' mentioned in the next stanza would then be that there is no such force – no heaven, divinity or providence – and that no one is in control. (b) In contrast to the boundlessness and plenitude of the natural world, how is it that there is a limiting principle within human beings (see Day, 155)? In this construal, the fault or wound is within us, an imperfection of human nature that keeps us from being wholly one with nature.

Given this semantic indeterminacy, the best way for the reader to proceed is to treat the speaker's utterance as if it were a poem, paying particular attention to images and figures. These will tell one not so much what the speaker thinks but rather what he feels and perhaps why he feels as he does. After all, from the point of view of lived experience, the distinction between a metaphysical and a psychological explanation of the control mechanism that inhibits love is without a difference; the explanations are equally demoralizing.

In the opening stanzas of the poem, one notices a certain idealizing or onward-and-upward tendency in the speaker that can be traced in the perceptual and tropic details:

> Help me to hold it [the thought]! First it left
> The yellowing fennel, run to seed
> There, branching from the brickwork's cleft,
> Some old tomb's ruin: yonder weed
> Took up the floating weft,
>
> Where one small orange cup amassed
> Five beetles, – blind and green they grope
> Among the honey-meal: and last,
> Everywhere on the grassy slope
> I traced it. Hold it fast!
>
> The champaign with its endless fleece
> Of feathery grasses everywhere!
> Silence and passion, joy and peace,
> An everlasting wash of air –
> Rome's ghost since her decease.
>
> Such life here, through such lengths of hours,
> Such miracles performed in play,
> Such primal naked forms of flowers,
> Such letting nature have her way
> While heaven looks from its towers!

The movement of this passage is from up close to distant, palpable to impalpable, definite to indefinite, actual to figurative: from yellowing fennel to an 'endless fleece/Of feathery grasses'; from ruinous tomb to 'An everlasting wash of air'; from blind, groping beetles to a figurative dove; from a real orange-cup to a symbolic rose. Moreover, the adjectives and nouns used to describe the champaign – 'endless', 'everywhere', 'everlasting', 'miracles', 'primal ... forms', 'heaven' – hint at a temporal parallel to the spatial movement: from the finite to the infinite, from the mutable to the permanent. And 'joy and peace' are two of the terms used in Paul's epistle to the Galatians to describe the fruits of the Spirit of God (5:22). (Galatians is echoed again three stanzas later: 'nor slave nor free' recalls Paul's insistence that 'there is neither bond nor free, there is neither male nor female: for ye are all one in Christ Jesus' [3:27–8] – a further indication of the speaker's desire for incorporeal oneness.)

But the aspiration that climaxes in stanza ix is negated in the following stanza:

> No. I yearn upward, touch you close,
>   Then stand away. I kiss your cheek,
> Catch your soul's warmth, – I pluck the rose
>   And love it more than tongue can speak –
> Then the good minute goes.

The speaker 'yearn[s] upward'; but there is another, stronger, movement in the poem, an ironic counter-movement to his frustrated desire for vertical ascent. It is the drift from the ordered to the random; from the 'floating weft' sustained by the air to the 'thistle-ball' randomly buffeted even by light winds; from a sense of transcendent context or design for human love to a contingent view ('Fixed by no friendly star'). By the end of the poem, the speaker seems not different from, but similar to, the blind beetles. He has grasped not the timelessness of spiritual love, but merely a 'good minute' that goes, just as the fennel runs to seed when its time comes and the rose dies when severed from its link with the earth. Conceptually, the speaker is left with contingency – his thoughts are like the random horizontal movement of the thistle-ball. Temporally, he is left with repetition, with tracing the same round over again. Tantalized many times in the past, he will presumably be equally tempted and frustrated in the future.

The speaker, one comes to realize, has been in flight from his temporal destiny. His finite heart has projected its longings for the infinite on the natural scene – not the near scene with its intimations of death and decay but the distant, endless-seeming expanse at the perceptual limit. He longs for identity with an everlasting natural world in order to overcome his mortality. He wants precisely the same thing from non-physical, soul-to-soul fusion with his beloved. The lesson in love of 'Two in the Campagna' is adumbrated in its title: though the speaker wants there to be *one* in the campagna, but there will always be two. As Shelley observed in a letter: 'I think one is always in love with something or other; the error, and I confess it is not easy for spirits cased in flesh and blood to avoid it, consists in seeking in a mortal image the likeness of what is perhaps eternal' (ii, 434).

5

'Andrea del Sarto' is a dramatic monologue, not a dramatic lyric. There is nothing lyrical about its subject – unhappy married love in middle age. The speaker has little of the earnestness and intensity that for Morris was the defining feature of Browning's love poetry. For Andrea the best is irretrievably in the past; he has dwindled from his 'kingly days' in the public spaces of the French court to impecunious domestic existence in 'the melancholy little house/We built to be so gay with'. What he sees when he looks out the window is that 'days decrease,/And autumn grows, autumn in everything'; 'A common greyness silvers everything'. As Andrea speaks to his inattentive wife Lucrezia, one senses that his enervated loquacity contains nothing he has not said before and will say again.

Andrea has two subjects on his mind; one is his art. He knows exactly how good a painter he is – that he possesses extraordinary technical proficiency but lacks the 'play, the insight and the stretch' of his more famous contemporaries, Leonardo, Michaelangelo and Raphael. Their works may drop earthward, but they themselves reach heights unknown to Andrea. In the phrase that the speaker of *Pauline* applied to Shelley in relation to himself, these painters are sun-treaders. In comparison, Andrea is 'the weak-eyed bat no sun should tempt/Out of the grange whose four walls make his world'.

The other subject is Andrea's marriage. What one learns from the poem about Lucrezia and her relationship with Andrea is first and foremost that she is beautiful, flawlessly so. It is clear that Andrea's attraction to her is rooted in her physical beauty, to which he responds sensuously and aesthetically: 'Your soft hand'; 'those perfect ears'; that 'perfect brow,/And perfect eyes, and more than perfect mouth'; 'Let my hands frame your face in your hair's gold,/You beautiful Lucrezia that are mine!' But there is irony in this last phrase (Andrean not authorial irony): Lucrezia is not his, nor does she care about his art. Several times in the poem Andrea blames his wife for their present situation: 'Had you ... given me soul'; 'Had you ... but brought a mind'; 'Had you there urged'; 'had you not grown restless'. At other times, God is identified as the responsible party ('I feel he laid the fetter'). But the principal fact of Andrea's life is his dissatisfaction not with Lucrezia or God, but with himself. His cruel remarks to his wife are in essence an aspect of his self-dramatizing, self-pitying, self-tormenting nature.

What keeps Andrea's monologue from becoming as tedious to the reader as it is to his wife is the complex perversity of his character. In a dramatic monologue, Ralph Rader has argued, the reader's understanding of the speaker is always either inferior or superior to the speaker's understanding of himself (either we do not understand the speaker's purposes as well as he/she does or vice versa). The first situation makes for serious apprehension, the latter for condescension. Concerning 'My Last Duchess', for example, Rader argued that a stronger reading of the poem results from the former assumption. In the case of 'Andrea del Sarto', I would say that it is the uncertainty as to which position the reader is in that creates much of the poem's interest and that until the closing section the reader cannot unequivocally say whether or not Andrea understands himself as well as we do (that is, cannot decide whether our knowledge of him is greater than his self-knowledge).

In the poem's final section, Andrea seems to take responsibility for his marriage and his creative failure. He even claims that what he has become is 'as I choose'. But did Andrea really choose to be the weak-eyed bat, to be the bird drawn by the fowler's pipe to the snare, to never wish deeper than he does? He may have come to *accept* that these qualities define them, but that is not the same as having chosen them. The claim to have chosen seems no less hollow and self-serving than the other summary statements he makes in the closing section. 'Let each one bear his lot': this maxim is part of Andrea's rationalization of his appalling treatment of his parents; and in any event he is incapable of taking his own advice. 'No doubt, there's something strike's a balance. Yes,/You loved me quite enough, it seems to-night': this moral reckoning is factitious. There is no balance; a few lines later he is again bitterly indicting Lucrezia. 'In heaven, perhaps, new chances, one more chance': surely not. The life Andrea has lived is the life he will live. Even in the New Jerusalem he sees himself enclosed within four walls, like the weak-eyed bat in present time.

The lesson in love? In the Victorian context, there is a home truth. As Mill observed in *The Subjection of Women*, differences of taste and education may 'detract greatly from the happiness of married life', even though the latter 'may stimulate the amatory propensities of men'. Moreover, 'dulness and want of spirit are not always a guarantee' of a wife's submission to her husband (392–3). There is also another lesson, a better one in the aesthetic sense of arising out of interrelationships

among the principal components of the poem (Andrea's art and his
wife) and in not being limited to a particular social construction. Earlier
in the poem Andrea had entreated Lucrezia to 'Let us but love each
other'. But is a person such as Andrea capable of love? The Duke in
'My Last Duchess' chooses never to stoop; Andrea chooses, or says he
chooses, never to extend his reach fully. If never stooping precludes
loving, is not the same thing true of the person who chooses never to
stand tall?

Thomas Hardy (1985) wrote that

> It is the incompleteness that is loved when love is sterling and true.
> This is what differentiates the real one from the imaginary, the
> practicable from the impossible, the Love who returns the kiss
> from the Vision that melts away. A man sees the Diana or the
> Venus in his beloved. But what he loves is the difference.
>
> (251)

Through a negative exemplum, Browning's 'Andrea del Sarto' similarly
suggests that love involves yearning and aspiration and that these qualities are rooted in incompleteness and imperfection. Like Andrea's art,
Lucrezia's beauty is 'faultless' – she is 'Placid and perfect'. There is no
imperfection or incompleteness; as a result there is nothing to call forth
the play, the insight and the stretch of love.

CHAPTER THREE

Tennyson's Delicate Vessels

> We do not remember anywhere to have seen the passion of love
> described with the combined intensity and refinement of some
> passages in [*Maud*] ... This kind of poetry which is almost a
> modern invention, and of which Mr. Tennyson is probably the
> greatest master, asks to be read ... in a mood in which reflection
> voluntarily adandons for a time its mental leadership; and thought
> follows instead of guiding, the current of emotion ... It is no
> argument against the high value of such results that 'feminine grace
> and tenderness' is the fullest commendation which a single phrase
> can give them.
>
> Coventry Patmore, 'Tennyson's *Maud*'

1

Prima facie, it might seem surprising to find 'feminine grace and tenderness' chosen as the best phrase to describe the love lyrics of *Maud*. The
speaker of Tennyson's monodrama, after all, is a violent, misanthropic
young man of 25 who is raised to vertiginous heights by his passion for
a girl of 16, whose brother he grievously wounds in a duel. In understanding Patmore's point, it is helpful to note that he reformulates the
distinction between poets of sensation and poets of reflection made by
Arthur Henry Hallam in his essay of 1831 on Tennyson's early poetry.
The 'fine organs' of the former kind of poet, Hallam said, 'trembled
into emotion at the slightest impulse from external nature'. So vivid was
'the delight attending the simple exertions of eye and ear' for such poets
that it became 'mingled more and more with their trains of active
thought, and tended to absorb their whole being into the energy of
sense' (1943, 186). And, as we have seen, in another place Hallam
(1981) spoke of the 'peculiar power' of 'sensuous perception' in his
friend's poetry and noted its similarity to 'the fragments of Sappho'
(401–2) – that is, to a distinctively feminine grace and tenderness.

It is also useful to compare Tennyson's poetry with that of Browning
– as Tennyson himself did. He once observed that Browning

> has a genius for a sort of dramatic composition and for analysing
> the human mind. And he has a great imagination. But a poet's
> writing should be sweet to the mouth and ear, which Browning's is

not. There should be a 'glory of words' as well as deep thought. This he has not got. In his last work he makes 'impulse' rhyme with 'dim pulse'.

(Page, 100)

On another occasion, after Browning had left the room, Tennyson remarked:

> It is necessary to respect the limits ... an artist is one who recognises bounds to his work as a necessity, and does not overflow illimitably to all extent about a matter. I soon found that if I meant to make any mark at all it must be by shortness ... To get the workmanship as nearly perfect as possible is the best chance of going down the stream of time. A small vessel on fine lines is likely to float further than a great raft.

(Page, 94)

Tennyson's distinction between himself and Browning holds true for their love poems. The former's are as a rule less discursive, more mellifluous and shorter. They are also less dramatic in that their centre of interest is more a state of consciousness than an attribute of personality or character. Another difference can be brought into focus by comparing sexual images and figures of the two poets. On the one hand, there is the female speaker of Browning's 'Count Gismond' recalling her future husband's rescue of her (his sword was covered with blood):

> Over my head his arm he flung
>   Against the world; and scarce I felt
> His sword (that dripped by me and swung)
>   A little shifted in his belt.

On the other, there is a detail in the description of Sir Lancelot as seen from her bower by the lovelorn Lady of Shalott in Tennyson's medieval poem: 'The helmet and the helmet-feather/Burned like one burning flame together'. In another pairing, we have on the one hand the first stanza of Browning's 'Meeting at Night' (the speaker is travelling to his beloved):

> The grey sea and the long black land;
> And the yellow half-moon large and low;
> And the startled little waves that leap
> In fiery ringlets from their sleep,
> As I gain the cove with pushing prow,
> And quench its speed i' the slushy sand.

On the other, here is the description of the dawn goddess Eos in Tennyson's 'Tithonus':

> Once more the old mysterious glimmer steals
> From thy pure brows, and from thy shoulders pure,
> And bosom beating with a heart renewed.

Thy cheek begins to redden through the gloom,
Thy sweet eyes brighten slowly close to mine,
Ere yet they blind the stars, and the wild team
Which love thee, yearning for thy yoke, arise,
And shake the darkness from their loosened manes,
And beat the twilight into flakes of fire.

Both Browning passages are indicative of his difficulty in expressing what Daniel Karlin (1993) calls 'erotic mutuality' (258). It is only male sexuality that is figured, even though the speaker of the first passage is a woman. In contrast, both of Tennyson's figures register a mutual response (in the second, Eos is warming to the male speaker in both senses of the phrase).

A virtuoso example of Tennyson's skill at simultaneously expressing both male and female sensibilities and points of view in a love relationship is the song from *Idylls of the King* of which Vivien makes cynical use in corrupting Merlin. It can be read either as male addressing a female or vice versa. In each case, certain features of the lyric that tend to pass unnoticed in one performance become luminous details in the other:

I think ye hardly know the tender rhyme
Of 'trust me not at all or all in all'.
I heard the great Sir Lancelot sing it once,
And it shall answer for me. Listen to it:

    'In Love, if Love be Love, if Love be ours,
Faith and unfaith can ne'er be equal powers:
Unfaith in aught is want of faith in all.

    It is the little rift within the lute,
That by and by will make the music mute,
And ever widening slowly silence all.

    The little rift within the lover's lute
Or little pitted speck in garnered fruit,
That rotting inward slowly moulders all.

    It is not worth the keeping: let it go:
But shall it? answer, darling, answer, no.
And trust me not at all or all in all.'

(iii, 406)

With a male speaker, this lyric reads as an invitation to erotic love with a discursive or pseudo-discursive argument. The thought guides rather than follows towards the goal of the beloved's yielding herself fully to the speaker – a capitulation that is made all the easier for her in that she can answer positively by saying no. But if a female speaker is the performer, one notices not so much the thought as the delicacy, even fastidiousness, of the images – a slight dissonance in sound and a single, barely visible mark of imperfection. And the former figure for want of faith becomes rich in implication. The rift in the lover's lute can be read as a trope for the insincerity (the unspoken intention to seduce) in the male lover's rendition of the poem, to which the female speaker is responding with a different performance of the same composition. In this construal, the emphasis on all or nothing becomes a plea for sincerity and a commitment of the lover's whole being, and reflects the vulnerability of the female beloved for whom love is not a thing apart but the whole of existence.

2

The finest examples of Tennyson's skill in blending male and female qualities in a love lyric are found in *The Princess*, which contains a critique of the traditional male love poem and three examples of how its limitations can be overcome. The subtitle of *The Princess* is 'a medley'. This refers to the pretext that there are several narrators; but it also calls attention to the mixture of narrative and lyric in the work. There are several lyrics and songs embedded in the narrative, plus six interludal songs sung by women between the 'rougher voices' of the male narrators. The story concerns a prince from the north who has been since early life betrothed to the princess of a southern kingdom whom he has never seen. Ida, the princess, has become an ardent feminist and founded a college for the education of women, from the grounds of which men are excluded on penalty of death. The prince and two of his friends journey to her country, disguise themselves as females, enter the college, and are made welcome. At one point the prince sings for the entertainment of a group that includes the princess a love song he has composed, aping the female treble as best he can:

> O Swallow, Swallow, flying, flying South,
> Fly to her, and fall upon her gilded eaves,
> And tell her, tell her, what I tell to thee.
>
> O tell her, Swallow, that thou knowest each,
> That bright and fierce and fickle is the South,
> And dark and true and tender is the North.
>
> O Swallow, Swallow, if I could follow, and light
> Upon her lattice, I would pipe and trill,
> And cheep and twitter twenty million loves.
>
> O, were I thou that she might take me in,

And lay me on her bosom, and her heart
Would rock the snowy cradle till I died.

Why lingereth she to clothe her heart with love,
Delaying as the tender ash delays
To clothe herself, when all the woods are green?

O, tell her, Swallow, that thy brood is flown;
Say to her, I do but wanton in the South,
But in the North long since my nest is made.

O, tell her, brief is life but love is long,
And brief the sun of summer in the North,
And brief the moon of beauty in the South.

O Swallow, flying from the golden woods,
Fly to her, and pipe and woo her, and make her mine,
And tell her, tell her, that I follow thee.

(ii, 235)

The prince's song is a traditional lyric of wooing with numerous conventional features: the use of birds as messengers, a common feature of Provençal love poetry; the seasonal analogy – as the natural world clothes itself with greenery in spring, so the beloved is urged to see that it is natural for her to clothe herself with the speaker's love; the *carpe diem* motif ('brief is life'); the speaker's self-figuration as made weak and vulnerable by his dependence on his lady's favour – a child wanting the snowy cradle of her breast, a small bird that can only pipe, trill, cheep, and twitter; and the erotic intimations – lying on the beloved's bosom, the rustle of clothing.

The prince's 'voice [rings] false' in two senses. There is the situational dissimulation of a robust young man feigning a female register; and there is the dissimulation of the male lover feigning weakness and defencelessness to secure his sexual goal. Princess Ida is not fooled by either. She remarks on the grating harshness of the recitation – more like a marsh-diver or a meadow-crake than a nightingale – and she trashes the lyric itself, which she recognizes as an example of 'mock-love'. She knows who is taking in whom. For her, 'O Swallow, Swallow' is 'A mere love-poem!':

We hold them slight; they mind us of the time
When we made bricks in Egypt. Knaves are men,
That lute and flute fantastic tenderness,
And dress the victim to the offering up,
And paint the gates of Hell with Paradise,
And play the slave to gain the tyranny.

(ii, 236)

That is to say, Ida identifies the aim of the male love lyric as gaining control of the body and spirit of the female addressee – to cause her to be 'Pinned down/by love' as Adrienne Rich puts it in her critique of Thomas Campion's 'When to the lute Corinna sings' ('Snapshots of a Daughter-in-Law').

Three examples of a different kind of love lyric are subsequently given in *The Princess*. As was noted in the first chapter, each is based on a traditional kind of male love lyric. But in each poem the female point of view in the love relationship is expressed or intimated. The first is 'Ask me no more' which answers Thomas Carew's 'Song [Ask me no more]', one of the most popular and frequently imitated love lyrics of the seventeenth century. Carew's song is itself a *responsio* – a male reply to an implied series of *ubi sunt* questions by a female speaker concerning the transience of natural beauty. These presuppositions are converted by the male speaker into extravagant praise of the beloved's beauty. Her cheek, her hair, her voice, her eyes, and her bosom are respectively associated with roses, bits of sunlight, the nightingale's song, stars, and the spicy nest of the phoenix. In this way, the female's attempt to turn the mind to lasting things is converted by Carew's male speaker into a subtle love invitation – *respice finem* becomes *carpe diem*. And in the last stanza, dying is given an erotic suggestiveness. As the speaker of 'O Swallow, Swallow' longs to die on the beloved's bosom, so does Carew's phoenix: 'unto you at last shee flies,/And in your fragrant bosome dyes'.

Tennyson's poem rescores the ask-me-no-more topos for a female voice and shifts the 'conceptual ground from knowledge to feelings' (Hollander, 63):

> Ask me no more: the moon may draw the sea;
>   The cloud may stoop from heaven and take the shape
>   With fold to fold, of mountain or of cape;
> But O too fond, when have I answered thee?
>   Ask me no more.
>
> Ask me no more: what answer should I give?
>   I love not hollow cheek or faded eye:
>   Yet, O my friend, I will not have thee die!
> Ask me no more, lest I should bid thee live;
>   Ask me no more.
>
> Ask me no more: thy fate and mine are sealed;
>   I strove against the stream and all in vain;
>   Let the great river take me to the main:
> No more, dear love, for at a touch I yield;
>   Ask me no more.

(iii, 279)

In Carew's lyric, the repeated syntactical formula is an insistent rhetorical cadence articulating a single-minded argument. In Tennyson's poem, in which thought follows instead of guiding the current of emotion, it becomes a delicate refrain that means something different each time it is repeated.

The question at the beginning of the second stanza – 'what answer should I give?' – shows that the speaker understands perfectly well that the male is asking for sexual love. So do the images in the first stanza – the female cloud enfolding and fitting itself to the male projections of land, the female moon drawing the masculine sea. (They further suggest that the sexual attraction is mutual, and that she is both aware of it and not entirely averse to being beguiled.) There is a similar equivocation in the two meanings of 'I will not have thee die' – dying as the lover perishing for want of the lady's bestowal of her love, but also dying as sexual consummation. In the last stanza, the meaning of 'Ask me no more' is that there is no need to entreat me further. Words are no longer needed because at a mere touch I am yours. The female speaker's defencelessness is not the male dissimulation of weakness (the chirping swallow, the dying phoenix), but rather the weakness of a delicate vessel in a strong current being irresistibly drawn to the masculine sea, just as in the earlier, initiatory phase of the lovers' mutual attraction the female moon had drawn the sea.

It is significant that at the end of the poem the decisive sense is touch. According to Luce Irigaray,

> the predominance of the visual, and of the discrimination and individualization of form [in western culture], is particularly foreign to female eroticism. Woman takes pleasure more from touching than from looking, and her entry into a dominant scopic economy signifies ... her consignment to passivity: she is to be the beautiful object of contemplation.
>
> (25–6)

In Carew's song, the female was precisely that. But in Tennyson's lyric, which displays a thorough understanding of Irigaray's point, the woman is as much a subject of sexual love as a sexual object. The visual sense (the male sense *par excellence*) becomes recessive at the outset, when the cloud obscures the individual forms of mountain and cape; and her entry into mutual erotic pleasure is signalled by a touch.

This same displacement from sight to touch occurs in the two other lyrics, where it is also a registration of the female sensibility in love relationships. The first, 'Now sleeps the crimson petal', is an invitation-to-love poem modelled on the Persian ghazal, which accounts for the exotic décor and the distichs with a refrain phrase ending the second line. The invitation is conveyed not through argument or encomium (as in Carew's song) but indirectly through descriptions of the particulars of the couple's sensory environment:

> Now sleeps the crimson petal, now the white;
> Nor waves the cypress in the palace walk;
> Nor winks the gold fin in the porphyry font:
> The fire-fly wakens: waken thou with me.
>
> Now droops the milk-white peacock like a ghost,
> And like a ghost she glimmers on to me.
>
> Now lies the Earth all Danaë to the stars,
> And all thy heart lies open unto me.
>
> Now slides the silent meteor on, and leaves
> A shining furrow, as thy thoughts in me.
>
> Now folds the lily all her sweetness up,
> And slips into the bosom of the lake:
> So fold thyself, my dearest, thou, and slip
> Into my bosom and be lost in me.

(ii, 284–5)

The temporal moment – the fall of night – is all important. When a bright object is seen against a dark background, there is an increase in the temporal integrating time needed for the eye to take in the object, as when a photographer uses a longer exposure in dim light. The result is a slower developing but deeper, more lasting visual impression. The objects of perception lose their distinctiveness of colour, outline and mass ('like a ghost') and merge into a continuum of glowing white or yellow spots against a black background that in this poem stretches from the proximate fire-fly and peacock to the distant stars and meteor.

At the same time, the slowness plus the concentration of attention has an ataraxic (tranquillizing, relaxing) effect. Boundaries become fluid and opposites tend to merge – for example, motion and stasis. 'Nor' becomes infiltrated by 'Now' as the cypress that is explicitly said not to wave, and the gold fin which is said not to wink, irresistibly begin to move in the mind's eye. Other features of the poem have a similar effect. There is the epistrophic 'me' with which each stanza closes and the anaphoric 'Now' with which each begins. The two words slowly pulsate with the subliminal erotic invitation to merge: 'Now ... me', 'Now ... me', 'Now ... me'. And within the images themselves there is a delicious sexual suggestiveness: the maid Danaë lying open to Zeus, who appeared to her in the form of a shower of stars and ravished her; the lily folding herself and slipping into the bosom of the lake; and the luminous meteor furrowing the sky. In this last figure, three pairs of terms are stated or adumbrated, and a fourth implied – a meteor gliding through the sky, a plough making a furrow, thoughts of her entering his mind, and (implicitly) the physical merging of the male entering the female.

As Elaine Jordan noted, the poem's erotic suggestiveness is androgynous: 'The speaker of the poem is male, but both lovers change as he is furrowed by her thoughts and becomes the lake into which she slips. Genital pleasure, passivity and activity, penetration and infolding, are mixed and doubled' (107). But more than mutual sexual pleasure is intimated in this marvellous lyric. The images also figure the psychological process of sympathetic identification with the beloved as described by Arthur Hallam (1943) in his 1830 essay 'On Sympathy'. In the 'modification of self-love' that 'all love is, in one sense', the 'soul' (Hallam's female-gendered word for what we would call self) comes to imagine a being external to it 'as a separate part of self, a state of her own consciousness'. There follows the 'desire ... to break down all obstacles, and to amalgamate the two portions of her divided substance ... to blend emotions and desires with those apparent in the kindred spirit' (137–40).

In the final stanza of 'Now sleeps the crimson petal', passive images and constructions give way to a gentle imperative. This is subtly emphasized by the enjambment at the end of the penultimate line, which had been prepared for by the enjambment in the third distich – a reminder that nothing in this celebration of complementarities and interminglings is single. In this stanza, an explicit connection is made for the first time between natural and human (bosom of the lake/my bosom), and the hitherto dominant sense of sight is extinguished in the encompassing fluidity of the tactile.

There is a similar displacement in the famous onomatopoeic lines at the end of 'Come down, O maid' (ii, 287–8), the last of the trio of feminized love lyrics in *The Princess*: 'The moan of doves in immemorial elms,/And murmuring of innumerable bees.' The avian moans and apine murmurings are aural modes of the same non-specular fluidity in which the lovers in 'Now sleeps the crimson petal' are 'lost'. Elsewhere in this invitation to love, argument and gentle exhortation are used to encourage the merging of male and female characteristics. The male speaker is not a 'passionate shepherd' in the aggressive way that Christopher Marlowe's was. He is associated with a sheltered valley, with home, and with children:

And come, for Love is of the valley, come,
For Love is of the valley, come thou down
And find him ...
So waste not thou, but come; for all the vales
Await thee; azure pillars of the hearth

Arise to thee; the children call, and I
Thy shepherd pipe.

And while the female addressee is a idealized, heroic figure, she is
implicitly criticized for being such. Moreover, when 'Come down, O
Maid' is read in the context of *The Princess*, there is an overlay of the
female voice. Princess Ida recites the poem in a 'low-toned' manner as if
she were speaking to herself and admonishing the male side of her
nature to succumb to the feminine side and thereby allow herself to be
fulfilled:

> let the torrent dance thee down
> To find [Love] in the valley; let the wild
> Lean-headed Eagles yelp alone, and leave
> The monstrous ledges there to slope, and spill
> Their thousand wreaths of dangling water-smoke,
> That like a broken promise waste in air.
> So waste not thou.

In this way, the poem may be said to contain a critique of the traditional male love lyric. The female addressee is positioned above the
lover but not exalted and idealized as are Petrarch's Laura and Sidney's
Stella. She is entreated to come down from the heights to her lover – not
to private, esoteric delights but to a domestic landscape at the centre of
which is a hearth and children – tokens of the sweetest of all Victorian
ideals, the companionate marriage.

The terms of such a marriage are set out in the narrative parts of *The
Princess*, Tennyson's oblique attempt to write a major contemporary-life
poem about the woman question in mid-nineteenth-century Britain. The
desirability of companionate marriage is shown through the depiction of
the development in self-knowledge of Princess Ida. At the beginning of
the narrative, masculine qualities are dominant in her – for example, the
desire to perform heroic acts and an overcultivation of the intellectual
powers. Ida's feminine or emotional side is correspondingly undeveloped.
This is mainly registered through her insensitivity to lyric poems/songs
and their emotive subjects. Her idea of poetry is instrumental: it should
be used to further great ends, to prophesy change and to celebrate freedom, force, growth and triumph in battle. She not only trashes love
poems; she also dismisses one of Tennyson's greatest lyrics, 'Tears, idle
tears', which she describes as 'moans about the retrospect' (ii, 234).

Ida only begins to change when the emotions of sexual love are
kindled in her. Once this happens, it is not long before 'Her false self
slipt from her like a robe,/And left her woman' (ii, 284). This disrobing
is accompanied by a good deal of discursive comment; but the emotional change in Ida is more effectively conveyed indirectly through the
lyrics she reads to the wounded prince as she nurses him ('Now sleeps

the crimson petal' and 'Come down, O maid') and through the powerful closing trope used by the prince:

> Look up, and let thy nature strike on mine,
> Like yonder morning on the blind half-world;
> Approach and fear not; breathe upon my brows;
> In that fine air I tremble, all the past
> Melts mist-like into this bright hour, and this
> Is morn to more, and all the rich to-come
> Reels, as the golden Autumn woodland reels
> Athwart the smoke of burning weeds.

(ii, 292–3)

3

In *Maud*, published eight years after the first edition of *The Princess*,
sexual love is a much more problematic proposition. A. S. Byatt and
John Killham were not wrong in saying that its principal love lyrics
describe 'the same kind of rich sensuous, timeless awakening to love'
as do 'Now sleeps the crimson petal' and 'Come down, O maid'
(Byatt, 75). But the plot of *Maud* involves more social impediments
than simply the woman question, and shows that there are psychological determinants of love relationships that can hinder or render
impossible the merging and blending of male and female qualities that
are the defining feature of the sexual love celebrated in *The Princess*.

Maud is a lyrical sequence in which, Tennyson explained, 'successive
phases of passion in one person take the place of successive characters'.
The one person, the 'I' of the work, is a 'morbid, poetic soul' (*Poems*, ii,
518). The crucial event in his early life has been his father's probable
suicide owing to financial catastrophe. 'I hate the dreadful hollow
behind the little wood', *Maud* begins, 'Its lips in the field above are
dabbled with blood-red heath'. The hollow is the place on the family's
small estate where the distraught father had met his end. Since the death
of his mother, the speaker has lived alone in an empty house and

> a morbid hate and horror have grown
> Of a world in which I have hardly mixt,
> And a morbid eating lichen fixt
> On a heart half-turned to stone.

(I, vi)

His view of the human condition reflects his psychological state. He is
obsessed with indications of the moral corruption of Victorian society.
And his philosophical position is that 'We are puppets' and that 'nature
is one with rapine ... The Mayfly is torn by the swallow, the sparrow is
speared by the shrike,/And the whole little wood where I sit is a world

of plunder and prey'. The best course for a man is 'not to desire or admire' but to try to attain a state of 'passionless peace'. It is for this reason he fears most of all 'the cruel madness of love' (I, iv).

The elements of 'feminine grace and tenderness' that Patmore found in the lyrics of *Maud* are indications of the extent to which the speaker's harsh views and attitudes are affected by his unpeaceful passion for the title character. The abrasiveness of his first utterances gives way to softer inflections. In the work's second lyric, having seen her 'cold and clear-cut face' as her carriage passed, he tries to persuade himself that Maud has 'neither savour nor salt' to appeal to his rough palate and that he has been unaffected by her. But subsequent lyrics register his attraction to her. In I viii, for example, he describes the first significant moment of eye contact between the two:

> She came to the village church,
> And sat by a pillar alone;
> An angel watching an urn
> Wept over her, carved in stone;
> And once, but once, she lifted her eyes,
> And suddenly, sweetly, strangely blushed
> To find they were met by my own;
> And suddenly, sweetly my heart beat stronger
> And thicker ...

Here, the masculine thump of the speaker's circulatory organ shows that the sight of Maud no longer leaves him heart-free, while the feminine blush that brings colour and warmth to Maud's cheek also brings sweetness to the verses. Four lyrics later, the speaker is exhilarated to the point of sounding light-headed:

> Birds in the high Hall-garden
>   When twilight was falling,
> Maud, Maud, Maud, Maud,
>   They were crying and calling.
>
> (I, xii)

And not long after, his delight in the plainness of the dresses Maud wears to discourage a suitor approved by her brother makes this morbid young man sound insouciant to the point of effeminacy:

> Now I know her but in two,
> Nor can pronounce upon it
> If one should ask me whether
> The habit, hat, and feather,
> Or the frock and gypsy bonnet
> Be the neater and completer;
> For nothing can be sweeter
> Than maiden Maud in either.
>
> (I, xx)

ıstead of a merging of male and female qualities, however, these and other lyrics show a temporary displacement of the former by the latter. To be sure, the presence of both qualities is an indication that Tennyson is once again engaged in a modernization of the traditional male love lyric. But the revisionary emphasis does not fall on merging. The delicate lyrical vessels of *Maud* carry a different cargo. In I, xv, the speaker reflects that

> So dark a mind within me dwells,
>   And I make myself such evil cheer,
> That if *I* be dear to someone else,
>   Then someone else may have much to fear;
> But if *I* be dear to someone else,
>   Then I should be to myself more dear.

And in another lyric he breaks off Carlylean ruminations on the need for a hero to transform society to express what he has come to recognize as his own deepest need. It is for self-transformation – 'for a man to arise in me,/That the man I am may cease to be' (I, x). These passages identify the core of the psychological plot of *Maud*. In 'Faith Healing', Philip Larkin observed that

> In everyone there sleeps
> A sense of life lived according to love.
> To some it means the difference they could make
> By loving others, but across most it sweeps
> As all they might have done had they been loved.

The speaker belongs to the latter group. The subject of *Maud* is the impact of this new sense of life on an alienated and morbid being.

There is a longstanding belief, beginning with Plato's *Phaedrus*, that love is a form of madness or divine mania. But the madness of the speaker of *Maud* is not owing to tradition or convention. Its sources lie in his own pathology, in 'some dark undercurrent woe' (I, xviii) that includes aggressive and violent elements. The love lyrics of *Maud* are revisionary in that they are both refurbishments of traditional topoi and tropes *and* expressions of the speaker's disturbed psychological condition. (In different ways, Eric Griffiths and Warwick Slinn also make this point.) Consider the common lyric practice of expressing emotion through the description of external objects – for example, the figurations of Maud's feet, a part of her anatomy to which the speaker is particularly attracted. In I, v, a simple simile is used – her feet are 'like sunny gems on an English green'. In I, xviii, the implied simile is considerably crisper: 'Just now the dry-tongued laurels' pattering talk/Seemed her light foot along the garden walk.' And in I, xxii, the trope of hyperbole is used. A sound seems to come

From the meadow your walks have left so sweet
  That whenever a March-wind sighs
He sets the jewel-print of your feet
  In violets blue as your eyes.

Alan Sinfield reasonably remarked that the 'notion that the small flowers as they bow before the breeze are displaying a reminiscence of Maud's footprint is extravagant but the delightfully acute visual perception reassures us that the speaker is in touch with the actual world' (478). But one would hesitate to say the same of the last two lines of the following quatrain:

I know the way she went
  Home with her maiden posy,
For her feet have touched the meadows
  And left the daisies rosy.

(I, xii)

Ruskin glossed the lines as 'only a lover's fancy; – false and vain' – that is, as a version of what he termed the 'pathetic fallacy', which occurred when 'violent feelings ... produce in us a falseness in all our impressions of external things' (*Works*, xviii, 142; v, 205). Tennyson's own explanation was emphatic: 'Anyone with eyes could surely have known how a lady's dress, brushing across the daisies, tilts their heads and lets us see the rosy under-petals.' He was equally curt when he remarked that he had seen 'the daisies rosy in Maiden's Croft, and thought of enclosing one to Ruskin labelled "A pathetic fallacy"' (Page, 68; H. Tennyson, i, 511). The critic and the poet are each half right: like a number of other figures in *Maud*, this one is an unsettling mixture of acute sensory perception *and* subjective projection. As the speaker himself remarks in a reflexive passage (II, ii), vividly particularized perceptual notations are a sign of a heightened subjective state.

The speaker's hyperacuity of perception is one indication that the impact of love on him is more complex and problematic than Tennyson allowed when he spoke of him as being 'raised to a pure and holy love which elevates his whole nature' and acquiring 'the unselfishness born of a great passion' (*Poems*, ii, 517–18). It is true that Maud is only 16 and seems utterly unselfconscious. But this does not make her a Laura or Beatrice figure who inspires in the lover exalted spiritual feelings. In Tennyson's study of love in the mid-nineteenth century, it rather means that Maud is not an equivalent centre of self – that she is not a subject of love, but a love object. It is therefore not surprising to find that the speaker sometimes exhibits possessive and even triumphalist feelings. Part of his delight in Maud's simple frocks, for example, is owing to the fact that she is dressing down for him. And Herbert Tucker has detected 'fantasies of erotic dominion' in I, xvi, that are said to prompt images of 'global hegemony' in the world-wide sunset blush of the next lyric, 'Go not, happy day' (419).

It is also well to remember that the originating moment of the protagonist's attraction to Maud – 'the germinal spot that is to develop itself into love', as George Eliot called it (194) – contains 'the least little touch of spleen' and that *Maud* opens abruptly with a reference to death in a dreadful hollow. Not that one is likely to forget this, given the repeated reminders of the collocation of death and love. There are, for example, the funereal angel weeping over Maud as she sits in church; the early morning mist surrounding Maud's home that seems to the speaker a 'death-white curtain' and makes him think of 'the sleep of death' (I, xiv); and the 'shining daffodil dead' that the speaker finds in his garden when he walks there at night in the attempt to rid his consciousness of the image of Maud's face – 'Pale with the golden beam of an eyelash dead on the cheek … Luminous, gemlike, ghostlike, deathlike' (I, iii).

When the speaker finally works up the courage to declare his love, he finds that it is returned. The result is 'I have led her home' (I, xviii), Tennyson's great expectation-as-virtual-fulfilment lyric, in which the love–death opposition is resolved. On the one hand, the poem is aria-like in its sweeping gestures (to the stars above and the cedars that seem to be sighing for Lebanon) and in its rhetorical embellishment:

> There is none like her, none.
> And never yet so warmly ran my blood
> And sweetly, on and on
> Calming itself to the long-wished-for end,
> Full to the banks, close on the promised good.
>
> None like her, none.
> …
>
> There is none like her, none.
> …

On the other hand, it has the intellectual content of an ode. Thought follows very closely the current of emotion and expands as the speaker's feelings expand. Under the powerful stimulus of reciprocated love, he reformulates his sense of human existence and his position in the universe. In the past it had seemed 'better to be born to labour and the mattock-hardened hand' – that is, to live unselfconsciously and unreflectively had seemed preferable to the development of intellectual powers in an age in which they tended to undermine traditional beliefs in purpose and providence. But now he feels that the power of love has transformed his sense of existence – that 'one simple girl' has become the 'countercharm of space and hollow sky'.

The speaker recognizes two ways in which the dusky strand of death is inwoven with his love: through his internal morbidity that makes a night's sleep seem a living death; and through his scientifically fostered sense of cosmic nothingness. But in his ecstatic mood, the sense of death as annihilation is balanced by the recognition that death does not negate love but rather makes it more precious:

> O, why should Love, like men in drinking-songs,
> Spice his fair banquet with the dust of death?
> Make answer, Maud my bliss,
> Maud made my Maud by that long loving kiss,
> Life of my life, wilt thou not answer this?
> 'The dusky strand of Death inwoven here
> With dear Love's tie, makes Love himself more dear.'

This recognition is an extraordinary moment in Tennyson's canon. A number of his other poems present an idealized view of human love as dependent upon immortality – In Memoriam, xxxiv, for example, in which it is insisted that without eternal life there can be no human love, only degrees of lust. But here, the premise is humanistic rather than theistic. Love becomes all the more precious in the predicate that there is nothing else that can provide a counterweight to the inevitability of personal extinction.

At the same time, as the lyric progresses it becomes apparent that the speaker cannot fully believe in his own good fortune. 'It seems that I am happy', he reflects, thus manifesting a degree of self-consciousness that inevitably qualifies that happiness. He may have 'have climbed nearer out of lonely Hell', but the end of the lyric makes it clear that he is not all the way out. He does retain the sense that the 'happy stars' are beating in time 'with things below' and that the swell of the sea is an 'enchanted moan' echoing and amplifying his own condition. But he is also aware of a different synergy – of

> some dark undercurrent woe
> That seems to draw – but it shall not be so;
> Let all be well, be well.

The climactic lyric in Maud is also the best known: 'Come into the Garden, Maud' (I, xxii). Her brother is giving a ball for the county gentry to which the speaker is not invited; indeed, the brother has forbidden Maud to have anything to do with him. But the lovers have arranged that he will wait in her garden and that when the guests have left she will 'Come out to your own true lover' so that he can see 'his own darling,/Queen Maud in all her splendour' (I, xx). When the lyric opens, he has already been waiting impatiently for some time and dawn is breaking:

> Come into the garden, Maud,
>   For the black bat, night, has flown,
> Come into the garden, Maud,
>   I am here at the gate alone;
> And the woodbine spices are wafted abroad,
>   And the musk of the rose is blown.

The beloved is not in hearing distance of this agitated, anapestic aubade. That her flowers act as her surrogate and are directly addressed suggests the influence of Persian love poetry, to which 'Now sleeps the crimson petal' was also indebted. But the oriental setting of that poem is replaced by an English garden, and its quietly assured tone by the speaker's exacerbated longing, the metrical expression of which is influenced by the rhythms of the dance music (polkas and walzes) being played inside the Hall. Maud dances there with her peers while the red and white flowers in her garden move in rhythm with the speaker's giddy anticipation of her arrival. During the night that is now ending,

> The slender acacia would not shake
>   One long milk-bloom on the tree;
> The white lake-blossom fell into the lake
>   As the pimpernel dozed on the lea;
> But the rose was awake all night for your sake,
>   Knowing your promise to me;
> The lilies and roses were all awake,
>   They sighed for the dawn and thee.

An earlier lyric had also been set in Maud's garden at dawn. In I, xiv, the speaker had come to stare at her bedroom window. At that time he heard 'the riverlet ... Running down to my own dark wood'. When he hears the same sound in I, xxii, the stream is said to run 'From the lake to the meadow and on to the wood,/Our wood, that is dearer than all'. The pronominal change is telling. The wood with the dreadful hollow behind it had earlier symbolized the speaker's morbidity. That it has become 'Our wood', a precious rather than a minatory place, signals the transformation that love has wrought in him. Another significant difference between the two dawn poems is that while 'the dim-gray dawn' of the earlier poem had made the speaker think of 'the sleep of death', the splendid midsummer dawn of xxii is eroticized. It makes him anticipate the 'long-wished-for end', the consummation of love, which is figured as swooning celestial extinction:

> For a breeze of morning moves,
>   And the planet of Love is on high,
> Beginning to faint in the light that she loves
>   On a bed of daffodil sky,
> To faint in the light of the sun she loves,
>   To faint in his light, and to die.

Tennyson said that 'Come into the garden, Maud' had, '& was intended to have, a taint of madness' (*Poems*, ii, 562n). The acute registrations of what the speaker sees and hears (the 'tear' falling from the passion-flower; the wheels of the departing carriages sounding 'Low on the sand and loud on the stone') are perhaps free of this taint. But not his equally acute registrations of what he does not in fact see and hear (Maud coming to him 'In gloss of satin and glimmer of pearls'; hearing words spoken by the roses, lilies and larkspur). And when his dizzying pitch of expectation culminates in the final stanza, it is with an image of death very different in implication from the earlier dawn *Liebestod*:

> She is coming, my own, my sweet;
> > Were it ever so airy a tread,
> My heart would hear her and beat,
> > Were it earth in an earthy bed;
> My dust would hear her and beat,
> > Had I lain for a century dead;
> Would start and tremble under her feet,
> > And blossom in purple and red.

This unwholesome exaltation marks the reappearance of the speaker's dark undercurrent woe. Like the recurrence of the desire to possess Maud earlier in the lyric ('"But mine, but mine," so I sware to the rose,/ "For ever and ever, mine"'), the speaker's imagined abasement in this stanza, which contains the last and most disturbing reference to the touch of her foot, foregrounds the psychological determinants of his existence. It also intimates that all will not be well when Maud finally comes into the the garden.

The turning point in the outer plot of *Maud* occurs in the white space after I, xxii, and is summarized in the next lyric (the first of the poem's second part). Maud comes but is followed by her enraged brother, who strikes the speaker, thus precipitating a duel. The brother is wounded, perhaps fatally, and the speaker forced to flee the country. The remainder of *Maud*, as Patricia Ball says, 'is really the aftermath of a poem whose theme is the way such a crisis came about' (144). The next lyric finds the speaker brooding in Brittany; the one after that reports the death of Maud. 'O that 'twere possible' (II, iv) finds the speaker in London among 'Hearts with no love for me'; and in the last poem of the second part he has become deranged and speaks from an asylum in which he is confined.

The single poem that comprises the final section of *Maud* balances the sequence's opening poem in having the condition of Britain as a principal subject. Early in the work (I, v), Maud had been overheard singing 'A martial song like a trumpet's call! ... Singing of Death, and of

Honour that cannot die,/Till I well could weep for a time so sordid and mean'. She now appears in a dream to the speaker, who is no longer institutionalized, and speaks to him 'of a hope for the world in the coming wars' – that is, in what came to be called the Crimean War. This dream inspires and reinvigorates the speaker, who persuades himself that the war effort will give his countrymen an other-regarding social purpose. It will offer the opportunity for 'the heart of a people [to] beat with one desire' – and for the speaker's stony heart to beat in time with it. In the poem's final lines, he affirms that

> It is better to fight for the good than to rail at the ill;
> I have felt with my native land, I am one with my kind,
> I embrace the purpose of God, and the doom assigned.

Tennyson's retrospective comment on the close of *Maud* was that the speaker has 'passed through the fiery furnace, and has recovered his reason, giving himself up to work for the good of mankind through the unselfishness born of a great passion' (*Poems*, ii, 517–18). This is surely tendentious. As numerous commentators have argued, the ending is much more equivocal than Tennyson allows and, as such, much more in key with all that has gone before in the work. For example, the ending shows that the speaker's violent, aggressive tendencies have survived his ordeal intact.

Most importantly, the conclusion of Tennyson's study of the effect of love on a morbid young man shows that the speaker has lost the sense of life lived according to love. He had once had this sense and had even felt the beginnings of its transforming power. But there is no suggestion in the poem that the transformation would have been completed had it not been for external circumstances. For Hallam, as we have seen, the sympathetic blending of lover and beloved presupposes on the former's part 'self-love' in a non-pejorative sense. The protagonist of *Maud* is lacking in this essential quality. As a result, the emotional movement recorded in the first part of the poem is less the flow of sympathetic desire seeking to amalgamate and blend than an oscillation between the desire to possess (to appropriate the other to his own self) and the desire for self-abasement. The latter is the psychological explanation of the speaker's preoccupation with Maud's feet, which he was moved to 'fall before ... and adore' in I, v and later imagined himself trembling under even after having lain for a century dead.

But the protagonist of *Maud* had at least known what he was missing. In one of his plainest and simplest lyrics, the one with the most feminine tenderness, he had identified and given memorably pathetic expression to the deepest need of his conflicted being:

O, let the solid ground
  Not fail beneath my feet
Before my life has found
  What some have found so sweet.
Then let come what come may,
What matter if I go mad,
I shall have had my day.

Let the sweet heavens endure,
  Not close and darken above me
Before I am quite quite sure
  That there is one to love me;
Then let come what come may
To a life that has been so sad,
I shall have had my day.

                                                   (I, xi)

CHAPTER FOUR

Unkissed Lips: Women and Love

How unhealthy it is to depend as I do so much on my own
thoughts and moods and feelings for employment, for excitement
... Shall I confess that I have nothing to do? It is disgraceful, I
know, but really what is there to occupy me, but going out, and
practising. I must try to cultivate that rhyming faculty which I used
to have, if it is not quite gone from me. But whatever I write will be
melancholy and self-conscious, as are all women's poems.

Alice Meynell, *aet.* 18

1

In book v of Elizabeth Barrett Browning's *Aurora Leigh*, the title character sits alone pondering the emotional costs of poetic vocation for a
woman:

How dreary 'tis for women to sit still
On winter nights by solitary fires
And hear the nations praising them far off,
Too far! ay, praising our quick sense of love,
Our very heart of passionate womanhood,
Which would not beat so in the verse without
Being present also in the unkissed lips
And eyes undried because there's none to ask
The reason they grew moist.
...
          To have our books
Appraised by love, associated with love,
While *we* sit loveless!

(440–76)

The passage has great resonance: some of its lines were used by Elizabeth Gaskell as the epigraph to her life of Charlotte Brontë; and poems
by a number of Victorian women poets centre on the antithetical relationship between being a poet and being loved.

Felicia Hemans's 'Woman and Fame' is an example (Leighton and
Reynolds, 7). Each of its first three stanzas develops a figure for fame in
the first four lines and contrasts it with a figure for the emotional needs
of women in a closing couplet: a potent draught in a charmed cup
versus sweet waters from 'affection's spring'; a wreath of laurel leaves
versus flowers 'from some kind hand'; trumpet notes versus 'words of

home-born love'. In each case, the former images are rejected in favour of the satisfaction of emotional needs. The last two stanzas of the poem, however, show that the rejection is notional rather than real, and that the subject of 'Woman and Fame' is a quarrel within the poet that she seems powerless to resolve. The 'sick heart' longs 'For aid, for sympathy – /For kindly looks to cheer it on,/For tender accents'. These fame cannot supply. Where then must 'the lone one turn or flee?' the speaker asks in the poem's closing lines. There is no positive answer; the pursuit of fame would seem to have left her with no emotionally satisfying alternative.

One reason for the opposition of love and fame for the women poets of the period is suggested by an observation in Mill's *Subjection of Women*. The higher degrees of artistic and intellectual occupations, Mill remarked, necessitate a degree of proficiency that presupposes 'long and patient drudgery, which, in the case even of the greatest natural gifts, is absolutely required for great eminence'. Whether the cause was 'natural or artificial [Mill thought the latter], women seldom have this eagerness for fame. Their ambition is generally confined within narrower bounds. The influence they seek is over those who immediately surround them. Their desire is to be liked, loved, or admired, by those whom they see with their eyes' (376). But when women did have both the desire for love and the impulse to creative fulfilment, a spur if not a precondition of which is the desire for fame, the result could be painful self-division and conflicted emotions, a condition that would find expression but not resolution in their poems.

This construal of the situation of the female love poets of the period is buttressed by Letitia Elizabeth Landon's monody, 'Stanzas on the Death of Mrs. Hemans'. After an opening celebration of its subject's poetic achievement, the sixth stanza begins: 'And yet thy song is sorrowful' – so much so that the monodist goes on to wonder whether her subject did not 'tremble at thy fame,/And loathe its bitter prize':

> Ah! dearly purchased is the gift,
>   The gift of song like thine;
> A fatal doom is hers who stands
>   The priestess of the shrine.
> ...
> Wound to a pitch too exquisite,
>   The soul's fine chords are wrung;
> With misery and melody
>   They are too highly strung.
> The heart is made too sensitive
> Life's daily pain to bear;
> It beats in music, but it beats
>   Beneath a deep despair.

It never meets the love it paints,
  The love for which it pines;
...
The meteor-wreath the poet wears
  Must make a lonely lot;
It dazzles, only to divide
  From those who wear it not.

                                    (Leighton and Reynolds, 44)

These stanzas, however, also suggest a different, non-gender-specific contextualization of its subject's suffering. They are typical of numerous nineteenth-century descriptions of the Romantic poet as a rhapsodist possessing an exquisite but isolating gift that allows him/her to feel more deeply than others and to envision ideal states, while at the same time causing both frustration and suffering because of the gap between vision and reality, desire and fulfilment. 'Our sweetest songs', said Shelley in 'To a Skylark', 'are those that tell of saddest thought'; Apollo, the god of poetry, said Swinburne in 'Hymn to Proserpine', is both 'A bitter god to follow [and] a beautiful god to behold'.

It is the self-pity of unrequited romantic love in Landon's monody, rather than the isolation of the lovelorn woman poet *per se*, that Barrett Browning criticizes in *her* monody on Landon, 'L.E.L.'s Last Question'. The question, asked in a letter written shortly before Landon's death, is given as the poem's epigraph: 'Do you think of me as I of you?' 'Love-learnèd', as Barrett Browning describes her, Landon 'had sung of love and love' until for her 'All sounds of life assumed one tune of love'. She was one of 'the Loving' who do little more than sit and 'listen for/The echo of their own love evermore'. Barrett Browning criticizes this ego-centric, debilitating love-longing by posing questions of her own:

           what are we that we should
      For covenants of long affection sue?
      Why press so near each other when the touch
      Is barred by graves?

Of the alternatives posed in Hemans's 'Woman and Fame', Landon had chosen human love. But in death the distinction is obliterated: 'None smile and none are crowned where lieth she.' For Barrett Browning, one's hopes should therefore centre not on earthly things, but on Christ ('He who drew/All life from dust, and for all tasted death') and His promise of life everlasting.

Published in 1844, 'L.E.L.'s Last Question' ends on the edge of the grave with Christian belief the only solace and support for the female poet. This is precisely the point at which Barrett Browning's *Sonnets from the Portuguese* begins. The work is a sequence of 44 sonnets, the subject of which is the germination and growth of love between herself,

then in her late thirties, and Robert Browning, six years her junior, with
whom she began an intense correspondence in January 1845 and married in September 1846. As 'L.E.L.'s Last Question' was an explicit
rebuke to the Hemans–Landon tradition of the lovelorn female poet,
Barrett Browning's sonnet sequence is an implicit rebuttal in that it tells
the story of how a female poet, unloved and resigned to her condition,
found love and happiness. The speaker at first thinks that she and her
younger, more vigorous suitor cannot be lovers because 'We are not
peers' – 'Unlike our uses and our destinies' (sonnets 9, 3). He radiates
life; she has a 'great heap of grief' hidden in her and 'frequent tears have
run/The colours from my life' (sonnets 5, 8). He is called to sing high
poems on 'some palace-floor'; her house has a broken casement and
bats and owlets living in the roof (sonnet 4). In short, 'O Belovèd, it is
plain/I am not of thy worth nor for thy place!' (sonnet 11).

She consequently attempts renunciation – but is unsuccessful. The
key realization is that 'love is fire' and is precious no matter what the
fuel. She 'stands transfigured, glorified aright' by the fire emanating
from her (sonnet 10). The turning point occurs when she accepts his
love: 'Here ends my strife. If *thou* invite me forth,/I rise above abasement at the word' (sonnet 16). After this, nothing much happens in the
remaining 28 sonnets of the sequence. Some poems record stages in the
lovers' growing intimacy – their letters, their first kiss, the exchange of
locks of hair, the granting of permission to use a pet name; and a
number of others offer additional figurations of the poet's recall to life
and love.

Some of these refigurations are implicitly reflexive. When the beloved
came into her life, for example, the poet thought herself 'like an out-of-
tune/Worn viol' that a good singer would be foolish to employ. She had
forgotten that 'perfect strains may float/'Neath master-hands, from in-
struments defaced' (sonnet 32). In a another sonnet, she longs

> to shoot
> My soul's full meaning into future years,
> That *they* should lend it utterance, and salute
> Love that endures, from Life that disappears!
>
> (Sonnet 41)

Passages like these make the writing of love sonnets one of the subjects
of the sequence and invite reflection on the kind of 'music' Barrett
Browning made – on her choice of verbal equivalents for the 'new
rhythm' into which her life was caught up by her love (sonnet 7) and on
her other presentational decisions.

One choice was *not* to write 'a novelistic poem of modern life', a
poem immersed 'in Victorian life', as Dorothy Mermin (1989) inexpli-
cably described the sequence (129–30). *Sonnets from the Portuguese*

has a society of two and its parameters are the walls of Barrett Browning's bedroom in her father's house on Wimpole Street. Indeed, it is the absence of Victorian life in the sequence that makes possible the spurious provenance of the sonnets being 'from the Portuguese'.

The key compositional choice was the one Barrett Browning usually made. It was the 'almost constant endeavour to be "striking"' that Patmore (1857) identified as her 'worst fault' as a poet (446). In *Sonnets from the Portuguese*, this effort has unfortunate results. One is the abundance of apostrophe, imperative address, declamation and other sweeping rhetorical gestures that are all the more noticeable in the absence of incident or dramatic tension. For Joan Rees, the effect is 'of somebody declaiming aloud and gesticulating melodramatically all by herself in a small retired room where, to our embarrassment, we have strayed' (151). Another result is the liberal use of recherché literary materials. In addition to the 'accumulation of medieval and Mediterranean stage properties, cypress trees, mandolins, minstrels, torches and so on' (149), there are the classical allusions. In the first sonnet Barrett Browning reminds the reader that she could read classical Greek (an unusual accomplishment for a Victorian woman) and alludes to both the resurrection of Adonis in Theocritus' fifteenth idyll and Athene saving the life of Agamemnon in the first book of the *Iliad*. The fifth sonnet alludes to Sophocles' Electra and the fortieth to the story of Polyphemus and Galatea in another Theocritian idyll. The smell of the lamp is even stronger in the nineteenth sonnet, which describes the colour of a lock of hair to be 'As purply black, as erst to Pindar's eyes/ The dim purpureal tresses gloomed athwart/The nine white Muse-brows'.

The most unfortunate presentational feature of the sequence is the indiscriminate figural embellishment that is occasionally crisp but more often soggy. Sonnet 11, for example, painfully conflates literal and figurative in speaking of 'trembling knees that fail/To bear the burden of a heavy heart'. A similar conflation mars sonnet 29, which contains the interesting psychological notation that the poet's constant thoughts of the beloved are so absorbing that they tend to come between her and him. *Per se*, the figuration chosen for this insight – 'wild vines' about a tree which eventually obscure it from sight – is unremarkable but serviceable. But Barrett Browning does not know when to stop: the beloved is addressed as 'O my palm-tree' and asked to 'instantly/Renew thy presence' by rustling his 'boughs' (which palm trees do not have) and setting his trunk free by causing the vines to 'Drop heavily down, – burst, shattered, everywhere!' In other sonnets the sogginess is the result of ramshackle prolixity of figuration. In sonnet 24, for example, we go from the 'world's sharpness' shutting in upon itself 'like a clasping knife', to the speaker leaning on the beloved and feeling 'as safe as guarded by a charm/Against the stab of worldlings, who if rife/Are weak to injure', and finally to 'the lilies of our lives' that 'Very whitely still ... may reassure'

> Their blossoms from their roots, accessible
> Alone to heavenly dews that drop not fewer,
> Growing straight, out of man's reach, on the hill.

The method of cornucopic allusion and figuration works much better in Barrett Browning's love letters to her future husband, where it facilitates the free play of her intelligence, and in her farraginous verse novel *Aurora Leigh*, a self-confident bravura performance that unscrupulously mixes genres, subjects and themes, and holds them all suspended in a fluency of discourse that makes use of what Hippolyte Taine, an early admirer of the poem, described as 'a system of notation ... created from instant to instant, out of anything and everything' (270). But in the enclosed space of a sonnet, and the comparatively brief compass of a seqeunce of 44 sonnets, this method makes for unsubtle, unrhythmic and pretentious effects.

To speak bluntly, in *Sonnets from the Portuguese* Barrett Browning was unable to make reciprocated sexual love *poetically* interesting – not even in the case of sonnet 43 ('How do I love thee? Let me count the ways'), the most widely known of all Victorian love poems. But while the aesthetic estimate of the work must be equivocal, the historical estimate is not in doubt. The sequence is a milestone in the love poetry of Victorian women in that it celebrates fulfilled sexual love – it is poetry from kissed rather than unkissed lips. And it does so through an energetic adaptation of the conventions of the male amatory sonnet sequence. Indeed, the main interest of Barrett Browning's love poems does not lie in the poems themselves. Glennis Stephenson, author of the one extended study of her love poems, is perfectly correct: their 'main interest ... lies in the ways in which they are influenced by, and concerned with, the social, cultural, and poetic conventions regarding women and love' (3).

2

On more than one poetic occasion, Christina Rossetti found it necessary to distance herself from the opinions and practice of Barrett Browning. One example is *her* poem on Landon, 'L.E.L.', which implicitly takes issue with the censure of the poet in 'L.E.L.'s Last Question'. The epigraph to Rossetti's poem ('Whose heart was breaking for a little love') alludes to the earlier poem's designation of Landon as 'One

thirsty for a little love'. And in the body of her poem Rossetti sympathetically evokes the love-hungry poet by speaking for her in tones of
heartbreaking pathos:

> Downstairs I laugh, I sport and jest with all:
>   But in my solitary room above
> I turn my face in silence to the wall;
>   My heart is breaking for a little love.
>   Tho' winter frosts are done,
>   And birds pair every one,
> And leaves peep out, for springtime is begun.

In both Barrett Browning's and Rossetti's poems, the only consolation for the terminally lovelorn poet is to trust in the Christian promise
of an afterlife. The former ends with a Protestant patriarchal 'He'
speaking from above 'the unshaken stars', while the latter poem gives
the final word to an Anglo-Catholic angel, who counsels patience and
speaks of eternal reward as a second spring. But unlike Barrett Browning's conclusion, Rossetti's seems pat and unearned. It might be said to
be effective aesthetically in that the spring imagery in the body of the
poem is repeated in a different key at the end. But on the conceptual
level, the consolation that flowers at the close does not have its roots
earlier in the poem. The problem of how a woman poet is to live
without love is finessed, not transcended.

In a note on the poem in his edition of his sister's poetical works,
William Michael Rossetti declared that 'L.E.L.' was obviously a personal poem. Just as in the poem the 'I' hides her real feelings when she
is downstairs, when the publishing stage came his sister is said to have
preferred 'to retire behind a cloud and so renamed the poem' (482–3). It
is true that the same sentiments found in 'L.E.L.' are also found in
numerous other poems in which Rossetti appears to be speaking *in
propria persona* – for example in 'The Heart knoweth its own bitterness': 'Weep, sick and lonely,/Bow thy heart to tears,/For none shall
guess the secret/Of thy griefs and fears.' But how could her brother be
so sure that 'L.E.L.' refers to herself and not to its title character? There
are, after all, a number of early poems of sorrowful love by Rossetti
that predate her first love experience with James Collinson – for example, 'Sappho' ('I sigh at sun-down'), written when she was only 16, and
the masterly 'Song [When I am dead my dearest]' written two years
later.

In any event, why need it be a case of either/or? It would seem an
essential aspect of Rossetti's practice as a poet to be both specific and
generic, personal and conventional – that is, to both reveal and conceal
herself. This strategy is both the subject of and is enacted in the delight-
ful 'Winter: My Secret', in which the hide-and-seek of an adolescent

stage of love experience is nicely caught – the stage when, as Robert Frost put in 'Revelation', 'We make ourselves a place apart,/Behind light words that tease and flout'. Rossetti's poem is addressed to a 'you' who may be taken to be both the would-be lover and the reader or critic desirous of getting behind the poet's 'mask'. For both, the revelation of 'my secret' would presumably imply her reciprocation of the love of her auditor.

Requited love, however, is precisely what one does not find in Rossetti's poetry. What one does find over and over again is the same self-consciously dolorous note: 'my tedious Grief' (ii, 109); 'It's a weary life' (iii, 231); 'A burden saddens every song' (i, 213); 'So tired am I, so weary of today,/So unrefreshed from foregone weariness,/So overburdened by foreseen distress' (ii, 139–40); 'I have no wit, no words, no tears;/My heart within me like a stone/Is numbed' (i, 68); 'Stripped bare of hope and everything … I sit alone with sorrow' (i, 209). Even Rossetti's well-known lyric, 'A Birthday', which is unusual in celebrating gain rather than loss, does so in a languorous, almost febrile way.

'Why should I seek and never find/That something which I have not had?' Rossetti asks in 'An "Immurata" Sister'. In one extraordinary poem, the sharply observed sonnet, 'A Triad', she adumbrated a socio-cultural explanation of her condition: that for the Victorian woman fulfilment through sexual love is available only inauthentically through the spirit-stifling institution of marriage:

> Three sang of love together: one with lips
> Crimson, with cheeks and bosom in a glow,
> Flushed to the yellow hair and finger tips;
> And one there sang who soft and smooth as snow
> Bloomed like a tinted hyacinth at a show;
> And one was blue with famine after love,
> Who like a harpstring snapped rang harsh and low
> The burden of what those were singing of.
> One shamed herself in love; one temperately
> Grew gross in soulless love, a sluggish wife;
> One famished died for love. Thus two of three
> Took death for love and won him after strife;
> One droned in sweetness like a fattened bee:
> All on the threshhold, yet all short of life.

The two who win death after strife are unmistakably the fallen woman (who 'shamed herself in love') and the lovesick woman poet (the snapped harpstring recalls Landon's figure of the fine chords of Hemans's soul being 'too highly strung'). The sluggish wife is a specimen of the Victorian type described by Patmore in his essay on 'The Social Position of Women'. Such women were brought up to regard securing a husband as the great goal of their existence: 'As a rule, [their] youth is spent in acquiring mere show-knowledge, and [their] life after marriage ... in vacant and aimless inactivity ... frivolity or insipid indolence' (532).

A number of other answers to the question posed in 'An "Immurata" Sister' have been biographical conjectures that lead one away from Rossetti's poems. A third kind of explanation, suggested by Angela Leighton, has the advantage of returning attention to the poems, the distinction of which is, after all, the principal reason that one cares to learn whatever can be known about the life-experience that informs them. Leighton notes that the 'winter secrets of [Rossetti's] life are not explained by [her] poetry, but they are uncannily repeated and echoed in it, till what looks like personal tragedy begins to appear as a highly worked invention and device' (163).

Monna Innominata, a sequence of 14 sonnets, is Rossetti's most highly worked love poem and exhibits at greater than normal length her remarkable fluency and her mastery of traditional forms – in this case the Petrarchan love sonnet. In the sequence one finds once again the mixture of revelation and concealment, of the specific and the generic. On the one hand, there is her brother William's editorial note: 'To any one to whom it was granted to be behind the scenes of Christina Rossetti's life ... it is not merely probable but certain that this "sonnet of sonnets" was a personal utterance – an intensely personal one' (462). On the other hand, there is the author's headnote, which explains that the work is the result of her imagining how a woman living in the time of the Troubadours or Petrarch and 'sharing her lover's poetic aptitude' might have written if she had recorded in verse her side of a courtly love relationship in which 'the barrier between them might be one held sacred by both, yet not such as to render mutual love incompatible with mutual honour'.

Monna Innominata is not only presented as supplementing the male line of amatory sonnets stemming from Petrarch and Dante (from whom the two epigraphs to each of its sonnets are drawn). As the closing sentences of the headnote indicate, Rossetti also envisions her sequence as a supplement to, and correction of, the practice of a contemporary writer of love sonnets. Had 'the Great Poetess of our own day and nation only been unhappy instead of happy', Rossetti suggests that 'her circumstances [might] have invited her to bequeath to us, in lieu of the "Portuguese Sonnets", an inimitable "donna innominata" drawn not from fancy but from feeling, and worthy to occupy a niche beside Beatrice and Laura'. In relation to Barrett Browning's sequence, then, *Monna Innominata* is intended as a demonstration of the potential of unfulfilled female love as the subject of a sonnet sequence. It may also be considerd an exemplification of how to observe poetic decorum and write a proper Italian sonnet as opposed to a 14-line pot-pourri.

A major compositional decision was where to begin the sequence. Rossetti chooses not to follow the poetic convention of love at first sight. She begins the sequence at a much later point in the love relationship, when the bloom is already off the rose. Indeed, in the second sonnet, the speaker admits that she cannot even remember when she and the beloved first met. She was so languorous, 'So dull to mark the budding of my tree', that even the moment of first physical contact, the touch of hand to hand, is unremembered. Nor is the reader given even a reprise of the intensities of early love or of any of the 'songs I sang/ When life was sweet because you called them sweet' (sonnet 1). Nor is there any account of the psychological dynamics of the developing relationship, like those detailed in the opening movement of *Sonnets from the Portuguese*.

Rossetti's first sonnet opens on a distinctly downbeat note: 'Come back to me, who wait and watch for you.' The beloved's visits have become infrequent. Since 'my world is you', the interstices between visits are filled with a longing that is more and more contaminated by a prospective pang at the brevity of the anticipated visit. But the female poet can do little creatively with this situation: 'We meet so seldom, yet we surely part/So often; there's a problem for your art!' (sonnet 7) – meaning his male poetic art. Her art is the attenuated music of regret – the antiphonal voice of her dovelike 'friendly cooings' from earlier in their relationship that were drowned out by his 'loftier song' (sonnet 4).

The encapsulation in the seventh sonnet of the subject of the first is one of a number of echoes, repetitions and gainsayings in the sequence. As with a musical composition, these repetitions with variations give aesthetic pleasure. They also supply a sense of structure and movement to the sequence, which helps disguise or compensate for the fact that virtually nothing happens over the course of the 14 sonnets other than a gradual intensification of regret, loneliness and unhappiness. The sequence might seem to describe a process, but it is in essence as static as 'L.E.L.'. There is only the simulacra of movement and change. For example, in the ninth sonnet, the volta in this sonnet of sonnets, the speaker is 'Thinking of you, and all that was, and all/That might have been and now can never be'. The last phrase suggests that something has happened, some crucial change in the relationship has occurred. But it occurs in the white space; it is not registered in the sequence either summarily or in a change of tone or emotional level. It is simply the *en passant* registration that what had been in principle temporary has become permanent; that the virtual has become the actual.

What future is there for the 'moon' (sonnet 1) when there is no longer a sun or for 'the helpmeet made for man' (sonnet 5) when there is no man? At the end of the tenth sonnet, there is the promise of heavenly rebirth (as

at the end of 'L.E.L.'): 'A little while, and life reborn annuls/Loss and
decay and death, and all is love.' But the cold comfort of this is pointed
up in the following sonnet: 'parting hopeless here to meet again,/Hopeless
on earth, and heaven is out of view'. In the twelfth sonnet, there is the
high-minded, self-effacing comfort of recommending to the absent beloved that someone of 'nobler grace' and 'sweeter face' take her place.
Since his pleasure is hers and his right is her right, his freedom, so she
says, makes her free: 'And you companioned I am not alone.'

But this is undercut in the penultimate sonnet, which recognizes that
it is in God and not herself that he must trust. This leaves the helpmate
'Helpless to help and impotent to do' – that is, denied even the assuage-
ments of vicariously other-regarding action. In the final sonnet, the
desolation is now total and unrelieved. The formal sign of this is that
there is no volta between octave and sestet – there being no place left to
turn. The speaker has gone beyond the wishful thinking of the end of
'L.E.L.' And she can no longer 'sing' – that is, find solace in the creative
activity of mind. The sequence ends with her in a terminally desolate,
irremissive and silent state of being:

> Youth gone and beauty gone, what doth remain?
>   The longing of a heart pent up forlorn,
>   A silent heart whose silence loves and longs;
>   The silence of a heart which sang its songs
>   While youth and beauty made a summer morn,
> Silence of love that cannot sing again.

Technically, Rossetti does not put a foot wrong in *Monna Innominata*.
But compositional and performative polish do not of themselves make
the work deeply engaging. Rossetti's sequence is different in degree
from her other love poetry; but it is not different in kind. It is another
example of her 'poetry of ennui' (Blake, 14) not only in its content but
also in its cumulative effect on the reader. In *Sonnets from the Portuguese*, Barrett Browning was imperfectly successful in making lyric
poetry out of requited love. In her amatory sequence Rossetti's success
in treating the subject of unhappy love is equally equivocal.

A highly self-conscious poet, Rossetti was herself aware of the limitations that her temperament imposed on her achievement as a love poet.
She may even be said to have provided a model of the reader's response
in 'Reflection', which invites being read as a poem about reading her
love poetry. Its male speaker is observing his beloved, whose invariable
posture is gazing through her chamber window: there 'she sits and
never answers … Who can guess or read her will?'

> Is it love she looks and longs for;
>   Is it rest or peace;
> Is it slumber self-forgetful

>In its utter ease;
>Is it one or all of these?
>...
>Is it day dream of a maiden,
>   Vision of a bride,
>Is it knowledge, love, or pride?

But the speaker eventually tires of his vigilant observation and loses interest:

>Now if I could guess her secret
>   Were it worth the guess? –
>Time is lessening, hope is lessening,
>   Love grows less and less:
>What care I for *no* or *yes*? –

3

The coextensiveness of the love poetry of Emily Dickinson with Victorian female love poetry is strikingly instanced in the similarities between her and her coeval, Christina Rossetti. For one thing, as Cora Kaplan has noted, both write a 'curious compacted lyric' that speaks 'directly to and about the psyche, expressing and querying feelings that are deliberately abstracted from any reference to, or analysis of, the social causes of psychological states' (61). For another, in the love poems of both, the male addressee is shadowy and unrealized and it is difficult if not impossibile to determine whether there is an autobiographical basis to poems that describe the interactions of a female speaker and a 'he'. And sometimes in the poems of both these intensely religious women the 'he' can as readily be construed to refer to God as to a man. Finally, both seem to have an inherent incapacity to be fulfilled or content, coupled with an equally strong longing to be so. Both, that is, answer to Dickinson's image of

>The Fruit perverse to plucking,
>But leaning to the Sight
>With the ecstatic limit
>Of unobtained Delight –

>(Poem 1209)

There is, however, at least one significant difference between the love poetry of the two poets. In his discussion of the condition of waiting-for-love in *The Culture of Love: Victorians to Moderns*, Stephen Kern makes use of Heidegger's distinction between inauthentic and authentic: 'Inauthentically, we *wait for* a future that will happen to us by force of circumstances over which we have no control. Authentically, we *anticipate* a future ... as our own responsibilty in the face of circumstance'

(11). Kern uses the former term to describe the characteristic waiting-for-love posture of Victorian women. I suggest that the term can also be usefully applied to the speakers of Christina Rossetti's love poems. Dickinson's waiting, on the other hand, was authentic rather than inauthentic because in her poetry she explored imaginatively the principal phases of the experience of sexual love and thus was able actively to choose renunciation rather than passively to endure her condition.

Poems concerning sexual love account for less than 10 per cent of Dickinson's total output, and no one would say that this grouping is among the most impressive clusters that can be made of her poems. But there are a number of compelling lyrics, the type and distinction of which come into sharp focus when they are arranged according to the successive phases of a love relationship. When they are, they become the Dickinsonian equivalent of Rossetti's *Monna Innominata*.

A number of poems show Dickinson's yearning and desire for heterosexual love coupled with hesitancy and trepidation that suggest a 'deep ambivalence about the role of love in her life' (Walker, 105). There are, for example, the extraordinary fabular or parabolic poems in which male sexual power is seen as potentially frightening or engulfing – 'The Drop, that wrestles in the Sea' (poem 284); 'I started Early – Took my Dog' (poem 520); 'My Life had stood – a Loaded Gun' (poem 754); and 'In Winter in my Room' (poem 1670). The best gloss for these poems is a letter Dickinson wrote when she was in her early twenties to her future sister-in-law:

> How dull our lives must seem to the bride, and the plighted maiden, whose days are fed with gold, and who gathers pearl every evening; but to the *wife*, Susie, sometimes the *wife forgotten*, our lives perhaps seem dearer than all others in the world; you have seen flowers at morning, *satisfied* with the dew, and those same sweet flowers at noon with their heads bowed in anguish before the mighty sun; think you these thirsty blossoms will *now* need nought but – *dew*? No, they will cry for sunlight, and pine for the burning noon, tho' it scorches them, scathes them; they have got through with peace.
>
> (*Letters*, i, 210)

On the other hand, there are poems that have as their subject prospective delight in sexual love. In poem 339, for example, the female speaker addressing her absent lover uses flower imagery that is boldly suggestive of female sexual arousal:

> I tend my flowers for thee –
> Bright Absentee!
> My Fuschia's Coral Seams
> Rip – while the Sower – dreams –

Geraniums – tint – and spot –
Low Daisies – dot –
My Cactus – splits her Beard
To show her throat –

Carnations – tip their spice –
And Bees – pick up –
A Hyacinch – I hid –
Puts out a Ruffled Head –
And odors fall
From flasks – so small –
You marvel how they held –

This poem is a reworking from the female perspective of the traditional type of male love lyric that catalogues the beauties of the beloved, for example Thomas Campion's 'There is a garden in her face'. Cynthia Griffin Wolff describes Dickinson's poem as 'a reconfigured blazon that retains the praise for a woman, but articulates it in the *woman's* own voice and on her own terms' (128). That is to say, the woman figuratively self-described in Dickinson's poem is a subject rather than an object of sexual excitement.

Another example of erotic excitement is found in poem 638:

To my small Hearth His fire came –
And all my House aglow
Did fan and rock, with sudden light –
'Twas Sunrise – 'twas the Sky.

The second half of this poem uses a natural image to convey a sense of the timeless-seeming quality of this exhilarating transport – it was 'no Summer brief – /With limit of Decay'; it was 'Noon – without the News of Night'. But the ecstasy of romantic love can be timeless only prospectively, as Dickinson well knew. The poetic vehicle for the expression of the timelessness of sexual love is the expectation-as-virtual-fulfilment lyric. Dickinson wrote two excellent poems of this type. Poem 211 asks the Eden of erotic fulfilment to 'Come slowly' and uses the image of bee and flower to figure both the humming pleasure of anticipation and its delirious consummation when 'the fainting Bee ... Enters – and is lost in Balms'.

The other poem uses the imagery of ship and harbour:

Wild Nights – Wild Nights!
Were I with thee
Wild Nights should be
Our luxury!

Futile the Winds –
To a Heart in Port –
Done with the Compass –

Done with the Chart!

Rowing in Eden –
Ah, the Sea!
Might I but moor – Tonight –
In Thee!

                                                          (Poem 249)

Although a 'thee' is addressed, this is not an invitation-to-love poem. The beloved is not physically present – the subjunctive in the second line indicates a contrary-to-fact condition. The poem's subject is anticipation, which is itself a paradisical state – 'Eden' is associated with the rowing, not the mooring. In the anticipated nights of luxuria, sexual pleasure for both participants is simultaneously figured with an almost Tennysonian subtlety: the boat mooring 'in Thee' has a phallic suggestiveness, while the boat sheltered from winds in a protective encompassing port has female connotations.

One of Dickinson's definition poems encapsulates her insight into the dynamics of erotic anticipation: 'Expectation – is Contentment – /Gain – Satiety' (poem 807). Another poem identifies the other principal psychological aspect of 'Gain' in a love relationship: 'To possess, is past the instant/We achieve the Joy' (poem 1036). The implications of transience for love relationships are explored in poem 322. In its first two stanzas, the ecstasy of what Browning called the infinite moment is rendered in natural and religious figures:

There came a Day at Summer's full,
Entirely for me –
I thought that such were for the Saints, –
Where Resurrections – be –

The Sun, as common, went abroad,
The flowers, accustomed, blew,
As if no soul the solstice passed
That maketh all things new.

But the extended moment does not last: 'The Hours slid fast – as Hours will,/Clutched tight, by greedy hands.' By the end of the poem, the parting lovers are exchanging crucifixes as 'Sufficient troth' that they shall be reunited beyond the grave in a marriage justified by the 'Calvaries of Love' they will have endured.

Another poem (poem 640) dramatizes the separation of lovers caused by an act of renunciation. It opens abruptly: 'I cannot live with You – /It would be Life' – that is, our union would make our love all-encompassing and exclusive and compete with the Christian plenitude of being that includes life everlasting. Three examples are given of the spiritual harm that the intense mutual absorption of romantic love would cause.

If he were to die first, how could she not claim 'my Right of Frost – Death's privilege'. If they rose together, his face would outshine that of Jesus and even if it did not, as in Catherine's dream in *Wuthering Heights*, she would grow 'homesick' in heaven and long to return to earth. And if she were saved and he were not, her celestial self 'were Hell to Me'.

But renunciation exacts a terrible price. At the close of poem 640, the poet is left with both 'Prayer – /And that white Sustenance – /Despair'. The aftermath of renunciation and its psychological cost is explored in poem 293:

> I got so I could take his name –
> Without – Tremendous gain –
> That Stop-sensation – on my Soul –
> And Thunder – in the Room –
>
> I got so I could walk across
> That Angle in the floor,
> Where he turned so, and I turned – how –
> And all our Sinew tore –
>
> I got so I could stir the Box –
> In which his letters grew –
> Without that forcing, in my breath –
> As Staples – driven through.

But the cost of renunciation is greater than that of a distress that can be fully healed by time. The remainder of the poem shows that the speaker's belief in a merciful God has been problematized by her experience. She is thus unable to be beguiled by the wishful thinking that makes the pain of separation a 'Sufficient troth' of future reward.

In another poem, the speaker is able to assess dispassionately her post-renunciation situation:

> I tie my Hat – I crease my Shawl –
> Life's little duties do – precisely –
> As the very least
> Were infinite – to me –
>
> I put new Blossoms in the Glass –
> And throw the old – away –
> I push a petal from my Gown
> That anchored there – I weigh
> The time 'twill be till six o'clock
> I have so much to do –
> And yet – Existence – some way back –
> Stopped – struck – my ticking – through

(Poem 443)

This poem recalls Rossetti's 'L.E.L.' – but only up to a point. Dickinson's speaker understands her situation and in this sense may be said to be in control of it. There is no sulking and no self pity. 'To simulate – is stinging work'; but the speaker does it both without hope of 'Reward' and 'With scrupulous exactness – /To hold our senses – on'.

A final poem has as its subject what has been learned through the imaginative exploration of the experience of sexual love.

> I learned – at least – what Home could be –
> …
> What Mornings in our Garden – guessed –
> What Bees – for us – to hum –
> With only Birds to interrupt
> The Ripple of our Theme –
>
> And Task for Both –
> When Play be done –
> Your Problem – of the Brain –
> And mine – some foolisher effect –
> A Ruffle – or a Tune –
>
> The Afternoons – Together spent –
> And Twilight – in the Lanes –
> Some ministry to poorer lives –
> Seen poorest – thro' our gains –
>
> And then Return – and Night – and Home –
>
> And then away to You to pass –
> A new – diviner – care –
> Till Sunrise take us back to Scene –
> Transmuted – Vivider –
>
> This seems a Home –
> And Home is not –
> But what that Place could be –
> Afflicts me – as a Setting Sun –
> Where Dawn – knows how to be –

(Poem 944)

Save for children, this imaginative projection has all the ingredients of the Victorian ideal of a companionate marriage, including sexual satisfaction. One critic suggests that Dickinson may have 'learned' about this state from reading *Aurora Leigh* and 'fantasizing the heroine's afterlife with Romney' (Eberwein, 105). But this is a frivolous notion. Dickinson extravagantly admired Barrett Browning's *magnum opus*, as we know from poem 593 ('I think I was enchanted'); and the elegiac poem she wrote after the posthumous publication of Barrett Browning's *Last Poems* includes the extravagant encomium: 'Not on Record –

bubbled other,/Flute – or Woman – /So divine' (poem 312). But Dickinson had nothing to learn from Barrett Browning either formally, stylistically or from the content of her poems. The effect on Dickinson of the older woman's poetry was surely the same as the effect on Gerard Manley Hopkins (1955) of studying masterpieces – it made him 'admire and do otherwise' (291).

Where, then, did Dickinson learn about phases of the experience of sexual love that she did not herself experience? The answer is that poets can create out of what they lack as well as out of what they possess – can imagine so intensely that they can for a moment 'esteem the fiction – real – [while] The Real – fictitious seems' (poem 646). In another poem (poem 518), this ability is figured as a male lover (the poem's speaker) dreaming of his beloved:

Her sweet Weight on my Heart a Night
Had scarcely deigned to lie –
When, stirring, for Belief's delight,
My Bride had slipped away –

This intensity of imaginative apprehension of the 'Dream – made solid' is in turn the reason for the intensity of the feeling of loss. Dickinson might have been refering to poem 944 ('I learned – at last – what Home could be') when she remarked to a correspondent: 'To lose what we never owned might seem an eccentric Bereavement but Presumption has its Affliction as actually as Claim' (*Letters*, ii, 532).

Like Hemans's 'Woman and Fame', Landon's monody on Hemans, and Rossetti's 'L.E.L.', Dickinson's moving sketch of the forsaken satisfactions of married love recalls the passage from *Aurora Leigh* with which this chapter began. But it does so in a way that bespeaks authentic choice. In her poem, sewing and playing or singing a tune are the limits of creative activity for a wife. And problems of the brain, like those explored in Dickinson's great poems of epistemological and metaphysical speculation, are shown to be similarly incompatible with the married state. The same point is exemplified at the macro-level by Dickinson's *Complete Poems*. She is unquestionably the foremost nineteenth-century woman poet in the English language, and there is every reason to think that unkissed lips were an enabling condition of her creative achievement.

CHAPTER FIVE

Clough's Compasses to Steer By

the notion of scrutinising the enthusiasm [of Love] sympathetically, yet scientifically, and estimating the precise value of its claims and assertions, probably never entered into any poetic soul before Clough.

Henry Sidgwick

1

In the seven years preceding his marriage in 1854 at age 35, Arthur Hugh Clough wrote three long poems of contemporary life, each of which is generically and formally different from the others. *The Bothie of Toperna-Fuosich: A Long-Vacation Pastoral* is written in hexameters. The '*bizarrerie* of the style [and] playful, mock-heroic key', Charles Kingsley noted in his review, gave Clough 'scope for all sorts of variations into the bucolic, sentimental, broad-farce, pathetic, Hebrew-prophetic, whatnot' (Thorpe, 40). In *Amours de Voyage*, Clough again employed hexameters, but there is nothing mock-heroic about what he called 'my 5 act epistolary tragi-comedy or comi-tragedy' (1957, ii, 546). The work is a verse novella, an Anglo-Saxons-in-Italy comedy of manners that anticipates those of Henry James and E. M. Forster. The unfinished *Dipsychus*, which also has an Italian setting (Venice this time rather than Rome), consists of a series of dialogues between the title character and a 'Spirit', interspersed with lyrics and soliloquies. While the work has obvious affinities with Goethe's lyric drama *Faust*, it as often calls to mind Byron's *Don Juan* and Gilbert and Sullivan's operettas.

What links these three works is that they are all reflective inquiries into sexuality, love and marriage in mid-nineteenth-century England. The central subject of *The Bothie* is mutual sexual attraction leading to marriage. For the protagonist of *Amours de Voyage*, sexual love is a momentous and problematic undertaking that he subjects to extended analysis. While these subjects are not the exclusive concern of *Dipsychus*, the title character and his alter ego dispute and dissect them so thoroughly that in the end romantic love leading to marriage ceases to be a real possibility for the poem's tormented protagonist.

2

The opening of *The Bothie* describes a festive dinner after an afternoon of Highland sports. The guests include a reading party of Oxford undergraduates, one of whom is Philip Hewson. By birth and education he is a gentleman, but with an inheritance so modest that he is 'Somewhat impaired in a world where nothing is had for nothing' (viii, 5). By conviction he is a 'radical hot, hating lords and scorning ladies,/Silent mostly, but often reviling .../Feudal tenures, mercantile lords, competition and bishops,/Liveries, armorial bearings, [and] the Game-laws' (i, 131–4).

Philip's radical thinking about Victorian mores becomes clear in his account of his sexual history in the second of the poem's nine parts (ii, 33–121). He had never, he says, 'properly felt the relation of man to woman ... the sexual glory' until he was one day strolling in some village fields:

> Chanced it my eye fell aside on a capless, bonnetless maiden,
> Bending with three-pronged fork in a garden uprooting potatoes,
> Was it the air? who can say? or herself, or the charm of the labour?
> But a new thing was in me; and longing delicious possessed me.

This 'mysterious secret' had not been imparted to him by 'prurient talk' or 'the growing distress, and celled-up dishonour of boyhood' (that is, masturbation – see Clough's *Oxford Diaries* lxi–lxii) or the social occasions in which he had been exposed to girls of his own station: 'balls, dances, and evening parties,/Shooting with bows, going shopping together, and hearing them singing ... performing dull farces of escort'. Indeed, if these females could only feel what he felt that day, Philip is sure they would abandon their artificial, doll-like mode of existence for a simpler one involving work that would allow them to

> feel the sap of existence
> Circulate up through their roots from the far-away centre of all
> things,
> Circulate up from the depths to the bud on the twig that is
> topmost!

It is important to note that Philip's radical views on the relation of man to woman are contested by Hobbes, the most reflective of the other undergraduates, and especially by the reading party's conservative tutor, 'the grave man, nicknamed Adam' (i, 20). The latter, for example, seeks to temper Philip's romantic idealizings by warning of 'the danger of pantry-flirtation' (iv, 261) and urging the view that a person can best find fulfilment in the station in life that God has placed him or her. This advice, however, does not at first keep Philip from becoming infatuated with Katie, a local girl. But he abruptly terminates their intimacy once he realizes what he takes to be the likely consequence – Katie's seduction and ruin. 'Modesty broken-through once', Philip believes, 'to immodesty flies for protection' (iv, 194). He even has dreams in which

> I am pacing the streets of the dissolute city,
> Where dressy girls slithering-by upon pavements give sign for
>   accosting,
> Paint on their beautiless cheeks, and hunger and shame in their
>   bosoms;
> Hunger by drink and by that which they shudder yet burn for,
>   appeasing, –
> Hiding their shame – ah God, in the glare of the public gas
>   lights.
>
> (iv, 175–9)

Philip's next infatuation is short lived. After this he arrives at the bothie (a hut or forester's cottage) of Daniel Mackaye, a former smith, soldier and schoolmaster, who has returned to his childhood home where 'on his pittance of soil he lived, and raised potatoes,/Barley and oats' (vi, 17–18). There he meets and is powerfully attracted to Mackaye's daughter Elspie. The inception and growth of their love is the subject of the last three parts of Clough's poem. At the beginning of these climactic sections a change in the conduct of the narrative is signalled by a narratorial intrusion in which the poet speaks of the difficulty of the task before him:

> Indirect and evasive no longer, a cowardly bather,
> Clinging to bough and to rock, and sidling along by the edges,
> In your faith, ye Muses and Graces, who love the plain present,
> Scorning historic abridgment and artifice antipoetic,
> In your faith, ye Muses and Loves, ye Loves and Graces,
> I will confront the great peril, and speak with the mouth of the
>   lovers,
> As they spoke by the alders, at evening, the runnel below them,
> Elspie a diligent knitter, and Philip her fingers watching.

To 'speak with the mouth of the lovers' means to write verisimilar dialogue, that is, to move from epic and mock-epic conventions to those of prose fiction – a shift that corresponds to the shift from male camaraderie in predominantly outdoor settings to domestic interiors in which female occupations and subjects (knitting, courtship protocols, declarations of love) are dominant. The 'great peril' is the risk of becoming novelettish; and it cannot be said that Clough has entirely avoided this pitfall.

Parts vii–ix go on for too long owing to the fact that, like the closing sections of many Victorian novels, they include a good deal of information, explanation and thematic amplification. There is Elspie explaining to Philip that he has misjudged Katie's character because he confused English with Highland ways and that in any event his infatuation was 'all delusion,/All a mere chance, and accident, – not proper choosing' (vii, 25–6). There is the account of the couple's engagement in glorious October weather – including their love talk and negotiations concerning social adjustments. While Elspie insists that 'I will not be a lady,/We will do work together', Philip accepts that 'in default of a [social] fight I will put up with peace and Elspie' (viii, 136–7; ix, 100).

Finally, before the couple leave to begin a new life on a farm in New Zealand, there is their wedding. As in the finale to George Eliot's *Middlemarch*, marriage is presented as the 'great beginning' of 'the home epic' in which mutual happiness will entail work for both parties and thus go against the grain of the social conventions and practices through which many young women (for example, Eliot's Rosamond Vincy) are 'spoilt for wives by the means to become so' (ix, 64). The union is endorsed by the tutor, and Hobbes supplies a striking emblem or 'allegory'. In Genesis, Jacob saw Rachel watering sheep at the well and kissed her. But he was forced by her father Laban to marry her sister Leah: 'this Rachel-and-Leah is marriage ... One part heavenly-ideal, the other vulgar and earthy'; and Laban is 'Circumstance, chance, the world' (ix, 199–201). And the omniscient narrator provides the closed ending characteristic of Victorian prose fiction, reporting that their married life was blessed by children and agricultural success and that 'the Antipodes too have a Bothie of Topér-na-fuosich'.

While none of this is uninteresting, the most original and powerful passages in the last three parts of *The Bothie* – indeed in the entire work – occur when Clough, while continuing to have his two leading characters speak for themselves, reverts to the epic mode and allows them Homeric similes to express their deepest emotional and sexual feelings. These extraordinary passages confirm the correctness of Philip's revolutionary idea concerning love: that 'the youthful instinct' (the sexual instinct) provides 'the compass to steer by' (ii, 193–6) and is the right guide to follow in the emotional life. *The Bothie* refines and qualifies the insistence in Clough's 'Natura Naturans' that sexual attraction precedes and is the *sine qua non* of human love. But it does not gainsay its primacy.

Indeed, a magnetic image is used by Elspie at the end of the first of the two similes she uses to describe her feelings for Philip as they sit outside the bothie beside a stream looking down a hillside to a 'salt sea loch'. She first calls attention to 'the high new bridge, they used to build at, below there'. In the figure she goes on to develop, she had been 'slowly with trouble' building herself – 'Painfully getting myself upraised one stone on another'. On the other side of the interpersonal divide, she has come to notice 'another fabric uprising, better and stronger,/Close to me, coming to join me'. This has led her to dream of arches and bridges and of 'a great invisible hand coming down' and dropping a key stone in the middle:

> ... I feel the great key stone coming in, and through it
> Feel the other part – all the other stones of the archway,
> Joined into mine with a queer happy sense of completeness,
>   tingling
> All the way up from the other side's basement-stones in the water,
> Through the very grains of mine: – just like, when the steel, that
>   you showed us
> Moved to the magnet, it seemed a feeling got hold of them both.
>
> (vii, 59–76)

This figure does suggest that, to revert to Philip's natural image, young woman as well as young men are able to feel the 'sap of existence' rising in them. But the fact that a second image (the steel and magnet) is required to complete the first, signals the limitations of bridge building as a trope for Elspie and Philip's mutual attraction. For one thing, it does not allow for interactive dynamics between male and female and thus necessitates an external agent – the invisible hand – to activate the current of sexual feeling.

The second image that Elspie uses is enormously more powerful and suggestive:

> You are too strong, you see, Mr. Philip! you are like the sea there,
> Which *will* come, through the straights and all between the
>   mountains,
> Forcing its great strong tide into every nook and inlet,
> Getting far in, up the quiet stream of sweet inland water,
> Sucking it up, and stopping it, turning it, driving it backward,
> Quite preventing its own quiet running: And then, soon after,
> Back it goes off, leaving weeds on the shore, and wrack and
>   uncleanness:
> And the poor burn in the glen tries again its peaceful running,
> But it is brackish and tainted, and all its banks disordered.
> That was what I dreamt all last night. I was the burnie,
> Trying to get along through the tyrannous brine, and could not;
> I was confined and squeezed in the coils of the great salt tide, that
> Would mix-in itself with me, and change me; I felt myself
>   changing;
> And I struggled, and screamed, I believe, in my dream. It was
>   dreadful.
>
> (vii, 124–37)

Imagery of commingling and merging had been used twice before in the *Bothie*, both times from the male point of view. Once when Philip had felt 'folded' into Katie; and again when, separated from her, he had wished he were dead because 'Spirits escaped from the body can enter and be with the living' and feel 'pure joy, as they mingle and mix inner essence with essence' (iv, 134, 43–5). But now sexual mingling is figured from the female point of view as a violent, unequal combining in which the female stream is molested and despoiled by the great salt tide. This extraordinary figuration of female apprehension of the emotional and psychological dynamics of sexual love leading to marriage has as its only equal among the materials of this study Emily Dickinson's trope, quoted in Chapter 4, of the sweet flowers at noon 'with their heads bowed in anguish before the mighty sun'.

At the end of part vii, however, the same figure is reinscribed by the psychologically omniscient narrator to show the positive resolution of Elspie's sexual/emotional awakening. Listening to her, Philip had released her fingers and 'recoiled, fell back, and shook, and shivered'. When she finishes, he announces he will leave the next day. But upon hearing this, it is Elspie who recoils. She takes Philip's visible hand, places it in hers, and kisses his fingers. Elspie is beginning to feel coursing through her the very force she just had compared to the vehement tide. As the masculine sea recedes, the feminine burn rushes after it:

> Felt she in myriad springs, her sources, far in the mountains,
> Stirring, collecting, rising, upheaving, forth-out-flowing,
> Taking and joining, right welcome, that delicate rill in the valley,
> Filling it, making it strong, and still descending, seeking,
> With a blind forefeeling descending, evermore seeking,
> With a delicious forefeeling, the great still sea before it;
> There deep into it, far, to carry, and lose in its bosom,
> Waters that still from their sources exhaustless are fain to be
>   added.
>
> (vii, 158–69)

What this equally extraordinary passage conveys is that the resolution and cure of Elspie's sexual apprehensions are found in sexual feeling itself, in her own uprising and outflowing emotions that, the figure suggests, are the first phase of the natural history of sexual love. As the mountain stream gathers force from its own interior sources and rushes forward to seek its destination in the great still sea and to be lost in its bosom, so does Elspie, directed and propelled by a force within her, come to be joined with Philip. What pings in the memory of the reader of Victorian love poetry is of course the close of Tennyson's master lyric of erotic mutuality, 'Now sleeps the crimson petal' (published in *The Princess* the year before the *Bothie* was written), in which a similar liquid enfolding figures the fulfilment of both male and female sexual longing.

Both of the figures used by Elspie are feminine in that touch is the dominant sense and metonymical rather than metaphorical in that their vehicles are drawn from the remote Highland glen in which she has been raised and in which she and Philip are sitting. In contrast, the epic simile that Philip uses in part ix to figure the effect in him of Elspie's love is masculine in that the dominant sense is visual and metaphorical in a way that is indicative of Philip's greater knowledge of the world and greater concern with the social context of their love:

> But as the light of day enters some populous city,
> Shaming away, ere it come, by the chilly daystreak signal,
> High and low, the misusers of night, shaming out the gas lamps, –
> All the great empty streets are flooded with broadening clearness,
> Which, withal, by inscrutable simultaneous access
> Permeates far and pierces, to the very cellars lying in
> Narrow high back-lane, and court and alley of alleys:
> He that goes forth to his walk, while speeding to the suburb,
> Sees sights only peaceful and pure; as, labourers settling
> Slowly to work, in their limbs the lingering sweetness of slumber;
> Humble market-carts, coming-in, bringing-in, not only
> Flower, fruit, farm-store, but sounds and sights of the country
> Dwelling yet on the sense of the dreamy drivers; soon after
> Half-awake servant-maids unfastening drowsy shutters
> Up at the window, or down, letting-in the air by the doorway;
> School-boys, school-girls soon, with slate, portfolio, satchel,
> Hampered as they haste, those running, these others maidenly
>   tripping;
> Early clerk anon turning out to stroll, or it may be
> Meet his sweetheart – waiting behind the garden gate there;
> Merchant on his grass-plat haply, bare-headed; and now by this
>   time
> Little child bringing breakfast to 'father' that sits on the timber
> There by the scaffolding; see, she waits for the can beside him;
> Mean-time above purer air untarnished of new-lit fires:
> So that the whole great wicked artificial civilized fabric, –
> All its unfinished houses, lots for sale, and railway outworks, –
> Seems reaccepted, resumed to Primal Nature and Beauty: –
> – Such – in me, and to me, and on me the love of Elspie.
>   (ix, 111–37)

Compared with those of Elspie, Philip's trope places their love and coming marriage in the wider domestic context of children, family and earning a living and in the larger historical context of mid-nineteenth-century constructive social endeavour. Indeed, his simile anticipates Ford Madox Brown's pictorial celebration of the same urban energies in 'Work'. But the principal signification of Philip's figure relates to the change in his inner being caused by 'the love of Elspie' – a single phrase that has two mutually inclusive meanings: both Philip's love of Elspie and her love of him. In Coleridge's use of the rising sun as a figure for the dawn of love in his letter dated 12 March 1811 to Henry Crabb Robinson, the sun of love is described as calling up 'the reek of the Marsh' (lust) and attenuating and transpiercing it until the viewer is conscious of light alone (154). Similarly, the opening lines of Philip's simile recall his earlier night vision of the 'streets of the dissolute city' with fallen women 'Hiding their shame ... in the glare of the public gas lights'. As the sunlight floods the city with 'broadening clearness' and shames away 'the misusers of night', so Elspie's love cleanses Philip of the dark sexual imaginings that had began with the celled-up dishonour of boyhood. Thus, Philip's simile both complements Elspie's elemental Lawrencian figures of male and female contestation and resolution and completes the tropic inscription of their dynamic affinity: Elspie has been sexualized by Philip's love; he has been refined and cleansed by hers.

3

Never again would Clough write anything so positive. *Amours de Voyage*, begun the year after *The Bothie* was published, is also concerned with sexual affinity, love, and marriage. But its perspective on these subjects is different because the central character is different. Philip and Claude are both educated and intelligent; both dislike middle-class values and social conventions, including those relating to relationships between the sexes – 'the general tender-domestic' as Claude calls it (i, 6). And both young men are in situations that offer opportunities to act independently. But while Philip is *engagé* politically and sexually, Claude is an intellectual – one of the 'contemplative creatures ... upon whom the pressure of action is laid so lightly' (ii, 14). He thinks rather than acts. Claude's letters from Italy to his friend Eustace back in England provide a pretext for the expression of his intensely self-centred reflections. Indeed, much of the time his letters read more like entries in a diary, which for all practical purposes they have become by the last movement of the poem: 'Yes, it relieves me to write, though I do not send' (v, 5).

The reason Claude gives for his non-involvement in the public sphere is that 'we are meant to look after ourselves' rather than the body politic. Nature intended, he says, that 'we cling to our rocks like limpets; Ocean may bluster,/Over and under and round us; we open our shells to imbibe our/Nourishment, close them again, and are safe, fulfilling the purpose/Nature intended' (ii, 2). A similar passivity is evident in his emotional life. Unlike Philip, for example, Claude shows no sexual interest in socially inferior females. He does, however, speak of 'the dream of romance ... the fever of flushed adolescence' (i, 9), and a 'vile hungering impulse, this demon within us of craving' (iii, 8) as conditions he has known and knows at first hand. And the extraordinary image he uses early in the poem to figure his attraction to Mary Trevellyn suggests there there is in him both the desire for sexual love and a powerful below-the-surface fear of it:

> Lo, with the rope on my loins I descend through the fissure; I sink,
>   yet
> Inly secure in the strength of invisible arms up above me;
> Still, wheresoever I swing, wherever to shore, or to shelf, or
> Floor of cavern untrodden, shell-sprinkled, enchanting, I know I
> Yet shall one time feel the strong cord tighten about me, –
> Feel it, relentless, upbear me from spots I would rest in; and
>   though the
> Rope sway wildly, I faint, crags wound me, from crag unto crag
>   re-
> Bounding, or, wide in the void, I die ten deaths, ere the end I
> Yet shall plant firm foot on the broad lofty spaces I quit, shall
> Feel underneath me again the great massy strengths of abstraction,
> Look yet abroad from the height o'er the sea whose salt wave
>   I have tasted.
>
> (i, 12)

Despite both this ambivalence and his superior attitude to her arriviste family, Claude has been attracted to Mary Trevellyn because she is untypical of the Victorian middle-class female in her social manner and intellectual poise. His attraction also has the advantage of providing food for thought:

> There are two different kinds, I believe, of human attraction:
> One which simply disturbs, unsettles, and makes you uneasy,
> And another that poises, retains, and fixes, and holds you.
> I have no doubt, for myself, in giving my voice for the latter.
> I do not wish to be moved, but growing, where I was growing,
> There more truly to grow, to live where yet I had languished.
>
> (ii, 11)

In *The Bothie*, Philip at one point had observed that 'Elements fuse and resolve, as affinity draws and repels them' (iv, 70); but he did not pursue the implications of this chemical analogy for emotional relationships. Claude does. The first thing he wants to determine is whether his attraction to Mary is a matter of 'affinity' or merely of what he calls 'juxtaposition'. The terms are derived from contemporary chemical theory. Affinities are 'the tendencies which certain elementary substances or their compounds have to unite and form new compounds' (Scott ed., 33). Not being the result of proximity, this process can be considerd a figure for romantic love rather than merely sexual attraction.

The concern with trying to distinguish between juxtaposition and affinity is not simply an intellectual's hair-splitting. It is of primary importance if marriage is taken seriously and if there is no belief in a supernatural force or sanction helping to determine one's destiny. For Patmore in 'The Wedding Sermon' (the concluding section of *The Victories of Love*) the case is quite different:

> A youth pursues
> A maid, whom chance, not he, did choose,
> Till to his strange arms hurries she
> In a despair of modesty.
> Then, simply and without pretence
> Of insight or experience,
> They plight their vows.

This is all right with Patmore because 'The thing proceedeth from the Lord ... Who never fails, if asked, to bless/His children's helpless ignorance/And blind election of life's chance'.

At one point Claude allows himself to wish for a divinity shaping his sexual future:

> Shall not a voice, if a voice there must be, from the airs that
>   environ,
> Yea, from the conscious heavens, without our knowledge or effort,
> Break into audible words? and love be its own inspiration?
>
> (ii, 12)

But Claude is not thinking well here. What he proposes is merely a sentimental rescoring of the providential guiding hand. If love is its own inspiration, then love is self-authenticating and any confirmatory voice must come from within, not without. As George Meredith wrote in 1861 to a friend who had sought his advice on whether to marry:

> Has she principle? has she any sense of responsibility? Has she courage? Enough that you love her. I believe that this plan of taking a woman on the faith of a mighty wish for her, is the best, and the safest way to find the jewel we are all in search of. As to love 'revealing' all the qualities in one great flash – do you believe it even in your present state?
>
> (1970, i, 105)

Love as a force, a feeling, an intuition, a sense of possibility, a mighty wish, a taking the plunge: this is precisely what Claude cannot tolerate. He cannot take the Carlylean advice of Eustase that '*Action will furnish belief*' (v, ii). Claude wants laboratory conditions for determining the quality and authenticity of love:

> I do not like being moved: for the will is excited; and action
> Is a most dangerous thing; I tremble for something factitious,

Some malpractice of heart and illegitimate process.

                                               (ii, 11)

Claude wants to conduct his emotional life in the same way he conducts his non-existent public life. But to do this would be to become an emotional limpet. What cannot authenticate and sustain love is thinking about it and analysing it – as Claude at one point seems to realize:

> *Hang* this thinking, at last! what good is it? oh, and what evil!
> Oh, what mischief and pain! like a clock in a sick man's chamber,
> Ticking and ticking, and still through each covert of slumber
>   pursuing.
> ...
> Take from me this regal knowledge;
> Let me, contented and mute, with the beasts of the field, my
>   brothers,
> Tranquilly, happily lie, – and eat grass, like Nebuchadnezzar.
>
>   (iii, 10)

Moreover, except in a Highland bothie in glorious early autumn weather, experiments in loving are affected not only by the excitement of the participants but also by social context. It is Claude's realization of this that precipitates his one decisive act, on which the slender plot of *Amours de Voyage* turns. Mary Trevellyn is a pleasure to converse with because, unlike most young ladies, 'she can talk in a rational way, can/ Speak upon subjects that really are matters of mind and of thinking' (ii, 10). But above all Claude is 'charmed' by her because 'she held me to nothing ... I could talk as I pleased ... *She* spoke not of obligations/ Knew not of debt' (iii, 9). But Claude is shocked to realize that his relations to Mary have made her family concerned with his 'intentions' about her and that what he had thought of as a special, naturally evolving relationship had to the eye of social convention been merely 'a permitted flirtation' – that is, a part of the middle-class courtship ritual – conducted under the 'vulgar eyes' of the Trevellyns (iii, 13). His reaction is abruptly to break off relations with the family – an act that he soon comes to regret. But by then the family has left Rome and despite his efforts miscommunication and mischance prevent him from recontacting them.

At the end of *Amours de Voyage*, Mary has the last epistolary word; but her point of view had rarely been given during the course of the poem. One would very much like to have heard as much from her as one did from Elspie in *The Bothie* – especially concerning the element of 'repulsion' that coexists with attraction in her feelings for Claude. Repulsion was the contemporary chemical term for the force between atoms of the same element. The implication, as J. P. Phelan has noticed, is that Claude and Mary 'are too similar to be genuinely compatible.

This finding links up with Claude's worries about the erosion of masculinity in the modern world' (16). Claude does reflect that his 'method of wooing' is not 'manly' and believes that women prefer 'the audacious, the wilful, the vehement hero [to] the timid, the sensitive soul' (ii, 14). But the absence of a fuller representation of Mary's point of view means that this most interesting aspect of their relationship is insufficiently developed.

In draft versions of *Amours de Voyage* Mary's point of view was developed. There are letters by her that detail her equivocal feelings for Claude. In one of them she appropriates 'Come down, O maid', one of Tennyson's invitation-to-love lyrics from *The Princess*, just as the narrator of *The Bothie* had appropriated the other, 'Now sleeps the crimson petal'. She urges Claude to 'come down to the path, come down my friend and my dear one,/Stand not upon the heights, that are dreary and lead you to nothing'. But in the same letter she remarks that there is something 'unwholesome' in Claude and expresses the fear she has been 'infected ... With his own tremors and doubts and sad paralytical temper'. And in another draft letter she reports that her experience with him has left her 'sadly disheartened' and alienated:

> ... the whole world seems changed, and instead of the fields and
>   the gardens,
> Nothing but ice and snow and a waste of sea surrounds me.
> All the old family ties, the quiet and simple affections,
> All that appeared so good and so happy and true and sufficient,
> Seem to be taken away, with nothing at all to replace them.
>   (Scott, ed., 62, 74)

That these striking letters were excised from the final version of the poem is one indication of Clough's difficulty in finding the right focus for the presentation of his central character. He must have eventually decided that the development of Mary's point of view would have led to the reader having a strongly negative reaction to Claude and thus detracted attention from the seriousness of his reflective inquiry into modern love. (This inference is consistent with Patrick Scott's analysis of the genesis of the poem in his edition.)

At the end of the final version, Claude is presented as being characteristically of two minds about the ending of his intimacy with Mary. On the one hand he feels like a coward who has 'slunk from the perilous field [where] the prizes of life are contested' (v, 5). On the other he reflects that 'After all perhaps there was something factitious' about his feeling for her (v, 8). Claude does, however, seem decisive and even impressive in rejecting the comfort and support of religion and putting his trust in knowledge. Ultimately he does not eat grass like Nebuchadnezzar. Instead, he rewrites another scriptural text:

Faith, I think, does pass, and Love; but Knowledge abideth.
Let us seek Knowledge; – the rest may come and go as it happens.
...
Knowledge is painful often; and yet when we know, we are happy.
Seek it, and leave mere Faith and Love to come with the chances.

(v, 10)

As for Hope, the third in the Pauline trio of what abides in 1 Corinthians 13: 'Who knows? Who can say? It will not do to suppose it' (v, 9).

4

Sexuality, love and marriage are not as exclusively the concerns of *Dipsychus* as they are of *The Bothie* and *Amours de Voyage*, but they do figure importantly. The work's title character has the same strong sexual urges as does Philip; but like Claude he is also an intellectual given to intense and incapacitating self-analysis. This is not articulated through letters but through debate between himself and an interlocutor. There are two personages in *Dipsychus*: the title character, whose name means 'double-minded', and the Spirit. Most of the time Dipsychus speaks in blank verse or regular lyrical stanzas; the utterances of the Spirit are more irregular and often vulgar; he uses coarse diction and two-syllable rhymes with a feminine ending that often make for farcical effects.

'What, whence, of whom?' is this Spirit, Dipsychus himself wonders: 'How am I to discover!/Myself or not myself? My own bad thoughts?/ Or some external agency at work/To lead me who knows whither' (i, 2). At times it seems that the Spirit is an external agency, the genius loci of the poem's worldly setting – the Venice of Byron, who is mentioned in the text and like whom the Spirit sometimes sounds. But other aspects of the Spirit suggest that he is the vocalization of demoralizing urges and thoughts that are an aspect of the speaker's divided psyche. Indeed, in the prose epilogue to the poem the poet suggests that 'the beauty of the poem' is that 'nobody can say' whether or not the spirit was an external voice: 'You see ... the thing which it is attempted to represent is the conflict between the tender Conscience and the World. Now, the over-tender conscience will of course exaggerate the wickedness of the world, and the Spirit in my poem may be merely the hypothesis or subjective imagination ... '

In scene 3 of part i, the subject is the conflict between the 'insidious lewdness' of Dipsychus' sexual desires for socially inferior females and his idealizing Victorian conscience. He wonders how, 'in the name of saints and saintly thoughts/Of mothers and of sisters and chaste wives' and of 'angel women-spirits' and 'innocent sweet children' he can be assailed by such desires. For the Spirit there is no problem: 'sin and shame', he urges, leave one 'much the same':

> 'Try all things' good and bad, no matter
> You can't till then hold fast the latter.
> If not, this itch will stick and vex you
> Your livelong days till death unsex you.

Dipsychus replies that while it might be possible for a man to feed the 'brute appetite' without being permanently tainted by the experience, the same is not the case for a woman.

> for oh, the sweet bloom of desire
> In hot fruition's pawey fingers turns
> To dullness and the deadly spreading spot
> Of rottenness inevitably soon
> That while we hold, we hate.

'Fiddle di diddle, fal lal lal!' is the Spirit's cynical reply, 'By candlelight they are not *pas mal*'. And when Dipsychus exclaims that he cannot believe that 'any child of Eve' was formed only to be 'swilled with animal delight/And yield five minutes' pleasure to the male', the Spirit devastatingly responds by reciting the song from Shakespeare's *As You Like It* about the lover and his lass who in the pretty springtime would lie betwixt the acres of the rye.

Dipsychus next looks to an idealized Victorian marriage as the solution to his conflict:

> O welcome then the sweet domestic bonds,
> The matrimonial sanctities; the hopes
> And cares of wedded life; parental thoughts,
> The prattle of young children, the good word
> Of fellow men, the sanction of the law,
> And permanence and habit, that transmute
> Grossness itself to crystal.

It is at first surprising to find that the Spirit agrees to help him 'map your life out on the plan/Of the connubial puritan'. The reason, one comes to see, is that there is more than one way for Dipsychus to damn himself. This is why the Spirit is himself two-sided – a 'compound of convention and impiety', in his self-description, a 'mongrel of uncleanness and propriety' (ii, 5). In scene 4 of part i, the Spirit leads Dipsychus into good society and urges him to make a 'virtuous attachment formed judiciously'. But Dipsychus has the same aversion as did Philip Hewson and Claude to properly brought up young ladies and to the 'pallid hotbed courtesies' that curb spontaneity and make one 'lose one's youth too early'. Indeed, when the subject of marriage comes up again in the second part of the poem, the Spirit has repeatedly to urge Dipsychus to 'submit, submit' to the world as it is: 'Oh! trust one who knows you,/ You'll make an admirable sposo' (ii, 2).

As the moment of his capitulation to the world nears, Dipsychus wonders if just possibly one could against all the odds find happiness in romantic sexual love as opposed to a conventional marriage:

> Then love; I scarce can think
> That these bemaddening discords of the mind
> To pure melodious sequence could be changed
> And all the vext conundrums of our life
> Solved to all time, by this old Pastoral
> Of a new Adam and a second Eve
> Set in a Garden which no serpent seeks.
> And yet I hold heart can beat true to heart:
> And to hew down the tree which bears this fruit
> To do a thing which cuts me off from hope,
> To falsify the movement of love's mind,
> To seat some alien trifler on the throne
> A queen may come to claim; that were ill done.
> What! to the close hand of the clutching Jew
> Hand up that rich reversion! and for what?
> This would be hard, did I indeed believe
> 'Twould ever fall. – But love the large repose
> Restorative not to mere outside needs
> Skin deep, but thoroughly to the total man,
> Exists I will believe but so so rare
> So doubtful, so exceptional; hard to guess
> When guessed, so often counterfeit; in brief
> A thing not possibly to be conceived
> An item in the reckonings of the wise.

(ii, 3)

This, the central passage in *Dipsychus* concerning love, comes to the demoralizing conclusion that it would be imprudent in the extreme to entertain the hope of fulfilment through sexual love. And once the sense of life lived according to love is extinguished, there is no alternative but to submit to the Spirit. 'Fear not, my lamb', he tells Dipsychus: 'whate'er men say/I am the Shepherd; and the Way' (ii, 5).

By the end of *Dipsychus*, one has come a long way not only from *The Bothie* but also from *Amours de Voyage* – a distance that is registered by parodies of passages in both earlier works. In the former, the epic simile of the sun entering a populous city had expressed the transforming effect on Philip Hewson of the love of Elspie. In *Dipsychus* (i, 4), when the Spirit observes that 'What we call love is good touched up with evil', the best that the title character can offer as a rejoinder is a negative reinscription of the same figure, one that includes polluting smoke and a 'vagrant miscreant [who] with a look/Transmutes me his; and for a whole sick day/Lepers me'. In *Amours de Voyage*, Claude had used his intellect rather than his emotions as the compass to steer by in his search for sexual love. However misguided this may have seemed, there was a certain impressiveness and dignity in his commitment to rationality. But in *Dipsychus* the possibility of reciprocated sexual love has become so problematized that the poem's protagonist finally chooses as his compass not knowledge but cynical calculation. The change is underlined by a gratuitous travesty of Claude's reflections in i, 5, when Dipsychus breaks into hexameters to proclaim that

> Life it is beautiful wholly, and could we eliminate only
> This interfering, enslaving, o'ermastering demon of craving
> This wicked tempter inside us to ruin still eager to guide us,
> Life were beautitude, action a possible pure satisfaction.

This is a unmistakable allusion to *Amours de Voyage* iii, 8. But unlike Claude's, each of Dipsychus' lines contains an internal rhyme – as the Spirit points out: 'Hexameters by all that's odious/Beshod with rhyme to run melodious.' But the internal rhymes do not make the lines melodious; they make them sound clumsy and sing-song and create an entirely farcical effect.

5

Patmore remarked that *The Bothie* was 'the only considerable poem of Clough's in which he seems, for a time, to have got out of his slough of introspection and doubt'. Noting the 'poetical power' of the poem's love-passages, Patmore guessed that, 'in the presence of a simple and amiable woman', Clough had felt 'a mystery of life which acted for a time as the rebuke and speechless solution of all doubts and intellectual distresses' (Patmore, 1913, 90). If so, the experience was not to be repeated. In 1854 Clough married Blanche Smith, a young women nine years his junior from the same station in life as the young women Philip Hewson and Dipsychus sought to avoid. As recorded in their correspondence, their three-year courtship and engagement was a protracted and painful process during which Clough displayed the qualities of character that Matthew Arnold described as his friend's 'morbid conscientiousness' (Lowry, 130).

Like the implied author of *Dipsychus*, Clough in his letters to Blanche seems to disbelieve in the possibility of fulfilment through sexual love. The most positive extrapolation that could be made both from these letters and from his unfinished poem would be something very close to the position that Coleridge ascribes to Wordsworth in his letter to Crabb Robinson of March 1811:

Wordsworth is by nature incapable of being in Love, tho' no man more tenderly attached – hence he ridicules the existence of any other passion, than a compound of Lust with Esteem & Friendship, confined to one Object, first by accidents of Association, and permanently, by the force of Habit & a sense of Duty.

For Coleridge, this attitude

will do very well – it will suffice to make a good Husband – it may even be desirable (if the largest sum of easy & pleasurable sensations in this Life be the right aim & end of human Wisdom) that we should have this, & no more – but still it is not *Love* – & there is such a passion, as Love.

(154)

CHAPTER SIX

Physic for Adults:
Meredith's *Modern Love*

Love makes clear the eyes that else would never see:
'Love makes blind the eyes to all but me and thee.'

Love turns life to joy till nought is left to gain:
'Love turns life to woe till hope is nought and vain.'
...
Love burns up the world to changeless heaven and blest:
'Love burns up the world to a void of all unrest.'

William Morris, 'Echoes of Love's House'

1

In the winter of 1861–62, George Meredith worked on a long poem, tentative titles for which were 'A Love-Match' and 'A Tragedy of Modern Love'. He was pleased to be creatively engaged, 'But the poem's morbid, and all about Love. So I despise my work, and sneer secretly at those that flatter me about it'. The finished work, a sequence of 50 16-line poems of four quatrains, was published in the spring of 1862 under the title *Modern Love* and a pre-emptive motto: 'This is not meat/For little people or for fools.' As he expected, Meredith received

> a severe drilling from the Reviewers ... A man who hopes to be popular, must think *from* the mass, and as the *heart* of the mass ... as a dissection of the sentimental passion of these days, [his work] could only be apprehended by the few who would read it many times. I have not looked for it to succeed. Why did I write it? – Who can account for pressure?
>
> (1970, i, 123, 145, 160)

The biographical pressure under which Meredith wrote had been building for more than a decade – ever since 1849 when at the age of 21 he had married Mary Nicolls, an intelligent and witty widow and mother six years his senior. The volume of poems Meredith published two years later included a number of idealizations of romantic love, among them 'Twilight Music', which speaks of the beloved's singing voice as bringing a sympathetic 'whisper from the stars' and blending 'divine delight with loveliest desire', and 'Love in the Valley' (first version), the one outstanding lyric he wrote during the early 1850s. For this amalgamation of the lyric of first love and the expectation-as-virtual-fulfilment lyric Meredith developed an original, trochaic- and caesura-based stanza, the emphatic rhythm of which seems as happy in itself as the maiden celebrated by the speaker is 'happy in herself' and in the April landscape of which she is part.

In time, the marriage began to deteriorate. Meredith's determination to pursue a literary career rather than obtain permanent employment meant that the couple had to live on a chronically insufficient income, the hardships of which were exacerbated by Mary's pregnancies and confinements, from which only one child survived – a son born in 1853. By the mid-1850s, violent quarrels had become a staple of their lives: 'Two highly strung temperaments', wrote Meredith's son by his second marriage, 'each imaginative, emotional, quick to anger, cuttingly satirical in dispute ... could not find domestic content within the narrow bounds of poverty and lodgings' (Meredith, 1912, i, 7).

In the late 1850s Mary began an affair with their friend, the minor pre-Raphaelite painter Henry Wallis, by whom she had a child. In 1858, the adulterous couple left England for Capri; the following year Mary returned alone. Despite her entreaties, Meredith refused to see his wife, though he did eventually allow their son to visit her. By 1861, Mary was seriously ill and increasingly distraught and remorseful. She often spoke of death and asked that some lines from a love lament by Tennyson be inscribed on her tombstone:

> Come not, when I am dead,
>   To drop thy foolish tears upon my grave,
> To trample round my fallen head,
>   And vex the unhappy dust thou wouldst not save.
>
>   (ii, 131)

Mary died of renal dropsy in October 1861. Later that month, Meredith informed a correspondent that he had just learned 'that one had quitted [the world] who bore my name: and this filled my mind with melancholy recollections which I rarely give way to' (1970, i, 108).[1]

2

The pitiful story of his marriage not only supplied the pressure that forced *Modern Love* from Meredith; it also furnished some of the poem's *fabula*. A marriage based on romantic love has undergone a heavy change. When the sequence opens, the husband has discovered that the wife has formed an attachment to another man. The husband himself subsequently becomes involved with another woman (whom he

refers to as 'Lady' or 'my Lady', the wife being designated 'Madam').
But this relationship does nothing to lessen the marital tension. Attempts at reconciliation prove equally unsuccessful. Only the death of
the wife terminates their conflicted relationship.[2]

The *sjuzet*, the artistic handling of this material, reflects the fact
that Meredith was a professional novelist as well as a gifted poet. The
point of view throughout is the tormented husband's. A few of the
sections at the termini of *Modern Love* are narrated in the third
person; these are the husband's impersonal retrospective representations and reflections. The first-person narration used in the great
majority of the sections is that of the husband as experiencing self
rather than as retrospective narrating self – that is, he describes scenes,
situations and his reflections on them as they occur or immediately
after. This means that there is no distance between a scene and its
narration. The reader is kept uncomfortably close to a nasty domestic
situation – so close that the effect is sometimes an expressionistic
distortion of the realistic surface.

Many of the 50 sections of *Modern Love* are vividly and economi-
cally realized scenes involving husband and wife. Some are social occasions in which the couple keep up appearances. A dinner party over
which they effortlessly preside is the subject of section 17:

> Went the feast ever cheerfuller? She keeps
> The Topic over intellectual deeps
> In bouyancy afloat. They see no ghost.
> With sparkling surface-eyes we ply the ball.

The couple play the surface game so well that, 'Enamoured of an acting
nought can tire,/Each other, like true hypocrites, admire'. Below the
surface, however, another game is being played: 'Hiding the Skeleton,
shall be its name.' This game is no laughing matter, as the allusion to
the ghost of murdered Banquo in *Macbeth* suggests. The couple's surface glitter is actually an ignis fatuus or will-o'-the-wisp – the 'corpse-
light' of decaying matter. On other occasions, it is less easy for them to
'act this wedded lie' (section 35). In section 21, for example, a visiting
friend who is deliriously in love announces that he has been accepted by
'most wondrous she' and asks for the blessing and advice of the 'wedded lovers':

> We question; if we dare! or if we should!
> And pat him, with light laugh. We have not winced.
> Next, she has fallen. Fainting points the sign
> To happy things in wedlock. When she wakes,
> She looks the star that thro' the cedar shakes:
> Her lost moist hand clings mortally to mine.

In most of the scenes in *Modern Love*, however, husband and wife are alone. These sections are tableau-like, a presentational style appropriate to the enforcèd ceremony of a love that has begun to sicken and decay and to the couple's self-conscious role-playing and dissimulation ('Each sucked a secret, and each wore a mask' [section 2]). There is little dialogue: either 'She will not speak. I will not ask' (section 22) or she wishes to communicate and he refuses to listen. While the wife seldom speaks and is presented only from the outside, acute notations convey a sense of *her* tormented inner being:

> She has desires of touch, as if to feel
> That all the household things are things she knew.
> She stops before the glass. What sight in view?
> A face that seems the latest to reveal!
> For she turns from it hastily, and tossed
> Irresolute, steals shadow-like to where
> I stand; and wavering pale before me there,
> Her tears fall still as oak-leaves after frost.
>
> (Section 22)

The principal setting in which husband and wife are alone together is the most intimate of domestic spaces – the bedroom. Each of the five sections with this setting exemplifies Tolstoy's dictum: 'A man goes through earthquakes, epidemics, the horrors of disease, and all sorts of spiritual torments, but the most agonizing tragedy he ever knows always has been and always will be – the tragedy of the bedroom' (Gorky, 383). *Modern Love* opens with an *in medias res* plunge into the marital pit:

> By this he knew she wept with waking eyes:
> That, at his hand's light quiver by her head,
> The strange low sobs that shook their common bed,
> Were called into her with a sharp surprise,
> And strangled mute, like little gaping snakes,
> Dreadfully venomous to him. She lay
> Stone-still ...
> Like sculptured effigies they might be seen
> Upon their marriage-tomb, the sword between;
> Each waiting for the sword that severs all.
>
> (Section 1)

In another section, the couple are guests at a country-house Christmas gathering: 'rooms are full: we can but get/An attic-crib. Such lovers will not fret/At that, it is half-said'. She takes the bed; he chooses the floor, where he successfully suppresses a 'dullard fit' of resentful sexual desire. But his punitive feelings, his desire for her debasement, find expression in a dream – a tableau within a tableau that employs the Victorian iconography of the remorseful fallen woman:

Out in the freezing darkness the lambs bleat.
The small bird stiffens in the low starlight.
I know not how, but shuddering as I slept,
I dreamed a banished angel to be crept;
My feet were nourished on her breasts all night.

(Section 23)

In a third bedroom scene, the husband's vindictive emotions find self-consciously theatrical expression. He enters the bedroom to confront his wife with two passionate love letters in her hand – one addressed to him and a more recent one addressed to her new love interest:

I think she sleeps: it must be sleep, when low
Hangs that abandoned arm toward the floor.
The face turned with it. Now make fast the door.
Sleep on: it is your husband, not your foe.
The Poet's black stage-lion of wronged love,
Frights not our modern dames: – well if he did!
Now will I pour new light upon that lid,
Full-sloping like the breasts beneath. 'Sweet dove,
Your sleep is pure. Nay, pardon: I disturb.
I do not? good!' Her waking infant-stare
Grows woman to the burden my hands bear.

(Section 15)

This tableau is artfully managed: arm and face, eyelid and breasts, are carefully arranged and lighted; and the precise moment depicted is simultaneously the wife's awakening from sleep and her recognition of his purpose. The scene's theatricality is further emphasized by the husband's self-parodic comparison of himself to Othello entering the chamber of his sleeping wife with the intention of murdering her.

This allusion exemplifies another presentational feature of *Modern Love* – the numerous literary and artistic references. These are narratorial rather than authorial references and instance the well-read husband's self-dramatizing and expressionistic proclivities. As Patricia Ball noted, 'posturing [and] theatricality of gesture' are features of a crisis in which 'sophisticated perceptions are submitted to primitive emotional pressures' (112). While they thicken the texture of *Modern Love*, these allusions do little to provide perspective on the marital situation represented in the text; they generate heat but little light. The same is true of the excess of signification in the language and figuration employed by the husband – portentous figures like the 'amber cradle near the sun's decline', within which 'Is lying a dead infant, slain by thee' (section 11), the numerous images of eating, drinking, tasting, sucking, and of snakes and serpents.

All these features of the text instance the husband-narrator's compulsive present-time devaluation and degradation of the experience of romantic love. He and his wife were once two reed-pipes filled with a god's 'mellow breath'; now they are played by a 'discord-loving clown' who puffs his 'gross spirit in them, worse than death' (section 8). In another section, the husband employs the image of hearts beating in unison like one timepiece set to another. It is the same quintessentially Victorian image of marital union found in Tennyson's *The Princess*, Browning's 'Two in the Campagna', and Patmore's 'Wedding Sermon'. But in *Modern Love* the image immediately mutates into a gross sexual allusion – the timepiece cannot stop but 'must for ever swell' (section 19). And while section 18 opens with a description of 'country merry-making on the green' – Jack and Tom paired with Moll and Meg, dancing to a fiddler, 'the nut-brown stream' of liquid refreshment – it ends very differently. Reflecting that he too has known 'rustic revels in my youth:/The May-fly pleasures of a mind at ease', the husband is led to exclaim: 'Heaven keep them happy.' But even as this benediction leaves his mouth, his mood is modulating into gratuitous and misanthropic cynicism:

> They must, I think, be wiser than I am;
> They have the secret of the bull and lamb.
> 'Tis true that when we trace its source, 'tis beer.

To the jaundiced eye and blighted sensibilities of the husband in present time, everything suggestive of romantic love appears polluted and degraded. What has happened to him? What is the cause of *his* degradation?

3

'Where came the cleft between us; whose the fault?' the husband asks himself; 'where began the change; and what's my crime?' (sections 8, 10). It is clear from these questions that he regards his wife's liaison with another man as a symptom rather than the cause of their present distress and that the answer to these questions must be sought elsewhere. Rod Edmond's (1988) new-historicist answer is that the fault is found in 'an historically specific social formation', the institution of Victorian marriage, 'which has come to define and distort love and sexuality' (209–10). This is surely tendentious. In *Modern Love*, as in Browning's *James Lee's Wife*, marriage is the ground on which romantic love is tested. Marriage (and income) remove the external obstacles to the fulfilment of sexual love, leaving only internal obstacles. Indeed, a principal aspect of the modern love studied in Meredith's poem is the freedom from institutional and social constraints. Other commentators have found an answer to the husband's questions in section 10, which has been thought to adumbrate a specific cause of the marital estrangement, for which there is a biographical parallel in Meredith's own marriage. In this section, the husband remarks: 'My crime is, that the puppet of a dream,/I plotted to be worthy of the world.' That is, he was not content to stay forever in 'Love's deep woods' and left them to attempt to make his mark in the world. Love being 'a thing of moods;/ Not like hard life, of laws', this caused a permanent fissure in his marriage. But this is a partial construal of the section. 'In Love's deep woods,/I dreamt of loyal Life: – the offence is there', the husband says, intimating that the originating cause of future discord is to be found in the dream of romantic love itself, rather than in his subsequent attempt 'to be worthy of the world'.

In present time, the husband 'plays the game of Sentiment' with his 'lady' – a game does not involve love but rather the gratification of ego and of sexual desire. 'I feel the promptings of Satanic power', he tells her, 'While you do homage unto me alone' (section 28). In the prelapsarian days with his wife, love was not a game in that they were not self-consciously playing parts. But the young lovers were sentimental in another way. *Modern Love* is as Meredith described it in the letter quoted above: 'a dissection of the sentimental passion of these days'. In another letter he glossed a line of Nature's speech in section 30:

> 'My children most they seem, when they least know me', says Nature. That is, while you lovers are acting Nature you are ignorant of her; and she has to cure you of your idealistic mists, by running the sharp thorn of Reality into your quivering flesh. Romance is neither in nor out of nature. It is young blood heated by Love or the desire for Love. It's true while it lasts – no longer.
>
> (1970, i, 129).

In Yeats's terser formulation ('Whence had They Come?'):

> Eternity is passion, girl or boy
> Cry at the outset of their sexual joy
> 'For ever and for ever'; then awake
> Ignorant what Dramatis Personae spake.

The 'sentimental passion of these days', then, consists in thinking that love has a lasting spiritual dimension, that it moves one permanently to a higher plane. It involves lovers thinking that idealistic mists are their proper habitat, that their love is not or should not be subject to temporal and circumstantial factors.

Romantic love is itself the disease – or rather its breeding ground, the specific affliction being the heart's 'cravings for the buried day' (section 50). Does *Modern Love* offer a remedy or antidote? Prima facie, the poem might seem to contain a prescription: to study the natural world and its operations and learn its lessons. There are two sections in which these lessons are spelled out. The first is section 13:

> 'I play for Seasons; not Eternities!'
> Says Nature, laughing on her way. 'So must
> All those whose stake is nothing more than dust!'
> And lo, she wins, and of her harmonies
> She is full sure! Upon her dying rose,
> She drops a look of fondness, and goes by,
> Scarce any retrospection in her eye;
> For she the laws of growth most deeply knows,
> Whose hands bear, here, a seed bag – there, an urn.
> Pledged she herself to aught, 'twould mark her end!
> This lesson of our only visible friend
> Can we not teach our foolish hearts to learn?

The answer at the end of this section is that it is very hard to 'Lose calmly Love's great bliss' when it is re-experienced in 'the renewed for ever of a kiss'. The same point is made in other sections. Over and over again, the husband looks back to the early days of his and his wife's love and laments the loss of its supernal radiance. 'Something more than earth/I cry for still', he exclaims in section 29:

> I cannot be at peace
> In having Love upon a mortal lease.
> I cannot take the woman [the lady] at her worth!
> …
> A kiss is but a kiss now! and no wave
> Of a great flood that whirls me to the sea.

In contrast, love-making in present time is figured as a gross mortal indulgence: 'But, as you will! we'll sit contentedly,/And eat our pot of honey on the grave.'

This devaluation might seem of itself to underline the urgency of learning a different, non-erotic kind of kissing – of learning 'to kiss the season and shun regrets', as 'Mother Nature' is beseeched to teach the speaker of Meredith's 'Ode to the Spirit of Earth in Autumn', another poem in the collection of 1862 that included Modern Love. But are we in fact meant to take section 13 straight and find a positive message in it? Or is the message ironized – that is, subject to the same withering scrutiny and distortion as seemingly everything else in the poem? Consider the seed bag and the urn: is there not something wrong with this alpha-omega figuration? Should it not be either a seed bag and a compost pile or a cradle and an urn? The mismatch looks like another expressive distortion suggesting an ironic, sardonic utterance. Moreover, the figuration calls attention to the breakdown of the human/natural analogy. Only humans revere their dead and treat their remains with dignity and solemnity. The acts of the bereaved attest to the fact

that there is a value or worth in human existence and human relationships that has no parallel in the world of nature.

In section 30, the natural prescription is written in a version of
phylogenetic discourse:

> What are we first? First, animals; and next
> Intelligences at a leap; on whom
> Pale lies the distant shadow of the tomb,
> And all that draweth on the tomb for text.
> Into which state comes Love, the crowning sun:
> Beneath whose light the shadow loses form.
> We are the lords of life, and life is warm.
> Intelligence and instinct now are one.
> But Nature says: 'My children most they seem
> When they least know me: therefore I decree
> That they shall suffer.' Swift doth young Love flee,
> And we stand wakened, shivering from our dream.
> Then if we study Nature we are wise.
> Thus do the few who live but with the day:
> The scientific animals are they. –
> Lady, this is my sonnet to your eyes.

The argument of the first 14 lines emphasizes the need for an intellectual
study of nature rather than simply for developing an affinity with natural
process. The emphasis is on thinking clearly and rationally – on 'more
brain' (section 48) as the answer to the vicissitudes of romantic love. But
the ending of the section introduces a complicating note. The final line
alludes to Shakespeare's sonnet 130 ('My mistress' eyes are nothing like
the sun'), his witty deflation of Petrarchan idealizations of the beloved.
But unlike Shakespeare's sonnet, this section seems to undermine the very
idea of love as an ennobling ideal in human existence and to replace it
with cynicism. Is this to be taken at face value? Is the answer to become a
'scientific animal' using a hedonistic calculus? In a study of Meredith's
pessimistic humanism, Arthur L. Simpson did not think so. He pointed to
the contrast between the 'intelligences' at the beginning of the section and
the 'animals' at the end, and to the change from the opening 'we' to the
concluding 'they', and argued that 'they' are 'not quite fully human, [are]
rationally safe but spiritually poor' and that taken as a whole the section
suggests that 'it is somehow better to shiver humanly in a hostile universe' than to become a scientific animal (350).

In addition, one ought to consider the places in *Modern Love* that
show the results of the application of intelligence. It is true that several
times the husband successfully attempts to act rationally as he struggles
to understand post-lapsarian or 'modern' love. In section 6, he will not
strike 'the world's coward stroke'; in section 19 he bleeds, 'but her who
wounds I will not blame'. But these are exceptions. Throughout

Modern Love, the husband is in the grip of powerful conflicted emotions that confuse his thought – 'What my drift?' 'Know I my meaning, I?' (sections 31, 40) – and undermine his humane principles. Sometimes the best he can do is 'strive to ape the magnanimity of love' (section 2); and for every constructive moment there are contrasting destructive moments. In section 14, for example, he says 'let me bear on the bitter ill'; but in the very next section he is the vindictive Othello of modern love. And in section 20, where he seems at pains to avoid applying a double standard, his rhetoric suggests braggart role-playing, not sober acknowledgement of his own past indiscretions. Moreover, where the husband seems most insightful is in numerous demoralizing insights into aspects of his situation that his intellect cannot rectify: 'In this unholy battle I grow base' (section 8); 'that hideous human game: – /Imagination urging appetite' (section 38); 'How rare from [our] own instinct 'tis to feel!/[We] waste the soul with spurious desire' (section 41).

All told, the husband's intellectual efforts amount to little in the face of his frequently violent emotions. In Meredith's work, it is passions, not intellect, that 'spin the plot' (section 43). No wonder, then, that the husband apostrophizes 'You burly lovers on the village green,/Yours is a lower, and a happier star!' (section 22); or that he reflects:

> If any state be enviable on earth,
> 'Tis yon born idiot's, who, as days go by,
> Still rubs his hands before him, like a fly,
> In a queer sort of meditative mirth.
>
>   (section 19)

4

The climax and conclusion of the husband's attempt at 'distraction' through involvement with his lady occur in section 39. It opens with his reporting that she has 'yielded' and rejoicing in the prospective enjoyment of the 'rose' of her mature sexuality that he imagines superior to the 'violet breath of maidenhood' (the early days of his and his wife's love). But the celebration is short lived: at the end of the section he is utterly deflated by seeing his wife with another man. What has happened is explained in the following section: 'The dread that my old love may be alive,/Has seized my nursling new love by the throat' (section 40). It is the confirmation of a suspicion the husband had earlier voiced:

> One restless corner of my heart or head,
> That holds a dying something never dead,
> Still frets, though Nature giveth all she can.

It means that woman is not, I opine,
Her sex's antidote.

(section 32)

In extremis, a possibility occurs to the husband: that he might 'achieve' peace 'By turning to this fountain-source of woe,/This woman [the wife], who's to Love as fire to wood' (section 40). The final ten sections of *Modern Love* record the results of this turn. In them, stagnation and oscillation between past and present give way to a forward movement that causes the reader to begin to wonder how the sequence will end. Is this mess of love capable of positive narrative, thematic and/or aesthetic resolution?

While there is more plotting and more incident in the closing sections, it is often difficult to determine precisely what is happening. One problem is posed by the white spaces between sections. It makes a difference whether there is a close temporal (and therefore presumably a causal) connection between sections, and it is sometimes not possible to determine the length of time is represented by the white space. This is particularly important in connection with the central difficulty of the closing phase of *Modern Love*: the husband-narrator's uncertain knowledge of, and possible unreliability concerning, both his wife's thoughts, motives and actions (especially those that concern the other man) and her knowledge of, or beliefs concerning, the state of her husband's relations with the lady. The effect of these obstacles on the reader is continuing uncertainty concerning what actually happens and why. The indeterminacy of meaning enacts at the level of the reading experience the epistemological uncertainty and the equivocal nature of modern love that the husband is experiencing at the narrative level.[3]

In section 41, it is reported that husband and wife have 'taken up a lifeless vow/To rob a living passion'. Houghton and Stange's gloss is that 'they have vowed marital fidelity without love' (644n), that is, they have agreed to end their affairs. This seems correct but incomplete. As the hands of the clock near midnight and the couple look like anything but 'a pair/Who for fresh nuptials joyfully yield all else', it becomes clear that their vow also includes the agreement to resume sexual relations, 'to make love according to the letter of their marriage-vows', as another editor puts it (Hanley, 109).

Earlier in *Modern Love* the husband had repeatedly felt a strong physical attraction to his wife, but had successfully struggled to resist the temptation of sex without love, which he clearly regarded as dishonourable and degrading (see sections 3, 5, 7, and 23). But now, at the beginning of section 42, 'I am to follow her' to bed. As the wife leaves the room, she has an 'air of cold/And statuesque sedateness' that calls to mind Pallas Athene. Once she is gone, 'The hands/Of Time now signal':

Within those secret walls what do I see?
Where first she set the taper down she stands:
Not Pallas: Hebe shamed! Thoughts black as death,
Like a stirred pool in sunshine break. Her wrists
I catch: she faltering, as she half resists,
'You love ... ? love ... ? love ... ?' all on an indrawn breath.

The handling of this bedroom scene is masterly. It is not possible to
determine whether the husband is imagining the scene or whether it is
actually occurring (though we know from the next poem that the couple do, so to speak, commit sexual acts). The effect is to suggest that
there is something voyeuristic or pornographic about the scene. On the
one hand, there is the domineering male; on the other, the half-pliant,
faltering and vulnerable female – Athena reduced to Hebe, the goddess
of youth who was dismissed as cupbearer to the gods because she 'fell
down in an indecent posture' (Lemprière, 265) while pouring at a
festival and was thus shamefully exposed to the male gaze.

In the final line of section 42 the wife is asking whether or not what is
taking place is an act of love. It clearly is not. The white space between
section 42 and section 43 contains the climactic moment in the sequence – the moment the husband and wife hit rock bottom. In section
43 it is made clear that their resumption of marital relations without
love has been a disaster:

Here is a fitting spot to dig Love's grave;
Here where the ponderous breakers plunge and strike,
And dart their hissing tongues high up the sand.
...
If I the death of Love had deeply planned,
I never could have made it half so sure,
As by the unblest kisses which upbraid
The full-waked sense; or failing that, degrade!
'Tis morning: but no morning can restore
What we have forfeited. I see no sin;
The wrong is mixed. In tragic life, God wot,
No villain need be! Passions spin the plot;
We are betrayed by what is false within.

The plunging waves striking the shore and the darting tongues of the
snake-like surf are suggestive images of sexual coupling that is 'unblest'
in the sense that it does not have the self-authenticating sanction of an
act of love. In an earlier section, the couple had kissed while taking part
in the drawing-room game called forfeits. It was one scene in the
'wedded lie' that they had performed so well before others (section 35).
But they cannot fool an audience that consists only of themselves. What
they have 'forfeited' in section 42 is the last shreds of their self-respect.
There is 'no sin' in a religious sense because there is no evidence of

Christian or any other supernatural belief in *Modern Love* (the 'God wot' is ironic – a derisive reference to a concept as vestigial as the verb). If there is no standard to transgress, then no one can be assigned moral blame for what has transpired. The active agent is a subterranean falseness within the self.

At the end of section 38, the husband had reflected that his feelings for his wife could be either those of 'Love, or Vileness! not a choice between,/Save petrifaction!' But in section 44, he is at last able to pity her. Time passes in section 45 and section 46. One summer day, the husband plucks a rose, smells it and is reminded of his lady and their time together. The reader is reminded of Nature casting a look of fondness on the dying rose with 'Scarce any retrospection in her eye' (section 13). That time may be healing the husband's wounds is further suggested when he comes upon his wife 'not alone' in what appears to be a dawn assignation. He takes her arm and declares his 'firm belief in her, ere she could speak'. Her reaction is equally striking: 'A ghastly morning came into her cheek,/While with a widening soul on me she stared.' What precisely is one to infer? Presumably that the wife has been unfaithful to their lifeless vow, is ashamed – and astonished at her husband's magnanimity in ignoring the prima-facie evidence of her misconduct. Is this unprecedented generosity the result of his having come to pity her? Does this betoken the beginning of a new post-romantic intimacy, perhaps even love, between them?

In section 47, the season is autumn:

> We saw the swallows gathering in the sky,
> And in the osier-isle we heard them noise.
> We had not to look back on summer joys,
> Or forward to a summer of bright dye:
> But in the largeness of the evening earth
> Our spirits grew as we went side by side.
> The hour became her husband and my bride.
> Love that had robbed us so, thus blessed our dearth!
> The pilgrims of the year waxed very loud
> In multitudinous chatterings, as the flood
> Full brown came from the West, and like pale blood
> Expanded to the upper crimson cloud.
> Love that had robbed us of immortal things,
> This little moment mercifully gave,
> Where I have seen across the twilight wave
> The swan sail with her young beneath her wings.

The couple here respond positively to a manifestation of nature that does not involve the recommendation that human beings either go with the flow or 'live but for the day'. What is suggested instead is a powerful compensation or mitigation of the 'tragedy' of modern love through felt participation in a natural continuum to which husband and wife are individually wedded and therefore mediately united. This section contains the only radiantly positive present-time moment in *Modern Love*. It is a version of the compensation for loss found in Wordsworth's Intimations ode, but with the termini reversed. In section 29, the husband had wondered

> Where is the ancient wealth wherewith I clothed
> Our human nakedness, and could endow
> With spiritual splendour a white brow ... ?

This recalls the famous Wordsworthian interrogation: 'Whither has fled the visionary gleam?/Where is it now, the glory and the dream?' Meredith's speaker was concerned with the loss of a quality that once invested the female other with 'spiritual splendour'; Wordsworth's with the disappearance of a 'celestial light' that once invested the natural world. That both have fled is the sad given of adult experience. In the Intimations ode, a human bond based on common mortality is one compensation for the lost radiance of youth. In section 47, a bond with the largeness of autumnal natural world is the compensation for the lost splendour of romantic love.

The original reading of the first half of the penultimate line of section 47 – 'And I still see' – had contained the intimation that this experience of expanded consciousness had been a defining or threshold moment in the couple's relationship and had effected a lasting change – that henceforth the crepuscular emblem of their relationship would be the protective swan with her young rather than the amber cradle containing a dead infant of section 11. Put discursively, the implication is that romantic love need not end in disillusionment and hatred but may become transformed into affectionate or companionate love, the precondition of which is the romantic lover's recognition of 'the non-ideal status of his love object' (Mitchell, 106) and that all human love is held 'upon a mortal lease' (section 29).

No wonder, then, that Meredith changed the line, for such resonances are out of phase with the dark, melodramatic finale of *Modern Love*. The opening of section 48 abruptly returns one from expanded vision to introverted complexities:

> Their sense is with their senses all mixed in,
> Destroyed by subtleties these women are!
> More brain, O Lord, more brain!

This crude gender stereotyping recalls the husband's earlier accusatory outbursts concerning his wife. It also ironically points up how little help his putatively superior intelligence has been in coping with his situation. The cause of frustration is a miscommunication. When the husband had poured out to his wife 'the pure daylight of honest speech', the wife had learned for the first time the details of his infatuation with his lady. But this had been 'the fatal draught, I fear'. Not realizing the relationship is over and perhaps trying to emulate her husband's fine gesture in section 46, she has run away in order to leave him free to act as he wishes. In the Victorian context, it is the act of a desperate woman – a lost woman. Like Lady Dedlock at the end of Dickens's *Bleak House*, the wife abandons her home and social position, and leaves herself vulnerable to the judgement of the 'hard world'.

In section 49, there is a return to third-person narration used at the beginning of *Modern Love*. This time, however, the narrator does not restrict himself to a close-up outside view of the action, as in the sequence's opening poem, in which he positioned himself at the foot of the marriage bed. In section 49, for the very first time, the husband-narrator offers an inside view of the wife:

> He found her by the ocean's moaning verge,
> Nor any wicked change in her discerned;
> And she believed his old love had returned,
> Which was her exaltation, and her scourge.
> She took his hand, and walked with him, and seemed
> The wife he sought, though shadow-like and dry.
> She had one terror, lest her heart should sigh,
> And tell her loudly she no longer dreamed.
> She dared not say, 'This is my breast: look in'.

The employment of psychological omniscience, however, does not make for total clarity concerning the wife's state of mind or the motivation for her final act – taking her own own life by means of an overdose – which is obliquely communicated in the bedroom scene that ends the section and brings the plot of *Modern Love* to its tragic conclusion:

> But there's a strength to help the desperate weak.
> …
> About the middle of the night her call
> Was heard, and he came wondering to the bed.
> 'Now kiss me, dear! it may be, now!' she said.
> Lethe had passed those lips, and he knew all.

5

In section 25, his wife's literary tastes had given the husband a fresh opportunity to torment her. Instead of the two love letters employed in section 15, he made use of a lightweight 'French novel' concerning a wife's adultery and eventual decision to return to her husband, which *his* wife had made the mistake of saying she found 'unnatural'. In the l, Edmond, the lover, comes to share the wife's 'devout chagrin' at their liaison. 'Blanc-mange and absinthe are his penitent fare' until 'his pale aspect makes her over-fond', at which point, 'to preclude fresh sin, he tries rosbif'. Having drolly rehearsed the novel's preposterous plot, the husband ironically concluded with a turn of the screw: 'My dear, these things are life:/And life, some think, is worthy of the Muse.'

This comment also contains a reflexive level of suggestiveness. The reader is implicitly invited to recognize the superior realism and greater seriousness with which *Modern Love* treats the subjects of romantic love, marriage and infidelity. The 'French novel' is a pastiche of the fashionable novel of the Second Empire as served up by Octave Feuillet, Victor Cherbuliez and Gustave Droz. Meredith had discussed examples of this kind of cross-channel confection in a review article written for the *Westminster Review* in 1857 (see Haight). To such productions he much preferred a novel by a more 'remorseless' realist: Flaubert's *Madame Bovary*. If adultery was to be treated in fiction, Meredith wrote, this was how to do it. Flaubert did not 'present the passion' tricked out with 'blandishing graces' or 'meretricious allurements' thereby awakening 'the sympathies of a vulgar prurience'. On the contrary, he subjected adultery to 'stern analysis ... No harm can come from reading *Madame Bovary*; but it is physic for adults, as the doctors say. The Author has no more love for her than an anatomist for his subject' (1857, 600–601).

The original epigraph to *Modern Love* – 'This is not meat/For little people or for fools' – echoes what Meredith said about *Madame Bovary* and suggests that he may have had Flaubert's work in mind as a model for his own dissection of sentimental passion. Certainly there are similarities between the two works. Prima facie, Matthew Arnold's description of Flaubert's novel could serve equally well as a description of Meredith's poem: 'a work of *petrified feeling*; over it hangs an atmosphere of bitterness, irony, impotence; not a personage in the book to rejoice or console us'. There are, however, telling differences of degree between the two works. Consider the last two sections of *Modern Love*, in which the husband-narrator speaks in the third person. The inside view of the wife given in the penultimate section is very different from the remorseless ironies of Flaubert's *style indirect libre*, which are applied to Emma Bovary (in Arnold's phrase) 'without pity or pause, as with malignity' (xi, 293). The husband's retrospective intimacy with the wife's thoughts suggests that, however imperfect his knowledge of her motives remained, he came to have a sympathetic insight into her tormented being.

In the final section of *Modern Love*, the husband–narrator is at a sufficient distance from the action not only to make several recapitulative generalizations (some of which I have cited above) but also to supply an end symbol for the entire work:

> In tragic hints here see what evermore
> Moves dark as yonder midnight ocean's force,
> Thundering like ramping hosts of warrior horse,
> To throw that faint thin line upon the shore!

The 'what' that 'evermore' moves is a figure for the uncontrollable destructive energies moving within human beings. In the formulation of section 43, 'what' is that which is 'false within', the imperfection that can bring the experience of romantic love to a tragic conclusion. The 'faint thin line' of ephemeral foam traced along the shore by the thunderous waves is a figure for the moments of post-romantic love tenderness between husband and wife (for which there are no analogues in *Madame Bovary*). One example is the wife's 'lost moist hand' clinging 'mortally' to her husband's in section 19. Another is the 'little moment' mercifully given in section 47. A third is the faint thin line of verse in the penultimate line of section 49: 'Now kiss me, dear! it may be, now!' The wife's last words intimate that physical contact between them is no longer degrading. Their final kiss is neither supernal like their early kisses, nor merely sexual like their embraces in section 43; it is the expression of a loving intimacy.

These moments of intense pathos are the reason that it was not totally inapposite when 30 years after *Modern Love* was first published Meredith removed his original motto, replacing it with a sonnet entitled 'The Promise in Disturbance' that reads more like an epilogue than an epigraph. These are its central lines:

> Now seems the language heard of Love as rain
> To make a mire where fruitfulness was meant.
> The golden harp gives out a jangled strain,
> Too like revolt from heaven's Omnipotent.
> But listen in the thought; so may there come
> Conception of a newly-added chord,
> Commanding space beyond where ear has home.

This passage suggests that Meredith wanted to emphasize the positive hints of a new kind of a post-romantic love by figuring them as a new chord emerging out of disharmony rather than merely as foam thrown up on the shore. The pathetic notes faintly heard in *Modern Love* are not a reason for rejoicing and not much consolation. But they do faintly intimate a conception of human love that can survive both the raptures of romantic love and the ravages of its decay.

Notes

1. For biographical informantion I have relied on Stevenson's biography and the articles by Perkus and Austin.
2. There are good introductions to *Modern Love* in the editions of Day Lewis, Hough and Regan. Of the numerous articles and chapters of books devoted to the poem, I have found most helpful those by Ball, Edmond (1988), Lucas, Mermin (1976) and Simpson.
3. For reconstructions of events in the closing sections of *Modern Love*, see Lindsay (85–6); Mermin (115); Edmond (221–4); Simpson, 352–4; Bartlett in Meredith (1978, ii, 1139); and Hanley (109–10). Critics are divided on the question of whether the work has a positive resolution: Regan (17–18), Golden (267) and Hanley (21) argue that it does; Simpson (352–4), Edmond (1988, 219 f) and Comstock (140–41) think otherwise.

CHAPTER SEVEN

The Old High Way of Love: Morris and Dante Rossetti

I had a thought for no one's but your ears:
That you were beautiful, and that I strove
To love you in the old high way of love;
That it had all seemed happy, and yet we'd grown
As weary-hearted as that hollow moon.
W. B. Yeats, 'Adam's Curse'

1

Dante Gabriel Rossetti was 28 and William Morris 22 when they met and became friends in 1856. In the autumn of the following year, Morris was one of the apprentices who worked with Rossetti decorating the walls of the Oxford Union's new debating hall with murals of subjects from Malory's *Morte d'Arthur*. That October, Rossetti met Jane Burden, a 17-year-old working-class girl whose father was employed in a livery stable, and persuaded her to model for a sequence of studies of Queen Guinevere. Tall and long-necked, with a pale ivory face, deep-set dark eyes, thick eyebrows and a mass of dark hair, Janey became for Rossetti and his group the incarnation of their medieval ideal of female beauty. She was the model for Morris's one easel painting, the portrait of 'La belle Iseult' (also known as 'Guinevere'), and the addressee of his poem 'Praise of My Lady', in which Morris adapted the medieval hymn of supplication to the Virgin Mary. Many of the features named in this litany are conventional attributes of the idealized female of courtly love lyrics; but as Georgiana Burne-Jones noted, the poem also offers a 'true' likeness, a 'faithful portrait', of Janey (i, 169):

My lady seems of ivory
Forehead, straight nose, and cheeks that be
Hollow'd a little mournfully.
Beata mea Domina!
...
Beneath her brows the lids fall slow,
The lashes a clear shadow throw
Where I would wish my lips to be.
Beata mea Domina!

Her great eyes, standing far apart
Draw up some memory from her heart,
And gaze out very mournfully;
 Beata mea Domina!

So beautiful and kind they are,
But most times looking out afar,
Waiting for something, not for me.
 Beata mea Domina!

Late in life, Rossetti told a confidant that he and Janey had been drawn to each other at that time but that he had felt himself too deeply committed to Elizabeth Siddal to pursue the relationship (Caine, 200–201; see Doughty, 649–50, 369). There was no obstacle in Morris's way; after Rossetti left Oxford, he fell in love with Janey. In February 1858, Swinburne, then an undergraduate at Balliol, mentioned in a letter Morris's 'having that wonderful and most perfect stunner of his to – look at or speak to. The idea of his marrying her is insane. To kiss her feet is the utmost man should dream of doing' (i, 18). Morris thought otherwise. He and Janey became engaged two months later; a year after that these two socially mismatched young people were married.

It is obvious that Rossetti's and Morris's relationship with Janey involves a male construction of the female. A late twentieth-century feminist discourse might read 'the Pre-Raphaelite reinvention of the idea of courtly love as a ruse designed to persuade non-aristocratic women that it is better to be adored than emancipated. Courtly sentiment ... helped to palliate unromantic Victorian patriarchal marriage, obfuscating the facts of male power and female subservience' (Cullingford, 34). E. P. Thompson's contextualization is more sympathetic. In his biography of Morris, this historian places the pre-Raphaelite idealization of the female and of love in the context of the medievalism that was 'one of the characteristic forms taken by the later flowering of the romantic movement in mid-nineteenth-century England ... It posed the existence, in the past, of a form of society whose values were finer and richer than those of profit and capitalist utility' (9). In their attitude to women there was on the one hand

> a persistent underlying element of respect for [their] personality and a yearning for a fully equal relationship of love and companionship between the sexes. On the other, there was an extreme idealisation of Love itself ... the woman was the 'soul' of the man, to be isolated and sheltered from the cares and realities of life.
>
>   (65)

This is surely the right inflection for Morris himself. He had grown up in bourgeois affluence, but while an Oxford undergraduate had read and been influenced by Carlyle's *Past and Present* and Ruskin's writings, including 'The Nature of Gothic'. And during a summer trip to the Continent, Morris had visited the French city of Rouen, 'then still in its outward aspect a piece of the Middle Ages; no words can tell you how its mingled beauty, history, and romance took hold on me' ('The Aims of Art', *Works*, xxiv, 85). As Morris (1984–96) explained to a young socialist in 1885: 'We were borne into a dull time oppressed with bourgeoisdom and philistinism so sorely that we were forced to turn back on ourselves, and only in ourselves and the world of art and literature was there any hope' (ii, 472).

In 1854 Edward Burne-Jones had described Morris 'as full of enthusiasm for things holy and beautiful and true, and, what is rarest, of the most exquisite perception and judgment of them. For myself, he has tinged my whole inner being with the beauty of his own' (i, 96). One element in Morris's feeling for Janey was no doubt the 'the chivalric drama of finding and transforming' (MacCarthy, 137) – of tingeing the inner being of the stable worker's daughter. And no doubt there was sexual desire as well. Like the radical Philip Hewson in Clough's *Bothie*, someone with Morris's social views would have found it difficult to become intimate with a middle-class girl expecting the conventional responses and reactions. Morris wanted to love with the all-or-nothing intensity he so admired in the love poems of Browning's *Men and Woman*:

> intense unmixed love; love for the sake of love[;] if that is not obtained disappointment comes, falling-off, misery ... I cannot say it clearly, it cannot be said so but in verse; love for love's sake, the only true love, I must say. Pray Christ, some of us attain to it before we die!
>
> (*Works*, i, 340–41)

It is harder to postulate what Janey might have thought about the transformation in her life between the fall of 1857 and her marriage less than two years later. Her point of view does not figure in contemporary representations of her. As Yeats (1986) observed in 1887: 'the heroines of all the neo romantic London poets, namely Swinburn, Morris, Rossetti ... are essentially men's heroines with no separate life of their own[;] in this different from Brownings' (i, 30). In 'Praise of My Lady', for example, the subject's 'full lips' are prominently featured: they are 'parted longingly' and seem 'made to kiss'. But they are not required to speak. This is another example of the close fit between the pre-Raphaelite ideal of beauty and the actual person. Janey was notoriously taciturn. Three decades later, Wilfrid Scawen Blunt, her lover during the late 1880s and early 1890s, noted in his diary that 'she is so silent a woman that except through the physical senses we could never have become intimate' (Faulkner, 1981, 29).

Janey did tell Blunt that 'I am not unhappy, though it is a terrible thing, for I have been with [Morris] since I first knew anything. I was 18 when I married – but I never loved him' (Faulkner, 1981, 39). But on another occasion, she remarked that her husband was 'the most magnanimous, the least selfish of men', and that she supposed if she were 'young again I should do the same again' (Longford, 323). Her statement that she never loved her husband, then, need not be taken to mean that she never cared for him. Nor is there any reason to think that she and Morris never experienced the fulfilment of romantic sexual love as it is represented in his 'Thunder in the Garden', a recollection-of-love lyric that is also one of the finest Victorian renderings of expectation as virtual fulfilment. The poem describes 'the ending of wrong' – that is, of the too-long deferred consummation of a love relationship – on a hot June afternoon with a thunderstorm impending. The male speaker's complete passivity is repeatedly instanced. It is 'she, the soft-clad' who 'Changed all with the change of her smile'. And yet there is reciprocity and mutual giving. She gives herself to the speaker, but the bestowal is a concomitant of her seeking the same gift:

> For her smile was of longing, no longer of glee,
> And her fingers entwined with mine own,
> With caresses unquiet sought kindness of me
> For the gift that I never had known.

The 'wild chance' of reciprocated sexual love breaks out at the same time as does the thunderstorm, which had also been holding itself 'aloof': 'I to myself was grown nought but a wonder,/As she leaned down my kisses to meet.' It is still afternoon when the storm ends. While the lovers wait for nightfall, she leads him into a garden of roses and lilies where 'nought was athirst'. There they wander until the moon appears:

> Then we turned from the blossoms, and cold they were grown
> In the trees the wind westering moved;
> Till over the threshold back fluttered her gown,
> And in the dark house was I loved.

There the poem ends; there is no need to describe what took place in the dark house, for the 'wonder' and 'marvel' of the consummation of their love has already been prospectively expressed.

In the early years of their marriage, during which their two daughters were born, the Morrises lived in Kent in the Red House, the Gothic home he had built for them. They seem to have been happy enough during this period. But in 1865, because of the demands of Morris's

> Some kindness out of all he asked of me
> And hoped his love would still hang vague and dim
> About my life like half-heard melody.

While the self-scrutiny that this poem presupposes may have helped Morris to understand his marital situation and to accept some responsibility for it, it did not cure his pain. Between 1865 and the early 1870s Morris wrote dozens of personal lyrics in the attempt to gain symptomatic relief of his distress.[1] For 'the wise men say', as a speaker in his dialogue poem 'Hapless Love' remarks, 'To talk of grief drives grief away' – one of these wise men being John Donne, who thought that if he could draw his love pains through 'rhyme's vexation, I should them allay' ('The Triple Fool').[2]

Morris's most sustained articulation of his position in a romantic marriage that had foundered is the sequence of poems of the months from *The Earthly Paradise*. J. W. Mackail, his first biographer, described these poems as containing 'an autobiography so delicate and so outspoken that it must needs be left to speak for itself' (i, 210). Mackail's adjectives are excellent – Morris's lyrics are delicate both in their descriptions of the natural world and the tact with which they adumbrate the marital situation. But they are also 'outspoken' in the candour with which his pitiful emotional state is laid bare.

Each poem contains three rhyme-royal stanzas describing with considerable crispness the English countryside in one of its monthly phases. Sometimes the speaker addresses the season, sometimes his silent beloved, and sometimes himself. Each poem turns on the contrast between living in the present through participation in natural process, and looking before and after and pining for what is not. The question implicitly posed by the sequence is whether the speaker can be cured of what Meredith's narrator in *Modern Love* called 'cravings for the buried day' (section 50)? Can an intimate responsiveness to nature's cycles teach him, in a phrase from another Meredith poem, 'to kiss the season and shun regrets'.

The answer in each and every poem in the sequence is *no*. 'March' and 'April', the first two, bring 'the hopes and chances of the growing year' and raise the possibility of living as do the birds, 'Unmindful of the past or coming days'. But the speaker cannot do so; he longs for a loveliness 'which never draweth nigh'. 'June' describes a day spent living in the present; but this state of being is a 'rare happy dream'. While 'August' describes an equally inviting natural scene, the poem ends not in contentment but in vexation: 'Ah, love! such happy days, such days as these,/Must we still mar them, craving for the best.' In 'October', the autumnal mood, made audible in the 'strange old tinkling tune' of church bells, is 'sweet, and sad ... Too satiate of life to

business interests, the family moved to London, where R
been living in seclusion since the death by her own hand o
Siddal in 1862. Around this time their marriage began to c
Morris's retrospective analysis – taking two passages of Old I
in *News from Nowhere* to have reference to his own ma
Thompson does – was that Romantic love did not modula
companionate marriage: 'Calf love, mistaken for a heroism tha
life-long, yet early waning into disappointment ...'; 'the unl
that comes of man and woman confusing the relations betweei
passion, and sentiment, and the friendship which, when things
softens the awakening from passing illusions' (*Works*, xvi, 57)
ever the reason, Janey seems to have been 'waiting for someth
for me'. By the late 1860s an intimacy had developed between
Rossetti – they went to parties together, and she became the pi
model for his paintings. To close friends, and to her husband, it l
clear that they were lovers.

2

Morris behaved towards his wife and Rossetti with understanding
generosity. He even took a joint lease with Rossetti on Kelmscott M
a remote Elizabethan house 30 miles from Oxford where Janey and
lover could be together out of the public eye. But Morris was devast
by his wife's affair and was further frustrated in being unsuccessfu
finding emotional solace in a relationship with Georgiana Burne-Jo
the wife of his closest friend, whose marriage was also under sti
owing to her husband's infidelity. Morris was in love with Georgia
or thought he was; but she remained faithful to her husband.

In one of the poems he wrote during this period, 'Why Dost Th
Struggle', Morris made a remarkable attempt to see his marital situ
tion from his wife's point of view: 'A childish heart ... loved me once
he imagines her thinking, 'and lo/I took his love and cast his love away

> A childish greedy heart! yet still he clung
> So close to me that much he pleased my pride
> And soothed a sorrow that about me hung
> With glimpses of his love unsatisfied –
> ...
> I wore a mask, because though certainly
> I loved him not, yet there was something soft
> And sweet to have him ever loving me:
> Belike it is I well-nigh loved him oft –
>
> Nigh loved him oft, and needs must grant to him

strive with death'. The sound intimates the promise of 'rest from life' and from 'Love which ne'er the end can gain'. But when the tune swells rather than wanes, so does the yearning heart: 'How can I have enough of life and love?' In 'November' a different antidote is offered: 'Look out upon the real world', the speaker tells himself – at the moon-blanched 'dread midnight' that contains no diurnal images or hopes and seems the 'changeless seal of change … Fair death of things that, living once, were fair'. But he is not strong enough to accept the given as sufficient. The same inability is once again instanced in the final stanza of 'December' which begins with what seems to be an acceptance of the comfortless present, but collapses into pitiful wishfulness as the speaker's resolve is once again contaminated by hope.

'February', the concluding poem, recapitulates what the preceding poems have repeatedly shown: that the speaker's emotional malaise, his debilitating and unmanly craving for a love that no longer exists, is irremediable. The aesthetic problem of effecting closure in a sequence that has cyclic natural process as its organizing principle is nicely solved. On a dismal late winter noon, the speaker imagines that on some May dawn in the future he will awake and, while thinking of days ahead, find that he sees 'nothing clear but this same dreary day' – the reason being that, despite the seasonal change, his condition will not have changed. On that future morning, he asks himself in the sequence's utterly dismal conclusion:

> Shall thou not wonder that it liveth yet,
> The useless hope, the useless craving pain,
> That made thy face, that lonely noontide, wet
> With more than beating of the chilly rain?
> Shalt thou not hope for joy new born again,
> Since no grief ever born can ever die
> Through changeless change of seasons passing by?

With Christina Rossetti's *Monna Innominata*, Morris's poems to the months are the most fully articulated Victorian poetic expressions of hopeless longing for an unrequited or lost love. Both works are also demoralizing on the psychological level and, despite the technical proficiency, not deeply engaging on the aesthetic level. In both of them there is 'something morbid' and 'something monotonous' – qualities that Matthew Arnold said were 'inevitably' found in poems describing 'situations, from the representation of which, though accurate, no poetic enjoyment can be derived'. They were those 'in which a continuous state of mental distress is prolonged … in which there is everything to be endured, nothing to be done' (i, 2–3).

It was suggested in Chapter 4 that the morbid and monotonous quality in Christina Rossetti's love poetry was caused by inauthentic waiting. In the case of Morris's poems to the seasons and the other personal lyrics he wrote around the same time, two explanations suggest themselves. One is that Morris is speaking from within an unhappy marriage – his beloved is not dead or absent but cohabitates with him. In the human rather than the natural present, there are intimate indoor moments in which the beloved's eyes momentarily seem to offer hope and thus renew his pain. Two of the 12 poems register such moments. In 'July', the blossom's scent

> Floated across the fresh grass, and the bees
> With low vexed song from rose to lily went,
> A gentle wind was in the heavy trees,
> And thine eyes shone with joyous memories;
> Fair was the early morn, and fair wert thou,
> And I was happy – Ah, be happy now!

A sexual element in the 'joyous memories' is intimated both by the bees and flowers and by the rose and lilies, which are emblems of sexual passion here as in 'Thunder in the Garden'. It does not matter whether the memories are of the previous night or of some earlier time; the July day is the epitome of the temporal span of their relationship. In that morning hour 'Peace and content were without us, love within'. Now thunder and wild rain are the atmospheric counterparts of their emotions. As for the future, while the setting sun will rise again,

> Who knows if next morn this felicity
> My lips may feel, or if thou still shalt live
> This seal of love renewed once more to give?

While the question is not rhetorical, the possibility of renewal seems slight given the poem's registration of the total passivity of the speaker. Felicity or a wasted life is entirely at the whim of the beloved and unaffected by natural process.

In 'January', the setting is the 'murky ending of a leaden day'. As she turns away from the window, a 'scarce-seen kindly smile' is noticed on the beloved's face, which seems 'Sent through the dusk my longing to beguile'. But then the lights in the room are turned on,

> And in the sudden change our eyes meet dazed –
> O look, love, look again! the veil of doubt
> Just for one flash, past counting, then was raised!
> O eyes of heaven, as clear thy sweet soul blazed
> On mine a moment!

But she does not look at him again: 'there she sitteth still,/With wide grey eyes so frank and fathomless'. The luminous moment has passed.

The other explanation is that in order for rhyme to allay love pains, the creative activity of mind needs to be fully engaged in the expression and representation of the pains. But writing poems, like all creative and compositional tasks, came easily to Morris. His creative engagement with his personal misery does not seem to have been intense enough to allow for a release from metronomic despondency for himself and a comparable lift for the reader. The poems of the months are fluent and three of them are more than that. But they are different only in tempo and not in kind from the 'narcotic strumming' of 'The Folk Singers' in Seamus Heaney's poem of that name, who 'pluck slick strings and swing/A sad heart's equilibrium'. Rossetti had a deeper commitment to the creative activity of mind. He was consequently able to do more poetically with his relationship to Janey during the most intense years of their affair than her tormented husband was with his.

3

With the 'regenerate rapture' of his love for Janey, poetry came back into Rossetti's life.[3] For the first time in six years he began to revise earlier poems and to compose new ones. Between 1868 and 1871, Rossetti wrote nearly 70 love sonnets recording his thoughts and emotions. In them, he adopted features of Dante's *Vita Nuovo* and the work of the other love poets he had translated in *The Early Italian Poets* (1861) – for example, the exalted spiritual significance assigned to love and the appearance of Love himself as an actor in the sequence. In *The House of Life* (1881) these sonnets were among the 101 that were arranged non-chronologically for the structural and thematic purposes of the work, as well as to detract attention from their biographical content (see Doughty, 378).[4]

Whether the love sonnets are better considered in this context or chronologically is a moot point. I believe the latter. If the 1868–71 sonnets are separated out from *The House of Life* and arranged in roughly chronological order, they have a different look and feel. This clustering avoids the architectural and astrological pretensions of *The House of Life*, a title that suggests a thematic and structural unity which the sequence only notionally possesses. Doing so also mitigates the cumulatively negative effect of the stylistic embellishments – the pretentious images, personifications, ornate detail, archaic diction, double epithets, polysyllabic Latinate words and heavy alliteration that caused Browning (1951) to complain:

> I have read Rossetti's poems – and poetical they are, – scented with poetry, as it were – like trifles of various sorts you take out of a cedar or sandle-wood box: you know I hate the effeminacy of his school, – the men that dress up like women – that use obsolete

> forms, too, and archaic accentuations that seem soft ... then, how I
> hate 'Love' as a lubberly naked young man putting his arms here
> & his wings there, about a pair of lovers – a fellow they would
> kick away in the reality.
>
> (336–7)

This clustering also helps to put the emphasis on the quality of individual poems, thus underlining the point of Rossetti's remark to Hall
Caine: 'You have too great a habit of speaking of a special octave,
sestette, or line. Conception, my boy, *fundamental brainwork*, that is
what makes the difference in all art. Work your metal as much as you
like, but first take care that it is gold and worth working' (Caine,
112).

Many of the sonnets focus on particular moments of intense feeling.
In a letter of August 1871, Rossetti observed that

> I hardly ever do produce a sonnet except on some basis of special
> momentary emotion; but I think there is another class admissable
> also – and that is the only other I practise, viz. the class depending
> on a line or two clearly given you, you know not whence, and
> calling up a sequence of ideas.
>
> (iii, 985)

Rossetti's sonnet on the sonnet (which prefaces *The House of Life*)
exemplifies the second kind of sonnet but describes the first:

> *A sonnet is a moment's monument, –*
>   *Memorial from the Soul's eternity*
>   *To one dead deathless hour. Look that it be,*
> *Whether for lustral rite or dire portent,*
> *Of its own arduous fulness reverent.*

The subject of several of these intense, arduously full moments is
sexual fulfilment. Determining to render these moments fully was a
bold decision given conventional Victorian taste. When a number of the
sonnets were first published in 1870, for example, they were excoriated
by Robert Buchanan in a review article entitled 'The Fleshly School of
Poetry'. Here, for example, are his remarks on 'Nuptial Sleep':

> Here is a full-grown man, presumably intelligent and cultivated,
> putting on record for other full-grown men to read, the most secret
> mysteries of sexual connection, and that with so sickening a desire
> to reproduce the sensual mood, so careful a choice of epithet to
> convey the mere animal sensations, that we merely shudder at the
> shameless nakedness.
>
> (891)

'Nuptial Sleep' uses two striking presentational strategies: a third person point of view and the choice of the post-coital rather than the

pre-coital or the orgasmic moment as the poem's subject (the past participle in the poem's original Latin title – 'Placata Venere' – emphasized this):

> At length their long kiss severed, with sweet smart:
>   And as the last slow sudden drops are shed
>   From sparkling eaves when all the storm has fled,
> So singly flagged the pulses of each heart.
> Their bosoms sundered, with the opening start
>   Of married flowers to either side outspread
>   From the knit stem; yet still their mouths, burnt red,
> Fawned on each other where they lay apart.
>
> Sleep sank them lower than the tide of dreams,
>   And their dreams watched them sink, and slid away.
> Slowly their souls swam up again, through gleams
>   Of watered light and dull drowned waifs of day;
> Till from some wonder of new woods and streams
>   He woke, and wondered more: for there she lay.

Responses to this sonnet have varied greatly; for example, while Buchanan despised it, Tennyson was deeply impressed by its 'passion and imaginative power' (H. Tennyson, ii, 505). My own response has always been equivocal. While I admire its boldness and the fundamental brainwork, the combination of *epuisé* sexuality (especially the labial fawning) and haphazard figural embellishment, including the kitsch Victorianism of the married flowers, gives a vulgarly titillating effect, as does the employment of a third-person narrator which puts the reader in the position of a voyeur. And then there is the swarmy ending of the poem, in which a nap restores to the male lover a sense of Edenic wonder over the recumbent other. Jerome McGann argues that in these lines 'the beloved appears to the eyes of the lover as a unique identity, wholly individuated despite the previous moments of mutual absorption' (182). But such idealizing commentary is hardly justified by the text – or the context. In his love sonnets one thing Rossetti was surely not interested in was the establishment of the individual identity of the female other. As in the *Vita Nuovo*, the point of view is restricted to that of the male lover. In 'The Portrait' (sonnet 10), the speaker says of one of his paintings of the beloved that the 'mouth's mould testifies of voice and kiss'. The love sonnets testify only to the latter. Like Morris's image of Janey in 'Praise of My Lady', the mouth of the beloved in Rossetti's love sonnets is made for kissing, not for communication.

The sestet of 'The Kiss' (sonnet 6) uses a different strategy for depicting the intensities of physical love:

> I was a child beneath her touch, – a man
>   When breast to breast we clung, even I and she, –
> A spirit when her spirit looked through me, –

> A god when all our life-breath met to fan
> Our life-blood, till love's emulous ardours ran,
>   Fire within fire, desire in deity.

This passage describes an orgasmically triggered expansion of consciousness. It is a strong realization of what in a letter Rossetti (1964–67) speaks of as 'the momentary contact with the immortal which results from sensuous culmination and is always a half conscious element of it' (ii, 727). This moment and its realization are close to, but not identical with, another kind of experience explored in the love sonnets that posed a different aesthetic problem: how to express and explore not the feeling of experiential transcendence (of being made immortal by a kiss), but rather the analogical feeling or intuition that particular intense moments of human loving are tokens or intimations of a greater love which extends beyond the temporal boundaries of an individual's life.

The aesthetic question is self-reflexively raised in 'Heart's Hope' (sonnet 5):

> By what word's power, the key of paths untrod,
>   Shall I the difficult deeps of Love explore?
> ...
> For lo! in some poor rhythmic period,
>   Lady, I fain would tell how evermore
>   Thy soul I know not from thy body, nor
> Thee from myself, neither our love from God.
>
> Yea, in God's name, and Love's, and thine, would I
>   Draw from one loving heart such evidence
> As to all hearts all things shall signify;
>   Tender as dawn's first hill-fire, and intense
>   As instantaneous penetrating sense,
> In Spring's birth-hour, of other Springs gone by.

The problem for Rossetti was how to do this effectively in the nineteenth century. While his love sonnets have a Dantesque *apport*, Rossetti cannot use 'the traditional religious symbolism' available to Dante 'since the symbols have been emptied of almost all their traditional religious content' (Hough, 1949, 81).

Rossetti's solution was the common Romantic one: to use natural facts drawn from 'the soul's sphere of infinite images' ('The Soul's Sphere', sonnet 62) as symbols of spiritual facts. But a distinction basic to symbolic perception in the nineteenth century has to be made. As Emerson explained in *Nature*, natural facts can symbolize spiritual facts in two senses of the latter term. They can be used metaphorically to figure emotional (including spiritual) states of feeling in the poet or another consciousness. At this level Rossetti is often successful, as has been recognized, for example, by Joan Rees who noted that his 'use of the natural world to provide images of elusive, fragile, deeply-affecting but scarcely graspable inner experiences is one of the most distinguishing marks of his poetry' (76). Examples are found in the last two lines quoted above from 'Heart's Hope' which figure the tender intensity of the emotional effect that Rossetti wants his love poems to have on the reader. The sestet of 'Soul-Light' (sonnet 28) contains another example:

> And as the traveller triumphs with the sun,
>   Glorying in heat's mid-height, yet startide brings
>   Wonder new-born, and still fresh transport springs
> From limpid lambent hours of day begun; –
>   Even so, through eyes and voice, your soul doth move
>   My soul with changeful light of infinite love.

The second way in which natural facts can symbolize is by figuring or intimating through analogy spiritual facts in the sense of transcendent or ideal essences – such as God or a life after death. But there is a problem endemic to symbolic perception in the nineteenth century: meaning does not inhere in the object but is conferred on it, or inferred from it, by the perceiver. This means that a natural fact will not have the same signification for everyone. More importantly, it means that the self-aware (as opposed to the naïve) symbolic perception of natural facts cannot confer certainty but only equivocal hints or 'doubtful knowledge' (in Shelley's phrase from the preface to *Alastor*). Rossetti's 'The Soul's Sphere' (sonnet 62) offers an apt illustration of the point. The (generalized) natural fact is 'some dying sun whose pyre/Blazed with momentous memorable fire'. How can the perceiver/poet determine with certainty whether this powerful image 'forecast[s]' [i.e. symbolizes]

> Visions of golden futures: or the last
> Wild pageant of the accumulated past
>   That clangs and flashes for a drowning man?

The frontier between the limit of the perceptible and what might lie beyond is thus a 'bitter bound' ('The Monochord' sonnet 79). In the figure from Paul's first epistle to the Corinthians that Rossetti used as the title for sonnet 34, analogical inference was seeing through a 'dark glass'. The octet to this poem poses strong questions concerning 'love, – the last relay/And ultimate outpost of eternity'. But the answer offered in the sestet is weak;

> Lo! what am I to Love, the lord of all?
>   One murmuring shell he gathers from the sand, –
>   One little heart-flame sheltered in his hand.
> Yet through thine eyes he grants me clearest call

> And veriest touch of powers primordial
>   That any hour-girt life may understand.

Here Rossetti is merely asserting, saying rather than showing; symbolic perception is replaced by the facile allegorical figuration and rhetorical embellishment in the form of notional synesthetic images.

The sestet is an example of what Elizabeth Bishop calls 'a great perversity'. It occurred when, in attempting to convey a sense of the spiritual dimension of love experience, a poet used 'the supposedly "spiritual" – the beautiful, the nostalgic, the ideal and *poetic*, to produce the *material*'. For Bishop, the right way for a love poet to express the spiritual is to use 'immediate, intense physical reactions, a sense of metaphor and decoration in everything – to express something not of them – something, I suppose, *spiritual*. But it proceeds from the material' (quoted in Millier, 65). This was the way Rossetti took in poems in which he was able to follow the self-advice of 'Love and Hope' (sonnet 43) to be content with the present and eschew analogical speculation concerning the future:

> Cling heart to heart; nor of this hour demand
>   Whether in very truth, when we are dead,
>   Our hearts shall wake to know Love's golden head
> Sole sunshine of the imperishable land;
>   Or but discern, through night's unfeatured scope,
>   Scorn-fired at length the illusive eyes of Hope.

The subject of several of Rossetti's love sonnets is present bliss, complete mutual satisfaction and contentment in the moment – when 'as soft waters warble to the moon,/Our answering spirits chime one roundelay' ('Heart's Haven', sonnet 22). In these poems, Rossetti found an answer to the aesthetic problem identified by other love poets – how to use words effectively when no words are needed. In *Astrophil and Stella* (sonnet 70), for example, Sidney's speaker, having vainly urged his muse to show his 'height of delight/In well raised notes', realizes that in love poetry 'Wise silence is best musicke unto bliss'. The same point is made in Louisa Bevington's 'Love and Language':

> Love that is alone with love
>   Makes solitudes of throngs;
> Then why not songs of silences, –
>   Sweet silences of songs.
>
> Parts need words: the perfect whole
>   Is silent as the dead;
> When I offered you my soul
>   Heard you what I *said*?

For Rossetti, the key to expressing present bliss was to situate his lovers in a natural setting and use natural description to express their state of being. In 'Youth's Spring Tribute' (sonnet 14), for example, as the April sun strikes down the glades, the beloved feels the lover's kisses 'as the Spring now thrills through every spray'. And 'Last Fire' (sonnet 30) describes a summer evening at the end of a day of 'sweet well-being of love and full heart's ease'. Human and natural are intermingled as 'this day's sun of rapture filled the west/And the light sweetened as the fire took leave'.

Rossetti's two finest celebrations of the sufficiency of present bliss are paradoxically two of his most powerful intimations of the spiritual dimension of love.

The Lovers' Walk (sonnet 12)

Sweet twining hedgeflowers wind-stirred in no wise
  On this June day; and hand that clings in hand: –
  Still glades; and meeting faces scarcely fann'd; –
An osier-odoured stream that draws the skies
Deep to its heart; and mirrored eyes in eyes: –
  Fresh hourly wonder o'er the Summer land
  Of light and cloud; and two souls softly spann'd
With one o'erarching heaven of smiles and sighs: –

Even such their path, whose bodies lean unto
  Each other's visible sweetness amorously, –
  Whose passionate hearts lean by Love's high decree
Together on his heart for ever true,
As the cloud-foaming firmamental blue
  Rests on the blue line of a foamless sea.

Silent Noon (sonnet 19)

Your hands lie open in the long fresh grass, –
  The finger-points look through like rosy blooms:
  Your eyes smile peace. The pasture gleams and glooms
'Neath billowing clouds that scatter and amass.
All round our nest, far as the eye can pass,
  Are golden kingcup-fields with silver edge
  Where the cow-parsley skirts the hawthorn-hedge.
'Tis visible silence, still as the hour-glass.

Deep in the sun-searched growths the dragon-fly
Hangs like a blue thread loosened from the sky: –
  So this wing'd hour is dropt to us from above.
Oh! clasp we to our hearts, for deathless dower,
This close-companioned inarticulate hour
  When twofold silence was the song of love.

Both of these pictorial sonnets have similar subjects – summer stillness and plenitude. In 'The Lover's Walk', the visual comprehensiveness requires a third person point of view. The lovers are leaning together and looking into each other's eyes. In their mutual absorption, they do not see their surroundings – but the viewer/reader does. The key compositional strategy is the human–natural mirrorings and doublings, which range from the close up to the distant: twining flowers and clinging hands; glades and faces similarly unventilated; skies mirrored in a stream like eyes reflected in eyes; light and cloud spanning the landscape as the lovers' smiles and sighs form the capstone of their arched bodies; their bodies leaning together along the line of the path as sky and sea blend along the horizon line.

In 'Silent Noon', on the other hand, the lovers are not gazing at each other but looking together in the same direction. There is a first person speaker and the reader/viewer sees what the recumbent lovers see from their 'nest'. There are instances of doubling at the beginning and end of the sonnet: the fingertips in the grass looking like 'rosy blooms' and the 'twofold silence' – natural and human. But the principal presentational strategy in 'Silent Noon' is to render the lovers' heightened consciousness through the representation of their vividly particularized sensations and perceptions of the natural scene: the rosy finger-points; the golden wild flowers edged by the silver cow parsley; the blue dragonfly; the oxymoronic alternations of 'gleams and glooms' in the pasture below in rhythm with the clouds above that 'scatter and amass'.

In both poems, these visual effects are amplified by figurative language. The synesthetic images – 'visible sweetness', 'visible silence' – are in the first instance (unlike those in 'The Dark Glass') registrations of perceptual intensity. But there is a figural suggestiveness also (synesthesia being both a quality of perception and a figure of speech). As David Riede notes: the fusion of two senses 'invokes an ideal beyond any actual sensual apprehension' (123). The metaphorical intensifications 'for ever' and 'deathless dower' have a similar twofold effect; these figures use duration as the vehicle, the tenor being intensity. But there is also the sense of a beyonding – a gradual etherealization or spiritualization of the love, its expansion temporally ('for ever') and spatially. This sense is also found in the superb simile in the last two lines of 'The Lover's Walk' – 'As the cloud-foaming firmamental blue/Rests on the blue line of a foamless sea' – in which sky and sea seem to have become intermingled. As Ortega y Gasset notes, as distance increases 'we no longer see one thing clearly and the rest confusedly … the duality of proximate vision is succeeded by a perfect unity of the whole visual field'. Distant objects become 'chromatic entities' and can acquire illusory or apparitional qualities, among them the aura of the infinite or the beyond (824–5).

Another example of beyonding is found in the remarkable sestet of 'Silent Noon', which is an exception to the rule that in a Rossetti sonnet a turn or volta occurs between the octet and the sestet, typically description

followed by reflection, question by answer, or problem by solution.
Here, for example, is a draft version of the sestet of 'Silent Noon':

> Think through the silence how when we are old
> We two shall think upon this place & day,
>   The beauty around us, & the beauty above,
> And clasp unto our hearts, when tempests lour,
> This close-companioned inarticulate hour
>   When twofold silence was the Song of love.

(Gates, 69)

What replaced this is an enormous improvement. Instead of reflections
on having something saved up for a rainy day, there is no volta but
rather a further intensification of the present moment and an expansion
of its significance – both of which hinge on the sonnet's single most
striking natural notation: the blue dragonfly.

To begin with, there is the micro-macro rhyming (both literally and
figuratively) of dragonfly and blue sky, of seasonal ephemera and the
abiding celestial. Here the dragonfly is a synecdochal symbol of the sky
– a part of the whole. At the same time, this natural object is an
allegory. The dragonfly seems suspended from the sky as this hour
seems dropped from above – that is, the dragonfly is taken as an
emblem of the lovers' connection with the transcendent, and as giving
their love a supernal sanction. The strong rhymes again emphasize the
point: above/love. And there is a similar reverberation in the third pair
of strong rhymes (dower/hour) – a sense of the permanent in the transitory.

But in the last line of 'Silent Noon' there is a startling temporal
reversal. Following a present imperative ('Oh! clasp we') we get not the
expected 'is' but 'was' – the word that Faulkner's Quentin Compson in
The Sound and the Fury called 'the saddest word of all'. It is possible
that the 'was' is vestigial – a trace of the early version of the sestet
quoted above. But it is none the less superbly apposite; it brings to the
grammatical surface of the poem the implications of a figure used in the
octet, the 'hour-glass' – the poem's one non-metonymic trope and one
manufactured object. The glass is 'still' in one sense (it makes no sound
and seems motionless) but not in another: the sand is moving and
measuring the passage of time. There is a ping of temporality, a dire
portent of transience. The temporal glass does not mirror and amplify
the lovers' enhanced sense of being; it intimates the inevitable cessation
of the visible silence of the present and their absorption in it.

There is one further felicity at the end of 'Silent Noon', which is of all
the love sonnets that came out of Rossetti's affair with Janey the fullest
exemplification of his conception of the sonnet as 'a moment's monu-
ment' to 'one dead deathless hour'. It is the implicitly reflexive element

that suggests Rossetti's awareness of what he has accomplished. In the sonnet, the 'inarticulate hour' and the silent song are made articulate and audible. It is as if the poet were alluding to Sidney's caveat and intimating his aesthetic triumph in expressing the bliss of sexual love. And this is not simply a flourish; it is an implicit restatement of a theme articulated in other love sonnets: that poems are 'Love's Last Gift' (sonnet 59) and that only 'Art's transfiguring essence' ('Transfigured Life', sonnet 60) can give permanence or immortality to the experience of romantic love.

4

In 'Love Enthroned' (sonnet 1) Rossetti placed the throne of Love far above the 'kindred Powers' of Truth, Hope, Fame, Youth and Life. Like Morris's contemporaneous *Love is Enough*, this sonnet seems the product of a 'state of compensatory fantasy' (Doughty, 541) unrelated to the Victorian experience of romantic love as fragile and contingent. In the particular case of Rossetti and Janey, the sonnet also fails to recognize what other sonnets do: that an illicit love relationship draws part of its intensity from the foreknowledge of its termination – of 'how brief [is] the whole/Of joy, which its own hours annihilate' ('Secret Parting', sonnet 45).

In 1872, Rossetti had a total nervous breakdown, including symptoms of paranoia and a suicide attempt. The causes included ill-health, his growing dependence on drugs, fear of public exposure of his affair with Janey, and delayed reaction to Buchanan's savage review (see Fredeman, 1970–71). After his recovery, the lovers spent less time together; by the mid-1870s their affair was over. It was terminated by Janey. When Blunt later asked her if she had been very much in love with Rossetti, she answered: 'Yes, at first, but it did not last long. It was very warm while it lasted. When I found that he was ruining himself with Chloral and that I could do nothing to prevent it I left off going to him – and on account of the children' (Faulkner, 1981, 30). There were further breakdowns in the late 1870s and until his death in 1882 Rossetti continued to suffer from drug dependence, depression and paranoia. Janey still modelled for him occasionally and they corresponded fondly. In 1878, for example, he wrote telling her that his studio was overflowing with her portraits, including those of her as Pandora and as Proserpine. One night in bed ten years after his death, Janey told Blunt that 'I never quite gave myself [to Rossetti] as I do now'. Perhaps if she had, Blunt reflected, Rossetti 'might not have perished in the way he did' (Faulkner, 1981, 30).

Morris died in 1896. In his later years, Blunt noted, he 'showed himself uniformly kind [to Janey] but without tenderness, treating her in a certain offhand way peculiarly his own' (Faulkner, 1981, 24). But there is also evidence of growing dependence and mutual fondness between them. In 1892, for example, when a house guest 'went up into the drawing room to say goodnight', he found Morris and Janey 'playing at draughts, with large ivory pieces, red and white. Mrs M. was dressed in a glorious blue gown, and as she sat on the sofa, she looked like an animated Rossetti picture or page from an old MS of a king and queen' (quoted in MacCarthy, 630).

In 1872, Morris had written in a letter that 'One thing wanting ought not to go for so much: nor indeed does it spoil my enjoyment of life always, as I have often told you: to have real friends and some sort of an aim in life is so much, that I ought still to think myself lucky'. But three years later he told the same correspondent that 'I am ashamed of myself for these strange waves of unreasonable passion: it seems so unmanly: yet indeed I have a good deal to bear considering how hopeful my earlier youth was, & what overweening ideas I had of the joys of life' (i, 173, 216). The one thing wanting, for which nothing could wholly compensate Morris, was love – 'real love' as described by a character in his unfinished novel of 1872: 'All is either love or not love. There is nothing between. Everything else – friendship, kindness, goodness, is a shadow and a lie' (73).

Notes

1. There is some disagreement over whether Janey or Georgiana is the subject or addressee of certain of these poems (see Mooney). But this does not effect their status as poetic expressions of unrequited love.
2. Coleridge was another. In his preface to *Poems on Various Subjects* (1796), he succinctly described the self-therapeutic dynamic in which release from psychological distress comes through its expression:

   After the more violent emotions of Sorrow, the mind demands solace and can find it in employment alone; but full of its late sufferings it can endure no employment not connected with those sufferings. Forcibly to turn away our attention to other subjects is a painful and in general an unavailing effort ...
   The communicativeness of our nature leads us to describe our own sorrows; in the endeavor to describe them intellectual activity is exerted; and by a benevolent law of our nature from intellectual activity a pleasure results which is gradually associated and mingles as a corrective with the painful subject of the description.
   (1966, ii, 1136)

3. The phase is from the sestet of 'The Monochord' (section 79):

> Oh! what is this that knows the road I came,
> The flame turned cloud, the cloud returned to flame,
>   The lifted shifted steeps and all the way? –
> That draws round me at last this wind-warm space,
> And in regenerate rapture turns my face
>   Upon the devious coverts of dismay?

William Michael Rossetti thought that the answer to these questions was the power of music (240–41). I follow Christina Rossetti and Oswald Doughty in reading 'The Monochord' as a poem of later love for which Music 'inspired the imagery rather than the theme' (Doughty, 436). To use Christina Rossetti's images, the 'common essence' or 'one thread' or single chord that 'vibrate[s] through all' the particulars mentioned in the poem is love (quoted in Doughty, 691) – the 'regenerate rapture' of Rossetti's love for Janey that is the cause of the sense of transport and wonder and the intimations of a transcendent force shaping his destiny.

4. For the reader's convenience, the numbers following titles or quotations from Rossetti's love sonnets are those assigned the sonnets in *The House of Life* (1881). The dates of composition are given by Fredeman (1965, 336–40).

CHAPTER EIGHT

Love Elegies: Patmore and Hardy

But is there any comfort to be found?
Man is in love and loves what vanishes,
What more is there to say?
                    W. B. Yeats, 'Nineteen Hundred and Nineteen'

1

Two of the finest Victorian achievements in love poetry are elegies occasioned by the death of a wife: Coventry Patmore's bereavement odes from *The Unknown Eros* and Thomas Hardy's *Poems of 1912–13*. The loss of the beloved in death had been a central subject of love poetry at least since Dante and Petrarch; but as Rod Edmond (1981) pointed out in a comparative discussion of the social context of the two Victorian works, 'love elegies on wives were rare before the nineteenth century', Milton's sonnet on his late wife and Henry King's 'The Exequy' being exceptions. Edmond also reviewed the internal evidence that the first poem in Hardy's sequence was influenced by two of Patmore's, which he rightly found to be of less interest than 'the similarities of approach and treatment growing out of their shared situation' (162, 152).

The fundamental similarities between the works, however, are not found in the social context but in the fact that they are elegies. Both move from the first intense emotions of grief and loss, through intervening stages, to the climactic moment when the mourner is able to assert either that the dead subject of the elegy in some way abides as a presence or that a compensatory equivalent has been identified. More particularly, what Peter Sacks says of the lyrics in Hardy's sequence is also true of Patmore's odes:

> Despite their stark, individual beauty, their apparently erratic and fragmented ordonnance ... and the perplexed wandering of their protagonist, these poems enact familiar tasks: proving the reality of loss, confronting guilt and anger, recollecting and then severing attachments to the dead, establishing substitutive figures for the lost object of love, curbing the mourner's desires by an act of self-purification that both redefines and reinforces his continuing identity.

(235)

What makes these and other similarities between the works particularly interesting are the differences between their authors. One of them
is biographical: in Patmore's case an exceptionally happy 15-year marriage; in Hardy's a 43-year childless union that was happy only in its
earliest phase. Another is religious belief, a particularly pertinent con-
sideration in an elegy. Patmore was a devout Christian with a predispo-
sition for theology; Hardy was intellectually as well as temperamentally
an agnostic. A third difference concerns matters of creative intelligence
and aesthetic calculation. While Patmore used an extraordinary verse
form of his own devising, Hardy employed a mix of traditional metres
and stanza forms. Like *In Memoriam*, Tennyson's elegiac sequence,
Hardy's *Poems of 1912–13* is a finished work of art composed of self-
contained lyric units, the whole of which is greater than the sum of its
parts. Indeed, Hardy's sequence is his major achievement as a lyric poet.
Patmore's bereavement odes, on the other hand, are embedded in the
larger structure of *The Unknown Eros*, and their clustering is in part a
critical construction in that not all of these odes appear in consecutive
order in the larger work. The whole of the bereavement odes being
notional, and the successive phases of the grieving process less clearly
delineated and linked, I have treated Patmore's cluster at lesser length
than Hardy's sequence, the parts of which are intricately interrelated
and of great cumulative power.

2

In 1847, Patmore (then 24) married Emily Augusta Andrews, the daughter of a nonconformist minister. Their differing religious persuasions –
he was high church Anglican – were reconciled when she accepted his
position minus its Roman Catholic tendencies. Their happy and fulfilling union, from which six children were born, deepened Patmore's
belief that married love was the symbol of God's love for men and
women and that 'it is only through marriage-love that we can understand the love of Christ' (Champneys, ii, 84). These views are reflected
in his lyrical narrative of a happy marriage, *The Angel in the House*
(1854, 1856).

In the late 1850s, the first symptoms of consumption appeared in
Emily. She was only 38 when she died of the illness in 1862. Two years
later, Patmore remarried, as Emily had encouraged him to do in her
will:

> I leave my wedding-ring to your second wife with my love and
> blessing ... also, I leave you my grateful acknowledgment of your
> goodness and love to me, my last prayer [being] that God may

bless and console you, my first, last, and only love. If in a year or two you are able to marry again, do so happily ...

But in the same year Patmore also became a Roman Catholic, as Emily had feared, believing that his conversion would preclude their future reunion in heaven. 'When I am gone', she had told Patmore in tears a few days before her death, 'they (the Catholics) will get you; and then I shall see you no more' (Champneys, i, 133; ii, 53).

For *The Angel in the House*, Patmore had employed iambic tetrameter, 'a swift and jocund measure', as he described it, 'full of laughter and gaiety, suitable, not to pathetic themes, but to a song of chaste love and fortunate marriage' (quoted in 1961, 83n). In the early 1860s, Patmore developed a new verse form. This was 'a lyrical ode, iambic in rhythm and retaining such hints of symmetry as assonance and irregular rhyme, but without stanzas or other predictable patterns, and with lines varying in length from two to sixteen syllables' (Turner, 109). The metrical liberties, Patmore believed, were suited to the variations of exalted feeling which alone could justify the use of the form.

A feature of the traditional lyrical ode, of which Wordsworth's Intimations ode was for Patmore the single 'generally satisfactory' example in English, seemed to be that

> each line, however many syllables it may contain, ought to occupy the same time in reading. This view is supported ... by the necessity which has invariably been felt for printing the lines in such a manner that the reader shall know, beforehand, the requisite period to be occupied in the delivery of the line, and in the pauses by which it is to be preceded and concluded.
>
> (*Poems*, xii–xiii).

But Patmore himself came to feel that there was no need for indentation: 'if the feeling justifies the metre, the ear will take naturally to its variations; but if there is not sufficient motive power of passionate thought, no typographical aids will make anything of this sort of verse but *metrical nonsense*' (1961, 28). He also believed that the rhymes in lyrical odes could not be 'too much scattered, but, to compensate for the scattering they should be so numerous as to be always *felt*' (Hopkins, 1956, 345).

The odes that Patmore wrote in this verse form and eventually collected in *The Unknown Eros* (1878) included nine that are expressions of his love for, and grief over the loss of, Emily: 'The Day after Tomorrow', 'Tristitia', 'The Azalea', 'Departure', 'Eurydice', 'The Toys', 'Tired Memory', 'If I Were Dead' and 'A Farewell'. If considered in the context of *The Unknown Eros*, the theme of which is (in Terence L. Connolly's formulation in his edition of Patmore's *Mystical Poems of Nuptial Love*) 'the human soul's attainment of union with God through love' (151), the bereavement odes can be read allegorically, using this-for-that conceptual transference in which supernatural meanings are attributed to human emotions and natural particulars. But if separated out and clustered, as they have been by their two best commentators, Patricia Ball and John Maynard, these poems may be seen to recount 'a single evolving experience' (Ball, 61) and 'the love story of a couple' (Maynard, 1993, 214). The clustering is unquestionably superior in bringing into sharp focus the distinction of individual poems and in placing the emphasis on Patmore's impressions rather than his convictions – the former and not the latter being, Hardy insisted, the mission of the poet to record.

'The Day after To-morrow', the first bereavement ode, is a variation on the expectation-as-virtual-fulfilment lyric. The variation is that in this poem of married love expectation has been previously fulfilled on numerous occasions. As is usual, the beloved is not directly addressed. But the sea is beseeched to

> Tell her I come;
> Then only sigh your pleasure, and be dumb;
> For the sweet secret of our either self
> We know.

The central passage in the poem articulates a paradox:

> … on the third [day] our lives shall be fulfill'd!
> Yet all has been before:
> Palm placed in palm, twin smiles, and words astray.
> What other should we say?
> But shall I not, with n'er a sign, perceive,
> Whilst her sweet hands I hold,
> The myraid threads and meshes manifold
> Which Love shall round her weave:
> The pulse in that vein making alien pause
> And varying beats from this;
> Down each long finger felt, a differing strand
> Of silvery welcome bland;
> And in her breezy palm
> And silken wrist,
> Beneath the touch of my like numerous bliss
> Complexly kiss'd,
> A diverse and distinguishable calm?
> What should we say!
> It all has been before;
> And yet our lives shall now be first fulfill'd.

While Ball correctly remarked that the terminus of 'The Day after To-morrow' is heavenly reunion and 'endless perfection' (62), it is difficult to disagree with Alice Meynell's observation that the poem is 'not readily understood to refer to reunion after death' (102). The reason is that both readers have a point: Patmore's ode is simultaneously about earthly *and* heavenly love. On the one hand, it is a rapturous expression of the never failing delight of sexual love in marriage – a restatement and enactment of what Patmore had written to Emily in the year after their marriage:

> each commemoration of our wedding-day is more than a renewal of that day; ... the bride and bridegroom have not been lost in the husband and wife ... the never-failing freshness and mystery of marriage is increased each year by the sum of all the love and joy which have arisen between us during its happy months.
>
> (Champneys, i, 135)

On the other, the poem is also an expression of the longed for and assured renewal of their love in the next world. As Patmore (1895) wrote in another place:

> When a Lover says and means that he has been 'made immortal by a kiss,' he states an unexaggerated truth. His immortality, or his capacity for immortality, *has* been increased and partly initiated by the experience; for our eternity is but the sum, simultaneity, explanation, and transfiguration of all our pure experiences in time.
>
> (49)

That is to say, 'The Day after To-morrow' is another Victorian exemplification of the longing/belief that sexual love implies and intimates a supernatural dimension.

Despite the assured tone of 'The Day after To-morrow', in terms of the psychological processes of grieving Patmore is still at the beginning. Indeed, nothing as positive is found in any later poem in the cluster. And by 'A Farewell', the last bereavement ode, reunion is only a long-term possibility, not a day-after-tomorrow certainty, and is figured not as sexual bliss but as tearful amazement.

In 'Tristitia', the poem following 'The Day after To-morrow', Patmore's grief is expressed through a theological fiction or pretext. If you should 'win God's perfect bliss' (that is, go to heaven), and I fail to do so because of the 'gracious-seeming sin' of striving to please you more than to please God, do not be sad in thinking of my 'dateless exile gray' on 'the mild borders of the banish'd world' where dwell those for whose spiritual state the theological term is *tristitia* – that is, sadness or melancholy caused by spiritual sloth. This is not sound Catholic theology, as Gerard Manley Hopkins pointed out to Patmore. Hopkins's (1956) correct conclusion was that Patmore's poem was not in essence theological, but rather 'the lovely expression of an overstrained mood' (341–2):

> Near the sky-borders of that banish'd world,
> Wander pale spirits among willow'd leas,
> Lost beyond measure, sadden'd without end,

> But since, while erring most, retaining yet
> Some ineffectual fervour of regret,
> Retaining still such weal
> As spurned Lovers feel,
> Preferring far to all the world's delight
> Their loss so infinite,
> Or Poets, when they mark
> In the clouds dun
> A loitering flush of the long sunken sun,
> And turn away with tears into the dark.

Part of Patmore's work of mourning is to purge the impure emotions of tristitia figured in the spurned lover and pining poet. The comparable task in Hardy's sequence will be to discharge his distaste for the person that his wife had become. But for Patmore, the task is rather to discharge connubial nostalgia and self-pity. The latter emotion is not avoided in two of the bereavement odes, 'The Toys' and 'If I Were Dead'. But it is overcome in two other poems which show that the key to the purging of these impurities was for Patmore to face up to the finality of death and thus to distance himself from the uxorious anticipations of 'The Day after To-morrow'.

In 'Departure' and 'The Azalea', the context of this recognition is pathetic. Odic form and tonal register are adapted to accommodate the rendering of two intimate domestic moments – Emily's death on a late afternoon in July and the widower's distressful awakening one morning in the bedroom he no longer shares with his wife. Each poem turns on a potentially sentimental contrast. In 'Departure', there is on the one hand 'the great and gracious' natural being of Emily, which is evident even in her final hours when she turns her talk to 'daily things',

> Lifting the luminous, pathetic lash
> To let the laughter flash,
> Whilst I drew near,
> Because you spoke so low that I could scarcely hear.

On the other hand, there are her appalling last moments:

> ... all at once to leave me at the last,
> More at the wonder than the loss aghast,
> With huddled, unintelligible phrase,
> And frighten'd eye,
> And go your journey of all days
> With not one kiss, or a good-bye,
> And the only loveless look the look with which you pass'd;
> 'Twas all unlike your great and gracious ways.

It is the understatement that keeps sentimentality at bay: the pretense, conveyed in tones of affectionate chastisement, that her final leave-taking was discourteous rather than ghastly.

In 'The Azalea', the title flower is a figure for the sexual fullness of Patmore's married life:

> There, where the sun shines first
> Against our room,
> She train'd the gold Azalea, whose perfume
> She, Spring-like, from her breathing grace dispersed.
> Last night the delicate crest of saffron bloom,
> For this their dainty likeness watch'd and nurst,
> Were just at point to burst.

At dawn, Patmore has a dream in which his wife is dead:

> [I] groan'd aloud upon my wretched bed,
> And waked, ah, God, and did not waken her,
> But lay, with eyes still closed,
> Perfectly bless'd in the delicious sphere
> By which I knew so well that she was near,
> My heart to speechless thankfulness composed.

But then the awful truth is realized: 'It *was* the azalea's breath, and she *was* dead!/The warm night had the lingering buds disclosed', and it was their aroma, rather than hers, that he sensed in the room. The last lines of the poem contain the additional information that Patmore had fallen asleep reading a letter in which his wife had written:

> 'So, till to-morrow eve, my Own, adieu!
> Parting's well-paid with soon again to meet,
> Soon in your arms to feel so small and sweet,
> Sweet to myself that am so sweet to you!'

The letter and its contents are not supererogatory; the self-contained, metrically regular *abba* quatrain both recalls in a different (female) key the sexual delight of the Patmores' marriage and ironically echoes and undercuts the confident anticipation of 'The Day after To-morrow'. That poem had an operatic authenticity; but in the undeclamatory, understated tones of 'Departure' and 'The Azalea' one feels even more strongly the quality and depth of Patmore's love for his lost wife.

In 'Beata' (originally 'Felicia'), the ode immediately preceding 'The Day after To-morrow' in *The Unknown Eros*, the radiance and rare loveliness of being of Emily were boldly troped as a celestial whiteness perceived by the lover through a prism that 'did with gladdest hues my spirit caress,/ Nothing of Heaven in thee showing infinite,/Save the delight'. In 'Eurydice', the stage of mourning has now been reached when the light has gone out. Beatific figuration is replaced by Orphic harrowing of the underworld – not the realm of gloomy Dis but a Victorian slum:

> I, dreaming, night by night, seek now to see,
> And, in a mortal sorrow, still pursue
> Thro' sordid streets and lanes

> And houses brown and bare
> And many a haggard stair
> Ochrous with ancient stains,
> And infamous doors, opening on hapless rooms,
> In whose unhaunted glooms
> Dead pauper generations, witless of the sun,
> Their course have run.

Finally, the dreamer wins his way

> To where, with perfectly sad patience, nurst
> By sorry comfort of assured worst,
> Ingrain'd in fretted cheek and lips that pine,
> On pallet poor
> Thou lyest, stricken sick,
> Beyond love's cure,
> By all the world's neglect, but chiefly mine.

Finding the lost beloved brings, 'After exceeding ill, a little good' – which according to Patmore was for Aristotle 'the essence of pathos' (quoted in 1938, 172). It is the last expression of pathetic feelings in the bereavement cluster, the reason for which is explained at the beginning of 'Tired Memory', the climactic poem in the cluster:

> The stony rock of death's insensibility
> Well'd yet awhile with honey of thy love
> And then was dry;
> Nor could thy picture, nor thine empty glove,
> Nor all thy kind, long letters, nor the band
> Which really spann'd
> Thy body chaste and warm,
> Thenceforward move
> Upon the stony rock their wearied charm.
> At last, then, thou wast dead.

Details of the passage allude to earlier poems: the reference to Emily's letters recalls the end of 'The Azalea'; the empty glove recalls the complexly kissed hand in 'The Day after To-morrow'; and the honey ironically alludes to the last line of the same poem: 'One sweet drop more in the measureless increase/Of honied peace.' Measureless increase was the exuberant wish; exhaustion and emptiness are the present reality.

The mourner has reached the stage of having no feeling for the lost wife: 'My heart was dead,/Dead of devotion and tired memory.' What he retains is merely 'fond, unfeeling prayer' and 'wilful faith, which has no joy or pain'. Finally, he announces to God that he yields his wife up, 'again to have her given,/Or not' as He wills:

> And that same night, in slumber lying,
> I, who had dream'd of thee as sad and sick and dying,

And only so, nightly for all one year,
Did thee, my own most Dear,
Possess,
In gay celestial beauty nothing coy,
And felt thy soft caress
With hitherto unknown reality of joy.

As in Hardy's sequence, the recovery of a vivid memory image of the lost loved one at her most attractive is the climactic moment of the elegiac process.

As was also to be the case with Hardy, a second marriage soon follows. In this world 'None thrives for long upon [even] the happiest dream', Patmore says at the beginning of the closing section of 'Tired Love'. The section describes how a later love came into his life through the mediation of the memory image of his first wife. He is drawn to a 'fair stranger' because he sees in her 'a strange grace of thee' and is 'by thy delusive likeness doubly drawn'. At the same time, she is drawn to him because her heart is touched by 'the pale reflex of an alien love,/So vaguely, sadly shown', that she senses in him. Thus he 'lived again ... But (treason was't?) for thee and also her'.

3

Emma Hardy died in November 1912. By that time, the fissure in their marital relationship that Thomas Hardy had first detected over three decades earlier had become a chasm. Since the mid-1890s, the Hardys' life at Max Gate, their house on the outskirts of Dorchester, had been a mutual repulsion, with each spouse spending as little time as possible in the presence of the other. Emma, moreover, had begun to engage in an active social life in which her husband took little part, and to criticize him openly in conversation and letters. And, as Michael Millgate reports, to 'her long-standing grievance against what she considered the socially demeaning aspects of her marriage were now added an enthusiasm for women's rights' largely based on 'personal resentment against her husband' and his treatment of her. By the year of her death, 'her mental instability – her shifts between paranoiac protest, childish playfulness, and aggressive religiosity – had become very marked, showing itself not only in her public and domestic behaviour, but also in the writings ... to which she now devoted so much of her time' (355–6, 477–8). After visiting the Hardys in September 1912, A. C. Benson recorded in his diary that he had found the 73-year-old Emma 'absurdly dressed, as a country lady without friends might dress herself on a vague recollection of some nymph in a picture by Botticelli'. There seemed something intolerable in the thought of Hardy having 'to live day & night with the absurd, inconsequent, puffy, rambling old lady ... his patience must be incredibly tried' (quoted in Millgate, 481–2).

No wonder that upon hearing of Emma's death a friend of Hardy commented that 'he'll feel relief at this' (Hardy, 1979, xiii). Just the opposite was in fact the case. Hardy was deeply distraught by his wife's death and overcome with remorse. His emotions were further stirred by finding two manuscripts among her effects. One was entitled 'What I Think of My Husband'. In it, between the early 1890s and a day or two before her death, Emma had recorded 'bitter denunciations' full of 'venom, hatred & abuse' of her husband and his family (Bailey, 24). The other was a 15,000-word document, entitled *Some Recollections*, written less than two years before her death, in which she had evocatively described her early life in Cornwall, concluding with an account of her 'life's romance'. It began 'on a lovely Monday evening' in March 1870 when she met the young architect from Dorset who had come to restore the church at Saint-Juliot, continued during their courtship against the spectacular backgrounds of the Atlantic coast of Cornwall, and climaxed with their union: 'The day we were married', Emma fondly recollected, 'was a perfect September day – 17th, 1874 – not a brilliant sunshine, but wearing a soft, sunny luminousness; just as it should be' (30, 33, 37).

During the winter of 1912–13, Hardy read and reread the diaries in which Emma had recorded the exacerbations of her married life. But he also carefully studied *Some Recollections*, even supplying annotations to the account of their first acquaintance. It is clear that these recollections stimulated Hardy's memory and abetted the natural tendency of any bereaved person (as he put it in a letter of 13 December) to forget 'all the recent years & differences ... the mind goes back to the early times when each was much to the other – in her case & mine intensely much' (Hardy, 1978–88, iv, 239). Later that winter, he decided to return to Cornwall after an absence of four decades in order to visit the scenes of their courtship and of Emma's early life. The poetic expression of Hardy's inner life in the months between Emma's death and his return from Cornwall in March 1913 is found in his elegiac sequence, *Poems of 1912–13*.

4

The first two stanzas of 'The Going', the sequence's opening poem, emphasize the suddenness of Emma's final departure. Her death was preceded by 'no hint' or word of goodbye for her husband; it was as if she were 'indifferent quite'. There was no moment of farewell, only the eerie synesthesia of the morning light hardening on the wall of Hardy's bedroom while unknown to him his wife was breathing her last in another room. In the third stanza, the scene shifts from indoors and morning to outdoors and evening:

> Why do you make me leave the house
> And think for a breath it is you I see
> At the end of the alley of bending boughs
> Where so often at dusk you used to be;
>   Till in darkening dankness
>   The yawning blankness
> Of the perspective sickens me!

In the uncertain light, the poet thinks for a moment that he sees his wife where he had often seen her. But there is nothing of Emma left to see. There is only the 'darkening dankness' of a December nightfall and a sickening absence at the focal point of a long familiar scene, a blankness that seems 'yawning' in two senses: gaping and abysmal; but also indifferent, neutral, unresponsive to human need.

In the fourth stanza, the poet turns his attention to the remotest past of their relationship – remote both in time and in space (the Atlantic coast of Cornwall):

> You were she who abode
> By those red-veined rocks far West,
> You were the swan-necked one who rode
> Along the beetling Beeny Crest,
>   And, reining nigh me,
>   Would muse and eye me,
> While Life unrolled us its very best.

Sacks noted that the remoteness of this image was internally suggested by the slightly archaic diction ('abode', 'beetling', 'nigh', 'the swan-necked one') and the overtones of chivalric romance. He could not 'help suspecting that Hardy's image of the young Emma is not just the construction of the old mourner but rather the equally fictive product of the young lover' (242). The essential point about the image, however, as will have become clear by the end of the sequence, is not to whom it should be assigned but rather that it is idealized rather than realistic, and dreamlike rather than visionary.

Since they had once experienced the 'very best' that life could offer, the poet wonders in the next stanza why in later years they did not 'seek/That time's renewal' through revisiting the places of their early love. Such wishful thinking is checked in the final stanza: 'All's past amend,/Unchangeable'. The speaker seems 'but a dead man held on end/To sink down soon':

> ... O you could not know
>   That such swift fleeing
>   No soul foreseeing –
> Not even I – would undo me so!

'The Going' had opened with an urgent intimacy of address:

> Why did you give no hint that night
> That quickly after the morrow's dawn,
> And calmly, as if indifferent quite,
> You would close your term here, up and be gone ...

These lines are the first indication of a complexity of reference that runs throughout *Poems of 1912–13*. They refer both to the suddenness of Emma's death and to her latter-day habit of abrupt departures, of being suddenly up and gone with no goodbye, of 'vanishing' without a word. This habit is the subject of 'Without Ceremony', the short sixth poem in the sequence, which uses 'vanish' to describe Emma's sudden departures from a room or from Max Gate, just as 'The Going' uses the same verb to describe her equally unceremonious departure from life. 'So', the later poem concludes,

>   now that you disappear
> For ever in that swift style,
> Your meaning seems to me
> Just as it used to be:
> 'Good-bye is not worth while!'

Hardy, on the other hand, like any elegist, has to believe that it is worthwhile to say goodbye. But before that can happen, he will need what he could not find in 'The Going' – a presence rather than an absence, perhaps a soft call heard or a visual image glimpsed, to which to say goodbye. The essential task of the following poems of the sequence will be to replace absence with presence – to traverse the distance both between the dead and the living and between the later years of the Hardys' marriage and the long ago days of their love by the red-veined rocks.

In the opening line of 'The Going' ('Why did you give me no hint that night ...?') a flicker of irritation and annoyance can be detected beneath the pathos. A similar subtext is found in the problematic semantics of the opening lines of the poem's penultimate stanza: 'Why, then, latterly did we not speak,/Did we not think of those days long dead ... ?' There are two ways of reading these lines: the first is wistful and incipiently sentimental – why in the later years of our marriage did we neither speak about or think of the early days of our love in Cornwall and (the stanza goes on to say) plan to revisit the region. In the other construal, the first line is an independent syntatic unit containing a reluctant

admission of the painful reality of their cohabitation during the preceding two decades (for which 'latterly' is a euphemism): why during those
years did we not speak to each other?

These embedded equivocations are the first indications, at the very
beginning of the sequence, that for his search to be successful Hardy
will have to acknowledge and work through the hostilities and temperamental antipathies of the later years of his marriage. This necessity, plus
what would seem to have been his difficulty even in intimating a degree
of responsibility on his part for what their marriage had become, can
also be felt in 'Your Last Drive', the second poem in the sequence and
the first of four in which Emma is given lines to speak. The poem opens
with the banal reflection that a mere eight days before she would be
buried there, Emma had driven by the place of her interment without
giving it a thought. In the third stanza, the speaker's utterance becomes
much more interesting:

> I drove not with you ... Yet had I sat
> At your side that eve I should not have seen
> That the countenance I was glancing at
> Had a last-time look in the flickering sheen,
> Nor have read the writing upon your face,
> 'I go hence soon to my resting place ...'

These awkward contrary-to-fact conditionals allow Hardy to intimate
something of Emma's perspective on their marriage without his having
directly to admit either his coldness to her or the fact that he was aware
of her bitterness. To say that he 'should not have seen' the premonitory
writing on her face because it would not have been there (Emma being
unaware that her days were numbered) is fatuous. What Hardy would
seem to want to say, but can express only indirectly and elliptically, is
that he should not have seen Emma's face if he had been there because
he would not have been looking at it, or at least not looking at it with
the sympathetic attention that is the prerequisite of reading someone's
mood.

In the poem's penultimate stanza, Emma speaks in flat and utterly
unconditional tones of her complete indifference as to whether or not
Hardy will miss her after her death. Why should she care (a reader
familiar with the biographical facts might well reflect), given Hardy's
terrible refusal to take notice of her physical suffering during the last
year of her life and of her acute physical and mental distress in the days
immediately preceding her death (see Gittings, 149–50)? In the poem's
closing stanza the speaker's confessional promptings are stilled. He
ignores both the direct thrust of the words he has given Emma to speak,
and their implications concerning himself, by choosing to understand
what she says only in the biological, not the psychological, sense: that

is, Emma will neither know nor care how Hardy feels because she is
dead. He then rather lamely addresses the 'Dear ghost', saying he will
continue to care for her anyway. But in the closing lines of this peculiar
and troubled poem, the speaker seems capable only of registering the
abiding 'fact' of death and the distance between Emma and himself.

The short third poem, 'The Walk', uses a two-stanza, then–now,
structure to convey a powerfully understated sense of loss – of the
crucial 'difference' between Emma alive and dead:

> You did not walk with me
> Of late to the hill-top tree
>   By the gated ways,
>   As in earlier days;
>   You were weak and lame,
>   So you never came,
> And I went alone, and I did not mind,
> Not thinking of you as left behind.
>
> I walked up there to-day
> Just in the former way:
>   Surveyed around
>   The familiar ground
>   By myself again:
>   What difference, then?
> Only that underlying sense
> Of the look of a room on returning thence.

There is no direct statement of the speaker's emotions. 'Of late' during
his walks Hardy had not thought of Emma as left behind: being weak
and lame she could not have come anyway. Moreover, he preferred her
absence to her presence, and did not think of her as belonging at his
side. Indeed, he presumably did not think of her at all. 'To-day' is a
different matter: the absence caused by Emma's death, unlike that caused
by her physical infirmities, is present at some underlying level of consciousness. The pressure of this difference is not directly expressed; it is
obliquely registered in the final two lines of the poem. The sense of
Emma's absence is like the uncanny awareness that something – perhaps the removal of an object not consciously noticed for years – looks
different about a long-familiar room. Everything seems as before, but
there is a disturbing sense of difference. This awareness, of course,
exists only in the human perceiver. But as phrased by Hardy, it is as if
the difference (the absence) were already there in the room waiting for
him – waiting to be confronted.

The elegiac subject is directly presented in the next two poems, 'Rain
on a Grave' and 'I Found Her Out There', in both of which Emma is
referred to in the third person rather than addressed in the second. This
is one indication of the elegist's desire to create a certain distance

between himself and his loss. One result of the change is that the making of consoling rhetorical gestures is facilitated. The third stanza of 'Rain on a Grave', for example, voices the conventional and essentially senitmental wish that he could have died instead of her or, better, that both were in the grave together. And the endings of each poem contain suggestions of consolation and recompense. Sacks identifies them as psychologically necessary moments of respite and associates them with the 'conventionally consoling' (245) but ultimately unsatisfying moments in earlier elegies. 'Rain on a Grave', for example, closes with the thought that the daisies that Emma loved 'with a child's pleasure/All her life's round' will soon be in bloom. There is the suggestion that she will become part of nature's annual resurrection and even the intimation of her terrestrial apotheosis into flowers showing 'Like stars on the ground'.

Such fond imaginings, however, can hardly provide more than mo mentary consolation for the grieving poet. In neither poem is the fact of Emma's absence confronted. In *Poems of 1912–13*, the movement from loss to recompense, absence to presence, is identical with the movement of memory from 'latterly' to the days of the early freshness of Hardy's and Emma's love. The spatial counterpart of this temporal journey is Hardy's journey to Cornwall. In 'After a Journey', the first Cornish poem in the sequence, Hardy speaks of 'our past' (the early days of his and Emma's love) as being located 'across the dark space wherein I have lacked you'. This dark space is both the distance between the dead and the living and that between the Dorset of later years and the Atlantic coast of Cornwall in the early 1870s. At the same time, it is a psychological dark space within the mind of the poet, one that resembles the *pays obscur* of which Proust's narrator speaks near the beginning of *A la recherche du temps perdu*. This is the dark region, 'the abyss of uncertainty' within the mind, through which it must go seeking a lost, dimly recalled radiance. Not only seeking, but also creating. The mind, says Proust's narrator, 'is face to face with something which does not yet exist, to which it alone can give reality and substance, which it alone can bring into the light of day' (49).

Before Hardy's westward journey can begin, the irritations and vexations of the later years must be put behind him. They surface again both in 'Rain on a Grave' and in 'Lament'. We have seen that the former poem ends with Hardy thinking of the lifelong 'child's pleasure' that Emma took in the return of the daisies. 'Lament' similarly speaks of her 'child's eager glance' at the shy snowdrops that signal the beginning of spring. To put the question bluntly: should one regard this and comparable delights of Emma's as childlike or childish? Aspects of both poems suggest the latter. In fact, another result of the distance created by the shift from 'you' to 'her' is that it enables Hardy to discharge more vigorously (though still indirectly) his animus for the latter-day Emma. In the opening lines of 'Rain on a Grave', for example, the 'ruthless disdain' with which the clouds 'spout' their discharge onto Emma's mound is projected on to the natural phenomena by the conflicted emotions of the poem's speaker. Furthermore, in the remainder of the first stanza and the following stanza the fast-paced, sing-song tone insinuates that Emma had an absurdly exalted self-image in thinking of 'her delicate head' as 'dishonour[ed]' by the impudent rain.

In 'Lament', irritation with Emma's behaviour comes through more clearly. The poem's ostensible subject, the then–now, living–dead contrast, is baldly and repetitively driven home by the sharp turn in the seventh line of each stanza (she would have ... but she is dead) and by the insistent closing trio of strong rhymes. But its implicit or psychological subject is Hardy's distaste for all aspects of his wife's social being – the bright hats, the welcoming smiles, the ardent dominance of her dinner table, her 'junketings', and the other stale things 'That used so to joy her,/And never to cloy her/As us they cloy' (the plural pronoun 'us' being a euphemism for 'me').

The next two poems, 'The Haunter' and 'The Voice', are very different. In the first half of this ravishing love duet, Emma is imagined to be speaking from just beyond the borders of the perceptible, the dark space between death and life having suddenly become the finest of fine lines. Her tones are hardly those of the Emma who had coldly insisted in 'Your Last Drive' that she cared not at all for her widower. The speaker of 'The Haunter' is rather an epitome of the Victorian ideal of the female as a self-effacing helpmate, subordinate to her spouse and desiring only to please and protect him:

> O tell him!
> Quickly make him know
> If he but sigh since my loss befell him
> Straight to his side I go.
> Tell him a faithful one is doing
> All that love can do
> Still that his path may be worth pursuing,
> And to bring peace thereto.

Prima facie, 'The Haunter' might seem a self-serving exercise in wish-fulfilment on Hardy's part, a sentimental alternative to confronting absence and acknowledging responsibility. But as with Emma's vanishing in 'The Going', there is a double reference. Here it is the way in which the difficulties of communication between ghost and griever are analogous to the non-communication of husband and wife in the later years of their marriage. Thom Gunn has called attention to Hardy's use of the ballad convention of the ghost of a woman haunting the living husband who cannot perceive her:

> It is an original but simple device that immediately suggests great complexities – the fact that she cannot communicate with him but wants to, and the fact that he knows it, corresponds to a common enough situation in human relationships and almost certainly to that of the Hardys' marriage in its later years.
>
> (42)

Moreover, the key point about this exercise in pathos is that it is one half of a duet and is incomplete without the answering voice of the following poem. Its words of comfort and implicit forgiveness are what Hardy would presumably have liked to hear from Emma's ghost had she been able to communicate with him. But as the answering poem makes clear, the grieving widower does not in fact hear the words of 'The Haunter'. He rather hears sounds that reverberate in his consciousness (the triple rhythm 'call to him ... all to him' of the former poem being echoed in the 'call to me ... all to me' of the latter) and that seem, but may not be, those of a human voice. The point at issue is not whether the ghostly Emma can be credibly imagined to be speaking consoling words, but whether there is anyone speaking at all.

The Voice

Woman much missed, how you call to me, call to me,
Saying that now you are not as you were
When you had changed from the one who was all to me,
But as at first, when our day was fair.

Can it be you that I hear? Let me view you, then,
Standing as when I drew near to the town
Where you would wait for me: yes, as I knew you then,
Even to the original air-blue gown!

Or is it only the breeze, in its listlessness
Travelling across the wet mead to me here,
You being ever dissolved to wan wistlessness,
Heard no more again far or near?

  Thus I; faltering forward,
  Leaves around me falling,
Wind oozing thin through the thorn from norward,
  And the woman calling.

Emma, the 'woman much missed', is imagined to be calling to the poet from the distant past, when 'their day was fair' and they were all to each other. In the second stanza, for both verification of the communication and intensification of the experience, the speaker asks the caller to reveal herself in visual as well as aural form, to be present to him in 'the original air-blue gown' worn at one of their first meetings, a vividly specific notation that is at the same time suggestive of a supernal radiance. As Derek Attridge notes, 'the speaker is no longer bemused by an aural image, but excited by a visual one, and the words lose their easy flow for the sharper contours of emotional utterance' (331). But this shift brings with it a self-reflexive doubt. In the third stanza, an alternative possibility is raised concerning what the speaker is hearing: not a voice from the freshness of the past urgently attempting to communicate with him, but only the listless and messageless breeze, the wife being 'dissolved to wan wistlessness' and even if not 'consigned to existlessness' (the first edition reading of this phrase) none the less no more to be heard 'far or near'.

The key word, then, in the first three stanzas of 'The Voice' is *or*. These stanzas present alternative possibilities – a visionary or a naturalistic explanation of a phenomenon – without choosing between them. But at the end of 'The Voice' a desperate insistence is required to keep the *or* operative. The first three lines of the last stanza are insistently negative: at the aural level, the metrical expectations established by the preceding stanzas are frustrated by the faltering of the rhythm; at the visual level, a young woman in an air-blue gown is replaced by an old man stumbling onward in a wet December landscape. The voice-like calling sound is naturalistically explained by the north wind's passage through the thorn tree, a sound 'oozing thin' like the secretion of a wound – a striking synesthetic image, used here, as in 'The Going', to convey a sense of utter desolation. But then, in the extraordinary last line of the poem, there is the desperate assertion of possibility: not the wind through the thorn, but 'the woman calling'. Not, one notes, the 'woman much missed' intimately addressed in the second person in the poem's opening line; but a more impersonal and distanced third-person figure, 'the woman', whose voice by the end of the poem comes, if at all, not from the air-blue past but through the leafless wet branches of the thorn.

'The Haunter' and 'The Voice' are the first unmistakable indications that Hardy's sequence is not only an elegiac poem; it is also a love poem. The 'great thing' about *Poems of 1912–13*, Joseph Brodsky has observed, 'is that they are not in memory of his wife but in memory of his bride':

> In other words, the infinity the poet ponders and fathoms in his cycle is not that of the posthumous life but rather the one that separates him from Emma Gifford as he [knew her] in Cornwall, in [the early 1870s]. It is Emma Gifford in her original air-blue gown whom he tries to make out through the dim, dark, now cold

telescope of Emma Hardy in 1912–13, and who haunts him all over the place. Now this is love poetry in the truest sense because it tells the reader how thick the lenses are, how far and unattainable the star is – in short, about what becomes of love, about what love adds up to or dwindles down to.

(1160)

After the visionary equivocations of the love duet, there are two domestic poems, 'His Visitor' and 'A Circular', each spoken by a different marriage partner. They are the last registrations in the sequence of the temperamental antipathy of the later years. Then comes 'A Dream or No', in which Hardy finds himself urgently impelled back into the past, to the time when Emma wore a simple air-blue gown, was not weak and lame, and cared for nothing but her immediate natural surroundings. The poem does not speak of a voice faintly calling but of a 'strange necromancy' that has brought dreams of the far distant past: of Saint-Juliot; of 'a maiden abiding/Thereat as in hiding'; and of a night long ago when

> lonely I found her,
> The sea-birds around her,
> And other than nigh things uncaring to know.

This necromancy has 'charmed' the speaker 'to fancy/That much of my life claims the spot as its key'. But after 40 years, do the 'maid' and the places associated with her have any correspondence with past reality:

> Can she ever have been here,
> And shed her life's sheen here,
> The woman I thought a long housemate with me?
>
> Does there even a place like Saint-Juliot exist?
> Or a Vallency Valley
> With stream and leafed alley,
> Or Beeny, or Bos with its flounce flinging mist?

To answer these questions Hardy revisited Cornwall in March 1913. The culminating poems in the sequence are set in the shore and country around Boscastle (designated 'Castle Boterel' in the sequence). The first of them, 'After a Journey', has been called the climactic poem in the sequence. It is not that, but it is the turning point. In the poem, the spatial journey to the west is shown to be coterminous with the temporal journey in search of lost time. In the revisited Cornish places a living sense of Emma as she was at first, and of the poet's love for her, are recovered in memory. The double reference of the word *haunt* in the poem is one of the ways in which a sense of the complementarity of the two journeys is conveyed. Hardy is visiting his and Emma's 'olden haunts', 'the spots we knew when we haunted here together' and where

Emma's ghost, whom the poet is able to glimpse, now haunts in the apparitional sense. The distance between the dead and the living (and between loss and recompense) that has been traversed by this point in the sequence can be gauged by comparing 'After a Journey' to earlier poems. For one thing, the apparition in 'After a Journey' has little in common with the romance image of 'the swan-necked one' of 'The Going'; nor is she wearing an air-blue gown or radiating a supernal aura. She is more matter of factly described as having 'nut-coloured hair,/And gray eyes, and rose-flush coming and going'.

But the key point is that the Emma of later years has been superseded by the Emma of early days – the dame by the maiden. This is signalled by the perceptual switch from aural to visual. This supersession and its implications were not at first fully grasped by Hardy. In the first edition version of the opening line of 'After a Journey', the speaker declared that he had come 'hereto' in order 'to interview a ghost'. This expectation explains why a question is asked of the ghost in the second stanza: 'What have you now found to say of our past … ?' As the following lines make clear, 'our past' refers to all 43 years of Hardy's and Emma's relationship. That is to say, the speaker seemed initially to regard the phantom he encounters in Pentargan Bay as a shade from the under-world possessing knowledge of all phases of her life. In the revised version of the poem's opening line, the presupposition of this question is suppressed. It is none the less vestigially present in the poem and functions in a way similar to the residual negative feelings detected by Eric Griffiths that run 'counter to the declarative surface of the poem, feelings contained in the unvoiced possibilities which lie within the written words'. For example, '"What have you found now to say of our past" contains a vexed "What is it *now*?"' (230–31). Both the unvoiced possibilities and the question asked of a ghost who can no longer answer are traces of Hardy's earlier conflicted feelings towards Emma that have now been superseded by those in the voiced enactment of the lines of 'After a Journey'. But they remain vestigially present in a way that adds greatly to the resonance of this pivotal poem.

The fact that the apparition in 'After a Journey' is 'voiceless' distinguishes the Emma of the closing section of the sequence from the aural apparitions in earlier poems. In the answering call to one of them, the speaker of 'The Voice' had been explicitly concerned with asserting the possibility of transcendence. From the point of view of the Cornish poems, one can begin to see that attempt as another false surmise born of deep emotional need. From 'After a Journey' on, there will be only visual apparitions of Emma, which by the end of the sequence will have become fully explicable as memory images having neither a supernatural nor a natural explanation, but a psychological one. Similarly, after this poem Emma is never again directly addressed; there is no more 'you' but rather 'she', 'one', 'the woman', and finally 'the ghost-girl-rider'.

'After a Journey', then, explicitly rejects certain possibilities. F. R. Leavis rightly insisted on its tough-minded acceptance of loss and diminution. Having tracked Emma through the years and the dead scenes, Hardy attains

> only a presence that is at the same time the absence felt more acutely ... The loneliness and desolation are far from being mitigated by the 'viewing' in memory; for the condition of the 'viewing' is Hardy's full realizing contemplation of the woman's irremediable absence – of the fact that she is dead.
>
>   (95–6)

None the less, as Leavis recognized, 'After a Journey' ends with an affirmation – one that is not desperately insistent like the ending of 'The Voice', but that contains a quiet, if plaintive, note of assurance. Here is the last stanza:

> Ignorant of what there is flitting here to see,
>   The waked birds preen and the seals flop lazily,
> Soon you will have, Dear, to vanish from me,
>   For the stars close their shutters and the dawn whitens hazily.
> Trust me, I mind not, though Life lours,
>   The bringing me here; nay, bring me here again!
>   I am just the same as when
>   Our days were a joy, and our paths through flowers.

What Leavis called the quotidian ordinariness of the opening lines further underlines the difference between the vision of this poem and the romance visions of the young Emma in 'The Going', 'I Found Her Out There' and 'A Dream or No'. Similarly, the homy figure of the stars closing their shutters, plus the dawn's unspectacular hazy whitening, assure that there will be no transcendent associations given to the coming of a new day. When the dawn comes, Emma Gifford, the voiceless ghost, will have to 'vanish', but not for the reasons that in later years Emma Hardy made her unceremonious exits, and not in the sense that she will pass permanently from the speaker's vision. She has to vanish because dawn is the canonical time for apparitions to disappear. The tone of the close of the poem suggests there is no reason to think that the visual image of the young Emma will not reappear.

It is true that Hardy does not say that she will appear again, but what he does say intimates as much: 'I am just the same as when/Our days were a joy and our paths through flowers.' He scarcely means to say that he is physically the same man at 73 as he was in his early thirties. But he does affirm that there is a continuity in time between the man who haunted Pentargan Bay with Emma long ago and who is now haunted by her in the same place. What he most wants to assert, however, is not continuity but identity: the full recovery of the love for Emma that he had felt in their early days – not (as the natural setting of the poem makes clear) an idealized romance love, but a particular love for a woman with nut-coloured hair, gray eyes and rose flush.

Hardy has fully traversed the dark space between late and early, has worked through the antagonistic emotions of later years. And as his emotions have become purified and simplified, Emma's image has become refined in his memory. This is beautifully intimated in the one-syllable epithet that is placed in the centre of the stanza's third line and receives the line's principal stress: 'Soon you will have, Dear, to vanish from me.' The same term had been used in an earlier reference to Emma's way of vanishing in 'Without Ceremony': 'It was your way, my dear,/To vanish without a word.' But there the uncapitalized 'dear' was part of a conventional form of marital address and in context had overtones of reserve and even displeasure. In contrast, the 'Dear' in 'After a Journey' resonates with an unqualified and loving tenderness.

The psychological ground is now prepared for the climactic poems of the sequence – 'Beeny Cliff', 'At Castle Boterel', and 'The Phantom Horsewoman'. The first describes a spectacular natural setting: the 'chasmal beauty' of the cliff, 'the opal and the sapphire of that wandering western sea', and the momentarily obscured sun breaking out again and transforming the 'dull misfeatured stain' of the ocean's surface – 'purples prinked the main'. And, riding high above the ocean's surface, the woman 'with her bright hair flapping free – /The woman whom I loved so, and who loyally loved me'. Donald Davie suggested that in this poem the colour purple is used in its Latin sense of the brightest and most vivid colouring, not as the name for a particular tint, and is used metaphorically, as a transferred epithet: 'the purples that prink the main as seen from Beeny Cliff are the spiritual light of sexual love' which the lovers project on to their surroundings (140). But the poem's subtitle is 'March 1870 – March 1913' and its last two stanzas turn on the then–now contrast. In 1913, Beeny Cliff and the ocean are 'still' every bit as spectacular as they were 43 years before. The continuity in sublimity of the physical scene is so intensely felt as to raise in the speaker's mind the possibility of the human analogy: in 1873, the love of Hardy and Emma was as intense as the setting was spectacular. If the latter quality is continuous, the speaker wonders, why not the former? Such is the wish in the penultimate stanza. The falseness of the surmise is the subject of the final stanza:

> What if still in chasmal beauty looms that wild weird western shore,

> The woman now is – elsewhere – whom the ambling pony bore,
> And nor knows nor cares for Beeny, and will laugh there
>   nevermore.

The poignant 'elsewhere' is an attempt to mitigate the collapse at the human level of the then–now analogy by simply saying that in 1913 Emma is not present at the scene. This finesse, however, is brutally negated by the last word in the poem, 'nevermore', the definitive ring of which is further accentuated by its position as the last in a trio of strong rhymes.

'At Castle Boterel' also describes a particular place with particular associations revisited by Hardy after 43 years and also turns on the then–now contrast. But the two poems end very differently. There is nothing sublime about the setting of 'At Castle Boterel', in which the expanse of ocean is replaced by quotidian drizzle, and the woman riding 'high above' by the speaker and a girlish form walking up a long incline beside a chaise from which they have alighted in order to ease the pony's load. But despite the unencouraging setting, the speaker does not come up empty-handed at the poem's end, with nothing recovered and no recompense for loss. In fact, 'At Castle Boterel' is the climactic lyric of *Poems of 1912–13* and contains the sequence's strongest assertion of gain, recompense and continuity, and of the survival of something human from the past.

But one must be clear about what is being affirmed. In the afterglow of his idealizing reading of 'Beeny Cliff', for example, Davie described 'At Castle Boterel' as having a spiritual and metaphysical dimension, as making 'a measured affirmation [that] love triumphs over time' and as asserting that Hardy's and Emma's early love was 'invulnerable to time' and change. Davie repudiated the psychological reading put forward by Hillis Miller in his *Thomas Hardy: Distance and Desire*. Miller, says Davie, 'writes a minus for every plus in the poem, and a plus for every minus' in saying that the poem explicitly records Hardy's recognition that Emma exists not as a ghost that anyone might see, but only in his own mind, and that the special moment of their love recorded in the poem was a transitory imprint on the permanent physical setting (154–5). For Davie, one might say, the glass is full; for Miller, it is prospectively empty. But for a reader who has carefully followed the progression of *Poems of 1912–13* and is attuned to the workings of memory, the glass may be seen to be simultaneously half-full and half-empty.

In the central stanzas of the poem, the speaker recalls over a distance of four decades what passed one night between himself and Emma as they walked up a steep incline:

> What we did as we climbed, and what we talked of
>   Matters not much, nor to what it led, –

Something that life will not be balked of
  Without rude reason till hope is dead,
    And feeling fled.

It filled but a minute. But was there ever
  A time of such quality, since or before,
In that hill's story? To one mind never,
  Though it has been climbed, foot-swift, foot-sore,
    By thousands more.

Primaeval rocks form the road's steep border,
  And much have they faced there, first and last,
Of the transitory in Earth's long order;
  But what they record in colour and cast
    Is – that we two passed.

And to me, though Time's unflinching rigour,
  In mindless rote, has ruled from sight
The substance now, one phantom figure
  Remains on the slope, as when that night
    Saw us alight.

The dash at the end of the first stanza's second line is another indication of Hardy's extreme reluctance to express directly his deepest emotions. The dash functions as an ellipsis for which a phrase must be silently supplied: what specifically Hardy and Emma spoke of during their climb is unimportant, as is to what it ultimately led (the later years of irreparable antagonism). What does matter is 'something' of great value that the lovers experienced that night and that human life cannot well do without. The next stanza attempts to describe this 'something'. Since 'it' is intangible and transitory (filling but a minute) the something cannot be concretely named; but it is felt to be a time of unparalleled 'quality'. Against the background of geological time (the primeval rocks of the road's border), many transitory human moments have come and gone; but his and Emma's brief moment was of such intense non-spatial and non-durational quality that the millennia-old rocks – the granite face of what the next stanza calls 'Time's unflinching rigour' – seem by comparison to shrink to the status of mere chroniclers.

There is no suggestion here or anywhere else in the poem of a metaphysical reality existing in some timeless realm apart from the memory of the poet. Miller is surely right in seeing that the quality celebrated in 'At Castle Boterel' has only a psychological reality, which is wholly contingent upon the continued existence of the ageing poet who will one day be ruled from sight by the mindless rote of time's unflinching rigour. But Miller is wrong to say that this transience and inevitable extinction are what 'At Castle Boterel' recognizes and records. The poem does no such thing. It rather affirms the psychological truth that a past experience of transporting quality is recoverable through memory, that its recovery is exhilarating, and that the quality is a token of the value of human love and its enhancement of human life. Emma is dead and all that remains of her is a phantom figure present in the consciousness of an old man. But while her substance has permanently vanished, a quality abides, recovered and refined, in that consciousness.

The concluding stanza of 'At Castle Boterel' syntactically recapitulates the simultaneously half-full, half-empty nature of the recovered memory of what happened that night. As the backward-looking speaker of the 1913 present drives away from Boterel Hill, his tone changes noticeably from the defiant and passionate affirmations of the poem's middle:

> I look and see it there, shrinking, shrinking,
>   I look back at it amid the rain
> For the very last time; for my sand is sinking,
>   And I shall traverse old love's domain
>   Never again.

Grammatically speaking, the 'it' in the first and second lines could be taken to refer to either the 'phantom figure' of Emma or the receding slope. The former reading reasserts the dominance of linear time, which had been momentarily suspended when the non-horizontal, ascending movement of the slow walk up the hill had led to the experience of a timeless moment. In this reading, the last stanza reaffirms the inexorable temporal movement away from the ever-receding past towards the grave of the ageing speaker who is at the part of the life cycle for which sand in an hourglass is the appropriate geological metaphor. On the other hand, if the 'it' is taken to refer to the receding slope (part of the terrain of old love's domain), the stanza's negative implications are considerably diluted. The speaker may then be taken to be simply stating what was in fact to be the case: that he would never again return to Cornwall. Why should he, since he had obtained from his journey what he had come for: a memory image of the Emma of earlier days? As the final poem in the 18-poem sequence shows, the 'phantom figure' of the young Emma is not left behind on the receding slope.

'The Phantom Horsewoman' recalls an observation Hardy had made in 1901:

> I do not think that there will be any permanent revival of the old transcendental ideals; but I think there may gradually be developed an Idealism of Fancy; that is, an idealism in which Fancy is no longer tricked out and made to masquerade as belief, but is frankly and honestly accepted as an imaginative solace in the lack of any substantial solace to be found in life.
>
>   (333)

I would myself prefer to use other terms, but it is essentially correct to say that the recompense for loss in the climactic sections of the *Poems of 1912–13* is an idealism of fancy, an imaginative or qualitative solace accepted in the lack of any substantial solace to be found in life. 'The Phantom Horsewoman' begins with the half-empty glass:

> Queer are the ways of a man I know:
>   He comes and stands
>   In a careworn craze,
>   And looks at the sands
>   And the seaward haze,
>   With moveless hands
>   And face and gaze,
>   Then turns to go ...
> And what does he see when he gazes so?

The 'he' is the aged poet who at the end of the previous poem, 'Places', was left standing beneaped and stale on the shore of 'to-day', and who is now seen standing solitary and careworn on an actual shore. But who is the speaker of the poem, the 'I'? One might be initially tempted to think that it is the shade of Emma regarding the 'he' from her ghostly realm, as was the case in two earlier poems. But Emma's ghost had been speechless ever since 'His Visitor'; and 'After a Journey' was the last poem in the sequence to make use of the fiction of her ghostly existence out there. Since then, Emma's image had been explicitly a memory image and it is as such that she appears – inside the poet's head, not outside it – in the closing stanzas of 'The Phantom Horsewoman'.

The 'I' and 'he' of the poem are two sides of the same person, each seeing a different part of the half-full, half-empty glass. At the beginning of the poem, the speaker is at a certain critical distance from himself, commenting on the queerness, even craziness, of a careworn man staring at the sand and haze but seeing only 'A phantom of his own figuring' that has no existence outside his head. It is, however, the other half of the speaker, the visionary 'he' rather than the sceptical 'I', whose point of view – whose vision – gradually comes to dominate the poem.

This carefully calculated transition is one of the poem's principal felicities. In its first two sections, the long and rhyming, typographically set-apart first and last lines of the unusual stanza form serve as a frame for the picture contained in the intervening lines. This distinction between frame and picture is analogous to that between 'I' and 'he'. As the poem progresses, both distinctions become blurred. The narrator's point of view moves from that of a neighbour or acquaintance ('Queer are the ways of a man I know') to that of a consensus spokesman for the outside view ('They say ... '), and finally to the psychological omniscience of a privileged inside view in the final two stanzas. In the penultimate, the frame–picture distinction begins to break down; by the final stanza it has disappeared:

> Of this vision of his they might say more:
>   Not only there
>   Does he see this sight,
>   But everywhere
>   In his brain – day, night,
>   As if on the air
>   It were drawn rose bright –
>   Yea, far from that shore
> Does he carry this vision of heretofore:
>
> A ghost-girl-rider. And though, toil-tried,
>   He withers daily,
>   Time touches her not,
>   But she still rides gaily
>   In his rapt thought
>   On that shagged and shaly
>   Atlantic spot,
>   And as when first eyed
> Draws rein and sings to the swing of the tide.

Time's derision and its unflinching rigour cannot touch this apotheosized memory image of the ghost-girl-rider. In the opening poem of the sequence, the poet's desolation had been registered in the disturbing figure of the morning light congealing on the wall and in his momentary illusion that he glimpsed his late wife in the darkening distance. Earlier tentative cures for the yawning blankness of Emma's loss had been found in images of her face dyed a romantic fire-red by the sunset ('I Found Her Out There'), of her shape gently fading into the hazy whiteness ('After a Journey') and of her high-riding figure against the background of the opal, sapphire and iris hues of the Atlantic ('Beeny Cliff'). But finally, in the culminating figure of the sequence, the visual image of Emma has been refined to a pristine freshness, 'drawn rose bright' – that is, etched and vividly coloured by the light of dawn.

There is one more thing to be said about the distinction between 'he' and 'I' in 'The Phantom Horsewoman': it shows at least a certain degree of self-consciousness on Hardy's part about the work he has written. Two nineteenth-century elegies had closed with explicitly reflexive references to the completed poem as being not only the funereal offering but also, at least in implication, a principal compensation for loss. 'Take at my hands this garland [the poem], and farewell', says Swinburne to the 'silent soul' of Baudelaire at the end of 'Ave atque Vale'; 'and this for his dear sake', says Whitman at the close of 'When Lilacs Last in the Dooryard Bloom'd' – *this* being the completed poem: 'Lilac and star and bird twined with the chant of my soul.' Hardy does not suggest either of these things at the end of his sequence. But he did make a very interesting comment on *Poems of 1912–13* in a letter written while he was preparing the sequence for first publication: some of the poems available for inclusion

> I rather shrink from printing – those I wrote just after Emma died, when I looked back at her as she had originally been, & when I felt miserable lest I had not treated her considerately in her later years. However I shall publish them as the only amends I can make ...
>
> (v, 37)

Poems of 1912–13 is Hardy's goodbye gift to Emma and their completion and publication are the culmination of the process of working back from the troubled later days of their marriage to a recovered sense of the untroubled early days of their love. It is only a small step from saying this to saying that the creative achievement of *Poems of 1912–13* is of itself, more than any single positive moment recorded in it, the principal recompense for the sudden loss that so undid the poet.

5

Poems of 1912–13 was first published in 1914 in the first edition of *Satires of Circumstance, Lyrics and Reveries*. In this edition, the sequence consisted of 18 poems concluding with 'The Phantom Horsewoman'. Hardy, however, subsequently added three poems to the end. It is hard to give much weight to the first two of them, 'The Spell of the Rose' and 'St. Launce's Revisited'. Their principal effect is to provide a temporal and psychological space between the closing poems of the 18-poem sequence and the last of the additional poems, 'Where the Picnic Was', which serves as a coda to the sequence. It describes Hardy's winter return to a Dorset hilltop where the previous summer he and his elderly wife had picnicked with two companions. A 'cold wind blows,/ And the grass is gray' in 'the forsaken place'. Only a 'burnt circle' of charred sticks remains as a 'last relic' of the occasion. Since then, the two companions have returned to urban life and one has died. This poem performs several important functions. It rounds off the sequence by returning to the part of England where the opening poems were set and further recalls these poems in turning on the same then – now, living–dead hinge as a number of them. The image of the burnt circle carries a similar suggestion of completeness both in itself and in recalling the Virgilian epigraph of the series: 'Veteris vestigia flammae', that is, 'traces of an old fire'.

The poem thus encourages one to compare the end of the sequence with the beginning and to note that the psychological condition of the speaker has changed appreciably in the interim. He is no longer grief-stricken and troubled; his vexatious emotions seem behind him; and he no longer looks forward to his own death, as he did at the end of the sequence's opening poem. Nor are there any suggestions of a 'careworn craze' or daily withering that appeared in the sequence as late as 'The Phantom Horsewoman'. To be sure, the season is not spring, and there are no suggestions of fresh fields and pastures new for the septuagenarian widower. But when he quietly observes that 'Yes, I am here/Just as last year', there is the suggestion of endurance and a continuing identity in time. And in the closing lines of the poem – 'And one – has shut her eyes/For evermore', there is the intimation that the process of saying goodbye enacted in the sequence has been positively completed and that Hardy is at peace with Emma's memory (just as he seems to be in his letter to her cousin). There is, moreover, the registration of a loving tenderness in the pause before the closing reference to the shut eyes of his late wife, and in the delicacy of 'For evermore', which is as unequivocal as, but so different in its resonances from, the harsh finality of 'nevermore' at the end of 'Beeny Cliff'.

'Where the Picnic Was', then, does not negate or even qualify the compensatory assertions made in the climactic poems of the sequence. It does, however, place these moments of visionary intensity in a longer temporal perspective that allows one to infer what was in fact the case: that life with Emma in the past, both the early days and the later days, will be succeeded by a life in the future without her. The enabling condition of this transition was the process of saying goodbye inscribed in the preceding poems of the sequence, which reaches its climax with the affirmation of human love as an abiding 'quality' superior to duration.

6

The coda to Patmore's cluster of bereavement odes is 'A Farewell'. Occasioned by his reception into the Roman Catholic church, the poem's premise is Emily Patmore's apprehension that her husband's conversion would result in their spiritual separation for all eternity:

> With all my will, but much against my heart,
> We two now part.
> My Very Dear,
> Our solace is, the sad road lies so clear.
> It needs no art,

> With faint, averted feet
> And many a tear,
> In our opposed paths to persevere.
> Go thou to East, I West.

Once again, the theological pretext serves to facilitate the expression of an apprehension or longing not dependent on Christian belief. Fear of a theological impediment to reunion makes this poem in effect into a nineteenth-century agnostic poem of doubtful knowledge concerning the afterlife – a poem, for example, like Hardy's lyric 'He Prefers Her Earthly', which is addressed to his dead wife.

The occasion of Hardy's poem is a spectacular 'after-sunset' which leads the speaker to wonder whether Emma dwells 'in that glory-show'. The answer is that 'You may; for there are strange, strange things in being,/Stranger than I know'. The speaker then reflects on the implications of the possibility:

> Yet if that chasm of splendour claim your presence
> Which glows between the ash cloud and the dun,
>   How changed must be your mortal mould!
> Changed to a firmament-riding earthless essence
>   From what you were of old:
>
> All too unlike the fond and fragile creature
> Then known to me ... Well, shall I say it plain?
>   I would not have you thus and there,
> But still would grieve on, missing you, still feature
>   You as the one you were.

The subject of these stanzas is contrasting impressions or preferences concerning a lost loved one. Hardy allows for the possibility of Emma's continued existence as an 'earthless essence' in an otherworldly realm. But his temperamental preference, expressed in intimate and loving tones to the absent loved one, is for her to have continued existence only in his memory, where she retains her earthly features. Between grief and transcendence, Hardy prefers to take grief and to continue to feature 'You as the one you were'.

Prima facie, the temperamental point of view in Patmore's poem is the opposite: he prefers his wife unearthly in the sense of surviving death, and he hopes for a future reunion. 'A Farewell', however, is a far cry from the assurance of absolute ecstasy found in 'The Day after To-morrow'. It is rather the case, as Ball put it, that 'A Farewell' moves towards 'a muted climax of imagined meeting which depends entirely, as the tense phrasing shows, on the resolute acquiescence in the completeness of separation' (83):

> We will not say
> There's any hope, it is so far away.

But, O, my Best,
When the one darling of our widowhead,
The nursling Grief,
Is dead,
And no dews blur our eyes
To see the peach-bloom come in evening skies,
Perchance we may,
Where now this night is day,
And even through faith of still averted feet,
Making full circle of our banishment,
Amazed meet;
The bitter journey to the bourne so sweet
Seasoning the termless feast of our content
With tears of recognition never dry.

'A Farewell' is a powerful vision of possibility sustained by its own longing and seasoned by loss. Its ravishing last line alludes to Milton's 'Lycidas' (which in turn alludes to Revelations 7:17 and 21:4), in which the saints in the Christian heaven 'wipe the tears forever from [the] eyes' of the lost loved one. But the 'bourne so sweet' envisioned by Patmore where the lovers may meet again is not the celestial Christian heaven, which is after all a place where none either marry or are given in marriage. It is, rather, a terrestrial place on the other side of this earth where the long night of separation may be succeeded by the day of reunion. Patmore prefers his late wife to be like the peach-bloom in evening skies – unearthly but perceptible; he prefers the feast of content to be 'termless' but not eternal; and he would clearly prefer his amazed recognition to be not of an 'earthless essence' but of a recognizable figure – of 'You as the one you were'.

Thus, in the light of 'A Farewell', the bereavement odes of the Roman Catholic convert can be seen to share something of fundamental importance with Hardy's agnostic sequence: they are both late-Victorian attempts to find a solution to what Georg Simmel identified as 'the great problem for the modern spirit ... to find a place for everything which transcends the givenness of vital phenomena within those phenomena themselves, instead of transposing it to a spatial beyond' (243).

CHAPTER NINE

Continuities

Yonder a maid and her wight
  Come whispering by:
War's annals will cloud into night
  Ere their story die.
      Thomas Hardy, 'In Time of "The Breaking of Nations"'

1

Hardy's antagonism to the doctrinal aspects of Browning's poetry is well known. As he bluntly remarked in a letter of 1899, the longer he lived the more did Browning seem '*the* literary puzzle of the 19th century. How could smug Christian optimism worthy of a dissenting grocer find a place inside a man who was so vast a seer & feeler when on neutral ground' (1978–88, ii, 216). Hardy's resistance to Browning's optimism, however, did not keep him from reading and rereading Browning's poems over a 60-year period, valuing them highly, and making some of them part of his vocabulary of feeling. In 1894, as numerous pencilled markings attest, his interest in Browning's poetry was intensified when Mrs Henniker gave him a volume of *Selections from the Poetical Works of Robert Browning*. It has been suggested that his reading of this volume influenced Hardy's decision to abandon the writing of novels and return to poetry (Pinion, 192). Certainly the unpoetical diction and rough rhythms, the elaborate stanza forms and forced rhymes, and the dramatic character of many of Hardy's poems suggest the example of Browning.

So does the younger poet's interest in the chances and mischances of a spark being struck between potential lovers. It is not surprising that 'The Statue and the Bust', which turns on the lost chances and wasted lives of two persons who long for each other but who never come together because the timing is never right, was Hardy's favourite among Browning's poems (Felkin, 30). But James Richardson goes too far in describing the work as 'the Browning poem he could most easily have written' (36). Any of the several Browning love poems that Hardy imitated equally deserves this designation: 'Love among the Ruins', for example, which is rescored in 'Ditty'; 'Youth and Art', from which 'The Opportunity' derives; or any of the poems that understrut 'Under the

Waterfall', an artificial exercise in the fulsome, worldly manner of some of Browning's amatory verse.

The love poem that had the most personal importance for Hardy, however, is one that he could never have written himself. 'By the Fire-Side', which celebrates the opposite of a lost chance, is one of Browning's most optimistic and idealizing love poems. An aged speaker looks far back in time to the crucial moment, the turning point, in his relationship with the woman who has been his beloved wife for many years. They had been walking in the Italian countryside one autumn day when something totally unanticipated and unlooked for had happened. They had 'caught for a moment the powers at play' in the forests around them: the sights and sounds, the lights and the shades had 'made up a spell' during which a quantum leap in the intensity of their mutual feeling had occurred. The 'bar' between them was broken and two became one: 'we were mixed at last/In spite of the mortal screen'. Until then, their relationship had been quotidian: a drawing together 'Just for the obvious human bliss,/To satisfy life's daily thirst/With a thing men seldom' fail to attain. But in a 'moment, one and infinite', their love had become transcendent. Two souls had mixed 'as mists do'; the lovers had felt themselves to be part of a beneficent 'general plan'; the 'gain of earth' had become 'heaven's gain too'.

Prima facie, it seems extraordinary that 'By the Fire-Side' could figure as anything but an anti-text in Hardy's work. Indeed, when the poem is cited in *Tess of the D'Urbervilles* and *Jude the Obscure*, Hardy's intellectual animus is manifest: Browning's positive becomes an ironic intensification of the novelist's negative. But in two of Hardy's personal poems, in both of which he looks back over decades to special moments in the early days of his and Emma's love, the example of 'By the Fire-Side' enables Hardy to bring into focus and to re-create two crucial moments in the most important love relationship of his life. Tom Paulin (51, 67) has noted the echo of lines from 'By the Fire-Side' ('Oh, the little more, and how much it is!/And the little less, and what worlds away!') in the final stanza of 'At the Word "Farewell"', which recalls a crucial moment in Hardy and Emma's leave-taking in Cornwall in March 1870.

The other poem is 'At Castle Boterel'. As we saw in the previous chapter, this poem attempts to describe a 'something' of great value that life cannot well do without. Intangible and transitory, the something cannot be concretely named. But 'it' can be identified as a time of unparalleled 'quality'. It 'filled but a minute' (like the 'moment, one and infinite' of Browning's poem); but in this sudden intensification of the lovers' apprehension of each other, in this mutual expansion of consciousness, duration is dissolved in presentness and quantity is replaced by quality. 'At Castle Boterel' affirms that intense moments of 'obvious human bliss' are exceptional and of lasting value. The infinite moment of 'By the Fire-Side', that is to say, is de-idealized and humanized in Hardy's poem. But both poems record experiences of gain; and it is partially through the mediation of Browning's antecedent text that Hardy was able to comprehend and to articulate a supreme moment in his experience of human love.

2

In February 1913, as Hardy was preparing to revisit Cornwall after his wife's death, D. H. Lawrence's first collection of poems was published. The emotions expressed in *Love Poems and Others*, and in the poems published three years later in *Amores*, were packed in the ice and salt of rhymed stanzas that bespoke the influence of the Victorian love poets, especially of Hardy himself. Indeed, R. P. Blackmur complained that some of Lawrence's early poems were 'so strongly under the influence of [Hardy] that there was very little room for Lawrence himself' (290). For example, if encountered out of context, who would not say that the opening stanza of 'Liaison' (from *Amores*) is from a Hardy poem:

> A big bud of moon hangs out of the twilight,
>   Star-spiders, spinning their thread,
> Hang high suspended, withouten respite
>   Watching us overhead.

And other poems, for example 'Lightning' (from *Love Poems and Others*), sound like Hardy mixed with elements of Browning – just as a number of Hardy's own poems do.

Some poems in these two volumes, however, show that Lawrence's love experiences were, or came to be, incompatible with the formal and metrical example of Hardy and the other Victorian love poets – for example 'Bei Hennef', which is unrhymed, metrically irregular, and too conflicted in content to allow for traditional lyric closure:

> You are the call and I am the answer,
> You are the wish, and I the fulfilment,
> You are the night, and I the day.
>   What else? it is perfect enough.
>   It is perfectly complete,
>   You and I,
>   What more — ?

> Strange, how we suffer in spite of this!

Since the 'you' in 'Bei Hennef' was Frieda von Richthofen Weekley, his future wife, Lawrence reprinted the poem in his third volume of love poems, the autobiographcal sequence *Look! We Have Come Through!* (1917), in which he broke sharply with the poetic practice of the Victorians. Lawrence later remarked that his free-verse manifesto, 'Poetry of the Present', 'should have come as a preface' to the volume (*Complete Poems*, i, 23). And its contents reflect the conviction he expressed in a letter of 1916:

> The essence of poetry with us in this age of stark and unlovely actualities is a stark directness, without a shadow of a lie, or a shadow of deflection anywhere. Everything can go, but this stark, bare, rocky directness of statement, this alone makes poetry to-day ... Use rhyme *accidentally*, not as a sort of draper's rule for measuring lines off.
>
> (1956, 83–4)

Lawrence described the story line of his sequence in a prefatory note:

> the protagonist throws in his lot with a woman who is already married. Together they go into another country, she perforce leaving her children behind. The conflict of love and hate goes on between the man and the woman, and between these two and the world around them, till it reaches some sort of conclusion, they transcend into some condition of blessedness.
>
> (*Complete Poems*, i, 191)

The telling of this story takes British love poetry into areas where it had not been before. For one thing, there are the unselfconscious descriptions of quotidian intimacies that register the serenity and quiet wonder of reciprocated sexual love – for example, the much-praised 'Gloire de Dijon' and 'Roses on the Breakfast Table', or the lesser known 'Green':

> The dawn was apple-green,
>   The sky was green wine held up in the sun,
> The moon was a golden petal between.
>
> She opened her eyes, and green
>   They shone, clear like flowers undone
> For the first time, now for the first time seen.

There are also the features that led Aldous Huxley to say that 'Reading these poems was like opening the wrong bedroom door', and W. H. Auden to remark that they made him feel 'like a peeping Tom' (quoted in Booth, xiv). One of these features is the frequent registrations of the sufferings inflicted by the conflict of love and hate, which are shown to be a permanent feature of the lovers' life together. Their conflict is emblematized in the Lawrentian version of Hardy's 'maid and her wight'

– the elemental opposition of the local young couple out walking in 'Sunday Afternoon in Italy':

> *She is marked, she is singled out*
>   *For the fire:*
> *The brand is upon him, look you!*
>   *Of desire.*
>
> *They are chosen, ah, they are fated*
>   *For the fight!*

Another new feature is the solemn celebrations of sexual consummation opening into new areas of being (for example, 'Paradise Re-entered', 'Wedlock' and 'Song of the Man Who is Loved'), the apotheosis of which is reached in 'the mad, astounded rapture' of the discovery of anal sex in 'New Heaven and Earth'.

But while there is much that is new in *Look! We Have Come Through!*, there is much that is continuous with the love poetry of the Victorians. Conrad Aiken described Lawrence's 'temperament' as revealed in the volume to be 'modern to a degree: morbidly self-conscious, sex-crucified, an affair of stretched and twanging nerves'. This placed him, said Aiken, in 'the psychological wing of modern poetry' together with T. S. Eliot and others who were 'in a sense lineal descendants of the Meredith of *Modern Love*' (98–9). This is by no means the only Victorian point of reference. A key aspect of Lawrence's belief in the value of sexual love, its transforming potential in an individual's life, is the subject of 'And Oh – That the Man I Am Might Cease to Be – ', the title of which is a paraphrase of a line in Tennyson's love sequence, *Maud*, of whose troubled protagonist the Lawrence of *Look! We Have Come Through!* is also a lineal descendant. Another poem in the sequence, 'On the Balcony', is a non-didactic reinscription of Arnold's 'Dover Beach':

> Adown the pale-green glacier river floats
> A dark boat through the gloom – and whither?
> The thunder roars. But still we have each other!
> The naked lightnings in the heavens dither
> And disappear – what have we but each other?
> The boat has gone.

And nothing in Lawrence's sequence is more centrally in the tradition of Victorian love poetry than the valorization not of orgasmic ecstasy *per se* but the supreme attachment of marriage as the proper goal of sexual love. 'Here I am ... come to me', Lawrence writes in 'A Bad Beginning',

> Not as a visitor either, nor a sweet
> And winsome child of innocence; nor
> As an insolent mistress telling my pulse's beat.

Come to me like a woman coming home
To the man who is her husband, all the rest
Subordinate to this, that he and she
Are joined together for ever, as is best.

The explanation of these continuities is that love poetry has, in Michael Ignatieff's term, a 'discursive past' as well as a formal and metrical past. Lawrence came to reject the latter but reformulated key aspects of the former, just as Hardy had adapted the infinite–moment discourse of Browning. In his late essay, 'Pornography and Obscenity', Lawrence did unequivocally reject one aspect of the discursive inheritance of love poetry – the idealization of the female:

All that pure and noble and heaven-blessed stuff is only the counterpart to the smoking-room story ... Away with such love lyrics, we've had too much of their pornographic poison, tickling the dirty little secret and rolling the eyes to heaven.
But if it is a question of the sound love lyric, *My love is like a red, red rose – !* then we are on other ground. My love is like a red, red rose only when she's *not* like a pure, pure lily.

(1978, 180–81)

Examples of this kind of idealization can certainly be found in Victorian poetry. But Lawrence's complaint about the traditional male love lyric itself has a Victorian precedent in the complaint of Tennyson's Princess Ida. And, as we have seen, one of the defining features of Victorian love poetry was the endeavour of male poets to represent the female point of view in love relationships – to make women subjects of love poetry as well as objects. The same intent is seen in the love poems of Lawrence that have female speakers – including two of the most compelling pieces in the first volume, 'Cruelty and Love' (later retitled 'Love on the Farm') and the Hardyesque 'Wedding Morn'. These lessons in love are further examples of the extent to which Lawrence's love poetry derives from, and is continuous with, that of the Victorians. More generally, they are another illustration of the continuity of love poetry that makes the remarkable achievements of the Victorian poets as accessible at the turn of the twenty-first century as they were to Lawrence in the early twentieth century.

List of Works Cited

Adcock, Fleur, ed. *Twentieth-Century Women's Poetry*, London: Faber, 1987.

Adorno, Theodor. *Notes to Literature*, ed. Rolf Tiedemann, trans. Shierry Weber Nicholsen, 2 vols, New York: Columbia University Press, 1991.

Aiken, Conrad. 'The Melodic Line: D. H. Lawrence', *Scepticisms: Notes on Contemporary Poetry*, New York: Knopf, 1919.

Armstrong, Isobel, ed. *Victorian Scrutinies: Reviews of Poetry 1830–1870*, London: Athlone, 1972.

———. 'Browning and Victorian Poetry of Sexual Love', *Robert Browning: Writers and their Background*, London: Bell, 1974.

———. *Victorian Poetry: Poetry, Poetics and Politics*, London: Routledge, 1993.

Armstrong, Isobel, Joseph Bristow and Cath Sharrock, eds. *Nineteenth-Century Women Poets*, Oxford: Clarendon Press, 1996.

Arnold, Matthew. *Complete Prose Works*, ed. R. H. Super, 11 vols, Ann Arbor: University of Michigan Press, 1960–77.

———. *Poems*, ed. Kenneth Allott, London: Longmans, 1965.

Attridge, Derek. *The Rhythms of English Poetry*, London: Longman, 1982.

Austin, Richard. 'George Meredith and Mary Nicolls', *Texas Quarterly* 21 (1978): 127–48.

Bailey, J. O. *The Poetry of Thomas Hardy: A Handbook and Commentary*, Chapel Hill: University of North Carolina Press, 1970.

Bakhtin, M. M. *The Dialogic Imagination: Four Essays*, ed. Michael Holquist, Austin: University of Texas Press, 1981.

Ball, Patricia, M. *The Heart's Events: The Victorian Poetry of Relationships*, London: Athlone, 1976.

Barrett Browning, Elizabeth. *Letters*, ed. Frederic G. Kenyon, 2 vols, London: Smith, Elder, 1898.

———. *Complete Works*, eds Charlotte Porter and Helen A. Clarke, 6 vols, New York: Thomas Crowell, 1900.

———. *Aurora Leigh*, ed. Kerry McSweeney, Oxford: Oxford University Press, 1993.

Bevington, Louisa. *Poems, Lyrics, and Sonnets*, London: Elliot Stock, 1882.

Blackmur, R. P. 'D. H. Lawrence and Expressive Form', *Language as Gesture: Essays in Poetry*, New York: Harcourt Brace, 1952.

Blake, Kathleen. 'Christina Rossetti's Poetry: The Art of Self- Postponement', *Love and the Woman Question in Victorian Literature*, Sussex: Harvester, 1983.

Booth, Roy. 'Introduction' to D. H. Lawrence, *Love Poems*, London: Kyle Cathie, 1993.

Brodsky, Joseph. 'The Poet, the Loved One, and the Muse', *Times Literary Supplement* (26 October–1 November 1990): 1150, 1160.

Brontë, Emily. *Wuthering Heights*, eds Hilda Marsden and Ian Jack, Oxford: Clarendon Press, 1976.

Browning, Robert. *Dearest Isa: Robert Browning's Letters to Isabella Blagden*, ed. Edward C. McAleer, Austin: University of Texas Press, 1951.

———. *Poems*. ed. John Pettigrew (with Thomas J. Collins), 2 vols, New Haven, CT: Yale University Press, 1981.

Buchanan, Robert. 'The Fleshly School of Poetry: Mr. D. G. Rossetti', *Victorian Poetry and Poetics*, eds W. E. Houghton and G. R. Stange, 2nd edn, Boston: Houghton Mifflin, 1968.

Buckler, William E. *The Victorian Imagination: Essays in Aesthetic Exploration*, Brighton: Harvester, 1980.

Burne-Jones, Georgiana. *Memorials of Edward Burne-Jones*, 2 vols, London: Macmillan, 1904.

Byatt, A. S. 'The Lyric Structure of Tennyson's *Maud*', *The Major Victorian Poets: Reconsiderations*, ed. Isobel Armstrong, London: Routledge, 1969.

Byron, Lord. *Don Juan*, ed. Leslie A. Marchand, Boston: Houghton Mifflin, 1958.

Caine, Hall. *Recollections of Rossetti*, London: Cassell, 1928.

Carew, Thomas. *Poems*, ed. Rhodes Dunlop, Oxford: Clarendon Press, 1949.

Champneys, Basil. *Memoirs and Correspondence of Coventry Patmore*, 2 vols, London: Bell, 1900.

Clough, Arthur Hugh. *Correspondence*, ed. Frederick L. Mulhauser, 2 vols, Oxford: Clarendon Press, 1957.

———. *Amours de Voyage*, ed. Patrick Scott, St Lucia: University of Queensland Press, 1974.

———. *The Bothie: The Text of 1948*, ed. Patrick Scott, St Lucia: University of Queensland Press, 1976.

———. *Oxford Diaries*, ed. Anthony Kenny, Oxford: Clarendon Press, 1990.

———. *Selected Poems*, ed. J. P. Phelan, London: Longman, 1995.

Coleridge, Samuel Taylor. *Complete Poetical Works*, ed. Ernest Hartley Coleridge, 2 vols, Oxford: Clarendon Press, 1966.

———. *Selected Letters*, ed. H. J. Jackson, Oxford: Clarendon Press, 1987.

Comstock, Cathy. '"Speak and I See the Side-lie of a Truth": The Problematics of Truth in Meredith's *Modern Love*', *Victorian Poetry* 25 (1987): 129–41.

Cook, Eleanor. *Browning's Lyrics: An Exploration*, Toronto: University of Toronto Press, 1974.

Culler, A. Dwight. *The Poetry of Tennyson*, New Haven: Yale University Press, 1977.

Cullingford, Elizabeth Butler. *Gender and History in Yeats's Love Poetry*, Cambridge: Cambridge University Press, 1993.

Curle, Richard, ed. *Robert Browning and Julia Wedgwood: A Broken Friendship as Revealed by their Letters*, New York: Stokes, 1937.

Davie, Donald. 'Hardy's Virgilian Purples', *Agenda* (Thomas Hardy Special Issue) 10 (1972): 138–56.

Day, Aidan, ed. *Robert Browning: Selected Poetry and Prose*, New York: Routledge, 1991.

Day Lewis, C. 'Introduction', *Modern Love*, London: Hart-Davis, 1948.

Dickinson, Emily. *Poems*, ed. Thomas H. Johnson, 3 vols, Cambridge, MA: Harvard University Press, 1955.

———. *Letters*. ed. Thomas H. Johnson, 3 vols, Cambridge, MA: Harvard University Press, 1958.

Doughty, Oswald. *Dante Gabriel Rossetti: A Victorian Romantic*, New Haven: Yale University Press, 1949.

Eberwein, Jane Donahue. *Dickinson: Strategies of Limitation*, Amherst: University of Massachusetts Press, 1985.

Edmond, Rod. 'Death Sequences: Patmore, Hardy, and the New Domestic Elegy', *Victorian Poetry* 19 (1981): 151–65.

———. *Affairs of the Hearth: Victorian Poetry and Domestic Narrative*, London: Routledge, 1988.

Eliot, George. *Essays*, ed. Thomas Pinney, London: Routledge, 1963.

Emerson, Ralph Waldo. *Nature*, in *Essays and Lectures*, ed. Joel Porte, New York: Library of America, 1983.

Faulkner, Peter. *Wilfrid Scawen Blunt and the Morrises*, London: William Morris Society, 1981.

Faulkner, William. *The Sound and the Fury*, New York: Modern Library, 1956.

Felkin, Elliott. 'Days with Thomas Hardy: From a 1918–19 Diary', *Encounter* 18 (1962): 27–33.

Fredeman, William E., 'Rossetti's *In Memoriam*: An Elegiac Reading of *The House of Life*', *John Rylands Library Bulletin* 47 (1965): 298–341.

———. 'Prelude to the Last Decade: Dante Gabriel Rossetti in the Summer of 1872', *John Rylands Library Bulletin* 53 (1970–71): 75–121.

————. ed. *The P. R. B. Journal: William Michael Rossetti's Diary of the Pre-Raphaelite Brotherhood 1849–1853*, Oxford: Clarendon Press, 1975.

Freud, Sigmund. 'Contributions to the Psychology of Love', *Standard Edition of the Complete Psychological Works*, ed. James Strachey, vol. 11, London: Hogarth, 1957.

Frost, Robert. *Collected Poems*, New York: Holt Rinehart, 1949.

Fussell, Paul. *Poetic Meter and Poetic Form*, rev. edn, New York: Random House, 1979.

Gates, Barbara. 'Revising *The House of Life*: A Look at Seven Unpublished Sonnets', *Victorian Poetry* 21 (1983): 65–78.

Gilbert, Sandra M. and Susan Gubar. *The Madwoman in the Attic: The Woman Writer and the Nineteenth-Century Literary Imagination*, New Haven: Yale University Press, 1979.

Gittings, Robert. *Thomas Hardy's Later Years*, Boston: Little, Brown, 1978.

Golden, Arline. '"The Game of Sentiment": Tradition and Innovation in Meredith's *Modern Love*', *ELH: English Literary History* 40 (1973): 264–84.

Gorky, Maxim. 'Lev Tolstoi', *Reminiscences of Tolstoi by his Contemporaries*, trans. Margaret Wettlin, Moscow: Foreign Languages Publishing House, n.d.

Griffiths, Eric. *The Printed Voice of Victorian Poetry*, Oxford: Clarendon Press, 1989.

Gunn, Thom. 'Hardy and the Ballads', *Agenda* (Thomas Hardy Special Issue) 10 (1972): 19–46.

Haight, Gordon S. 'George Meredith and the *Westminster Review*', *Modern Language Review* 53 (1958): 1–16.

Hallam, Arthur Henry. *The Writings of Arthur Hallam*, ed. T. H. Vail Motter, New York: Modern Language Association, 1943.

————. *Letters*, ed. Jacob Kolb, Columbus: Ohio State University Press, 1981.

Hanley, Keith, ed. *Selected Poems of George Meredith*, Manchester: Carcanet, 1983.

Hardy, Emma. *Some Recollections*, intro. Robert Gittings, Oxford: Oxford University Press, 1979.

Hardy, Thomas. *Collected Letters*, eds Richard Little Purdy and Michael Millgate, 7 vols, Oxford: Clarendon Press, 1978–88.

————. *Complete Poetical Works*, ed. Samuel Hynes, 3 vols, Oxford: Clarendon Press, 1982–85.

————. *The Life and Work of Thomas Hardy*, ed. Michael Millgate, Athens: University of Georgia Press, 1985.

Heaney, Seamus. *Death of a Naturalist*, London: Faber and Faber, 1966.

Hecht, Anthony. *The Hard Hours: Poems*, New York: Atheneum, 1968.

Hickok, Kathleen. '"Intimate Egoism": Reading and Evaluating Noncanonical Poetry by Women', *Victorian Poetry* 33 (1995): 13–30.

Hindus, Milton, ed. *Walt Whitman: The Critical Heritage*, London Routledge, 1971.

Hollander, John. *Melodious Guile: Fictive Pattern in Poetic Language*, New Haven: Yale UP, 1988.

Hopkins, Gerard Manley. *Letters to Robert Bridges*, ed. Claude Colleer Abbott, London: Oxford University Press, 1955.

———. *Further Letters*, ed. Claude Colleer Abbott, 2nd edn, London: Oxford University Press, 1956.

Hough, Graham. *The Last Romantics*, London: Duckworth, 1949.

———.'Introduction', *Selected Poems of George Meredith*, London: Oxford University Press, 1962.

Houghton, Walter E. *The Victorian Frame of Mind, 1830–1870*, New Haven: Yale University Press, 1957.

Houghton, Walter E. and G. Robert Stange, eds. *Victorian Poetry and Poetics*, 2nd edn, Boston: Houghton Mifflin, 1968.

House, Humphry. 'Pre-Raphaelite Poetry', *Pre-Raphaeliteism: A Collection of Critical Essays*, ed. James Sambrook. Chicago: University of Chicago Press, 1974.

Ignatieff, Michael. 'Lodged in the Heart and Memory', *Times Literary Supplement* (15–21 April 1988): 411–13.

Irigaray, Luce. *This Sex Which is Not One*, Ithaca: Cornell University Press, 1985.

Jarrell, Randall. *Poetry and the Age*, New York: Vintage, 1955.

Johnson, Wendell Stacy. *Sex and Marriage in Victorian Poetry*, Ithaca: Cornell University Press, 1975.

Jordan, Elaine. *Tennyson*, Cambridge: Cambridge University Press, 1988.

Kaplan, Cora. 'The Indefinite Disclosed: Christina Rossetti and Emily Dickinson', *Women Writing and Writing about Women*, ed. Mary Jacobus, London: Croom Helm, 1979.

Karlin, Daniel. 'Browning's Poetry of Intimacy', *Essays in Criticism* 39 (1989): 47–64

———. *Browning's Hatreds*, Oxford: Clarendon Press, 1993.

Keating, Peter. [Review of A. Leighton and M. Reynolds, eds. *Victorian Women Poets*] *Times Literary Supplement* (26 January 1996): 27.

Kern, Stephen. *The Culture of Love: Victorians to Moderns*, Cambridge, MA: Harvard University Press, 1992.

Killham, John. 'Tennyson's *Maud* – The Function of the Imagery', *Critical Essays on the Poetry of Tennyson*, London: Routledge, 1960.

Larkin, Philip. *Collected Poems*, ed. Anthony Thwaite, London: Faber and Faber, 1988.

Lawrence, D. H. *Love Poems and Others*, London: Duckworth, 1913.

————. *Amores: Poems*, London: Duckworth, [1916].

————. *Selected Literary Criticism*, ed. Anthony Beal, New York: Viking, 1956.

————. *Complete Poems*, eds Vivian de Sola Pinto and Warren Roberts, 2 vols, New York: Viking, 1964.

————. *Phoenix: The Posthumous Papers*, ed. Edward D. McDonald, Harmondsworth: Penguin, 1978.

Leavis, F. R. 'Reality and Sincerity: Notes on the Analysis of Poetry', *Scrutiny* 19 (1952–53): 90–97.

Leighton, Angela. *Victorian Women Poets: Writing Against the Heart*, New York: Harvester Wheatsheaf, 1992.

Leighton, Angela and Margaret Reynolds, eds. *Victorian Women Poets: An Anthology*, Oxford: Blackwell, 1995.

Lemprière, John. *Lemprière's Classical Dictionary of Proper Names*, 3rd edn, London: Routledge, 1984.

Lindsay, Jack. *George Meredith*, London: Bodley Head, 1956.

Litzinger, Boyd and Donald Smalley, eds. *Browning: The Critical Heritage*, New York: Barnes and Noble, 1970.

Longford, Elizabeth. *A Passionate Pilgrim: The Life of Wilfrid Scawen Blunt*, London: Weidenfeld and Nicolson, 1979.

Lowry, Howard Foster, ed. *The Letters of Matthew Arnold to Arthur Hugh Clough*, Oxford: Clarendon Press, 1968.

Lucas, John. 'Meredith as Poet', *Meredith Now: Some Critical Essays*, ed. Ian Fletcher, London: Routledge, 1971.

MacCarthy, Fiona. *William Morris: A Life for Our Times*, London: Faber and Faber, 1994.

Mackail, J. W. *The Life of William Morris*, 2 vols, London: Longmans, 1899.

Maynard, John. '"Can't One Even Die in Peace?" Browning's "A Serenade at the Villa"', *Browning Society Notes* 6 (1976): 3–10.

————. *Victorian Discourses on Sexuality and Religion*, Cambridge: Cambridge University Press, 1993.

McGann, Jerome J. 'Dante Gabriel Rossetti and the Betrayal of Truth', *Critical Essays on Dante Gabriel Rossetti*, ed. D. G. Riede, New York: G. K. Hall, 1992.

Mellor, Anne K. *Romanticism and Gender*, New York: Routledge, 1993.

Meredith, George. 'Belles Lettres and Art', *Westminster Review* 68 (1857): 585–604.

————. *Letters*. ed. W. M. Meredith, 2 vols, New York: Scribner's, 1912.

————. *Letters.* ed. C. L. Cline, 3 vols, Oxford: Clarendon Press, 1970.

————. *Poems.* ed. Phyllis B. Bartlett, 2 vols, New Haven, CT: Yale University Press, 1978.

Mermin, Dorothy. 'Poetry as Fiction: Meredith's *Modern Love*', *ELH: English Literary History* 43 (1976): 100–119.

————. *Elizabeth Barrett Browning: The Origins of a New Poetry.* Chicago: University of Chicago Press, 1989.

Meynell, Alice. *The Second Person Singular and Other Essays*, London: Oxford University Press, 1922.

Meynell, Viola. *Alice Meynell: A Memoir*, London: Jonathan Cape, 1929.

Mill, John Stuart. *The Subjection of Women* in *Sexual Equality: Writings by John Stuart Mill, Harriet Taylor Mill, and Helen Taylor*, eds Ann P. Robson and John M. Robson, Toronto: University of Toronto Press, 1994.

Miller, J. Hillis. *Thomas Hardy: Distance and Desire*, Cambridge, MA: Harvard University Press, 1970.

Millgate, Michael. *Thomas Hardy: A Biography*, New York: Random House, 1982.

Millier, Brett C. *Elizabeth Bishop: Life and the Memory of It*, Berkeley: University of California Press, 1993.

Milton, John. *Complete Poems and Major Prose*, ed. Merritt Y. Hughes, New York: Odyssey, 1957.

Mintz, Steven. *A Prison of Expectations: The Family in Victorian Culture*, New York: New York University Press, 1983.

Mitchell, Juliet. *Women: The Longest Revolution: Essays on Feminism. Literature and Psychoanalysis*, London: Virago, 1984.

Mooney, Susan. 'William Morris: Biographical Gleanings 1865–1875', *Journal of the William Morris Society* 8 (August 1989): 2–12.

Moore, Tom. *Poetical Works*, ed. A. D. Godley, London: Oxford University Press, 1919.

Morris, William. *Collected Works*, ed. May Morris, 24 vols, London: Longmans, Green, 1910–15. Repr. New York: Russell and Russell, 1966.

————. *The Novel on Blue Paper*, ed. Penelope Fitzgerald. London: Journeyman Press, 1982.

————. *Collected Letters*, ed. Norman Kelvin, 4 vols, Princeton, NJ: Princeton University Press, 1984–96.

Newman, John Henry. *Newman the Oratorian: His Unpublished Oratory Papers*, ed. Placid Murray, Leominster: Fowler Wright, 1980.

Ortega y Gasset, José. 'On Point of View in the Arts', *Partisan Review* 16 (1949): 822–36.

Page, Norman, ed. *Tennyson: Interviews and Recollections*. London: Macmillan, 1983.

Pater, Walter. 'Aesthetic Poetry', *Victorian Poetry and Poetics*, eds W. E. Houghton and G. R. Stange, 2nd edn, Boston: Houghton Mifflin, 1968.

Patmore, Coventry. 'The Social Position of Women', *North British Review* **14** (1851): 515–40.

———. 'Tennyson's *Maud*', *Edinburgh Review* **102** (1855): 498–519.

———. [Review of Barrett Browning's *Poems* and *Aurora Leigh*] *North British Review* **26** (1857): 443–62.

———. *The Rod, The Root, and the Flower*. London: Bell, 1895.

———. *Principle in Art: Religio Poetae and Other Essays*, London: Duckworth, 1913.

———. *Mystical Poems of Nuptial Love: The Wedding Sermon, The Unknown Eros*, ed. Terence J. Connolly, SJ, Boston: Bruce Humphries, 1938.

———. *Poems*, ed. Frederick Page, London: Oxford University Press, 1949.

———. 'Essay on English Metrical Law': A Critical Edition with a Commentary. ed. Sister Mary Augustine Roth. Washington, D.C.: Catholic University of America Press, 1961.

Paulin, Tom. *Thomas Hardy: The Poetry of Perception*, London: Macmillan, 1975.

Perkus, Gerald H. 'Meredith's Unhappy Love Life: Worthy of the Muse', *Cithara* **9** (1970): 32–46.

Peterson, Linda H. 'Sappho and the Making of Tennysonian Lyric', *ELH: English Literary History* **61** (1994): 121–37.

Phelan, J. P. 'Introduction' to A. H. Clough's *Selected Poems*, ed. J. P. Phelan, London: Longman, 1995.

Pinion, F. B. *Thomas Hardy: Art and Thought*, London: Macmillan, 1977.

Poovey, Mary. *Uneven Developments: The Ideological Work of Gender in Mid-Victorian England*, Chicago: University of Chicago Press, 1988.

Proust, Marcel. *Remembrance of Things Past*, trans C. K. Scott Moncrieff and T. Kilmartin, 3 vols, London: Chatto and Windus, 1981.

Rader, Ralph W. 'The Dramatic Monologue and Related Lyric Forms', *Critical Inquiry* **3** (1976): 131–51.

Rees, Joan. *The Poetry of Dante Gabriel Rossetti: Modes of Self-Expression*, Cambridge: Cambridge University Press, 1981.

Regan, Stephen. 'Introduction', *Modern Love*, Peterborough: Daisy Books, 1988.

Rich, Adrienne. *Poetry and Prose*, eds Barbara Charlesworth Gelpi and Albert Gelpi, New York: Norton, 1993.

Richards, Bernard. *English Poetry of the Victorian Period 1830–1890*. London: Longman, 1988.

Richardson, James. *Thomas Hardy: The Poetry of Necessity*, Chicago: University of Chicago Press, 1977.

Riede, David G. *Dante Gabriel Rossetti Revisited*, New York: Twayne, 1992.

Rilke, Rainer Maria. *Rilke on Love and Other Difficulties*, ed. John J. L. Mood, New York: Norton, 1993.

Rossetti, Christina. *Poetical Works*, ed. William Michael Rossetti, London: Macmillan, 1904.

————. *Complete Poems: A Variorum Edition*, ed. R. W. Crump, 3 vols, Baton Rouge, LA: Louisiana State University Press, 1979–90.

Rossetti, Dante Gabriel. *Poems and Translations 1850–1870*, London: Oxford University Press, 1959.

————. *Poems*, ed. Oswald Doughty, London: Dent, 1961.

————. *Letters*, ed. Oswald Doughty and John Robert Wahl, 4 vols, Oxford: Clarendon Press, 1964–67.

Rossetti, William Michael. *Dante Gabriel Rossetti as Designer and Writer*, London: Cassell, 1889.

Ruskin, John. *Works* (Library Edition), eds E. T. Cook and Alexander Wedderburn, 39 vols, London: George Allen, 1903–12.

Sacks, Peter. *The English Elegy: Studies in the Genre from Spenser to Yeats*, Baltimore, MD: Johns Hopkins University Press, 1985.

Saintsbury, George. *A History of English Prosody*, 3 vols, New York: Russell and Russell, 1961.

Shaw, Marion. *Alfred Lord Tennyson*, Atlantic Highlands, NJ: Humanities Press, 1988.

Shelley, Percy Bysshe. *Complete Poetical Works*, ed. Thomas Hutchinson, London: Oxford University Press, 1960.

————. *Letters*, ed. Frederick L. Jones, 2 vols, Oxford: Clarendon Press, 1964.

Sidgwick, Henry. 'The Poems and Prose Remains of Arthur Hugh Clough [1869]', *Miscellaneous Essays and Addresses*, London: Macmillan, 1904.

Sidney, Sir Philip. *Selected Poems*, ed. Catherine Bates, London: Penguin, 1994.

Simmel, Georg. 'Eros, Platonic and Modern', *On Individuality and Social Forms: Selected Writings*, ed. Donald N. Levine, Chicago: University of Chicago Press, 1971.

Simpson, Arthur L. 'Meredith's Pessimistic Humanism: A New Reading of *Modern Love*', *Modern Philology* 67 (1970): 342–56.

Sinfield, Alan. 'Tennyson's Imagery', *Neophilologus* 20 (1976): 466–79.

Slinn, E. Warwick. *The Discourse of Self in Victorian Poetry*, London: Macmillan 1991.

Stephenson, Glennis. *Elizabeth Barrett Browning and the Poetry of Love*, Ann Arbor, MI: University of Michigan Institute of Research Press, 1989.

Stevenson, Lionel. *The Ordeal of George Meredith*, New York: Scribner's, 1953.

Swinburne, A. C. *Collected Poetical Works*, 2 vols, London: Heinemann, 1924.

———. *The Swinburne Letters*, ed. Cecil Y. Lang, 6 vols, New Haven, CT: Yale University Press, 1959–62.

Taine, Hippolyte. *Notes on England*, trans. Edward Hyams, London: Thames and Hudson, 1957.

Tennyson, Alfred. *Poems*, 2nd edn, ed. Christopher Ricks, 3 vols, Berkeley, CA: University of California Press, 1987.

Tennyson, Hallam. *Alfred Lord Tennyson: A Memoir*, 2 vols, London: Macmillan, 1899.

Thompson, E. P. *William Morris: Romantic to Revolutionary*, New York: Pantheon, 1977.

Thorpe, Michael, ed. *Clough: The Critical Heritage*, London: Routledge, 1972.

Tucker, Herbert F. *Tennyson and the Doom of Romanticism*, Cambridge, MA: Harvard University Press, 1988.

Turner, Paul. *English Literature 1832–1900 Excluding the Novel*, Oxford: Clarendon Press, 1989.

Valency, Maurice. *In Praise of Love: An Introduction to the Love Poetry of the Renaissance*, New York: Macmillan, 1961.

Walker, Nancy. 'Voice, Tone, and Persona in Dickinson's Love Poetry', *Approaches to Teaching Dickinson's Poetry*, eds Robin Riley Fast and Christine Mack Gordon, New York: Modern Language Association, 1989.

Whitman, Walt. *Complete Poetry and Collected Prose*, ed. Justin Kaplan, New York: Library of America, 1982.

Wolff, Cynthia Griffin. 'Emily Dickinson', *The Columbia History of American Poetry*, ed. Jay Parini, New York: Columbia University Press, 1993.

Wordsworth, William. *Poetical Works*, eds E. de Selincourt and Helen Darbishire, 5 vols, Oxford: Clarendon Press, 1940–49.

Woudhuysen, H. R. 'Sales of Books and Manuscripts', *Times Literary Supplement* (11 December 1992): 28.

Yeats, William Butler. *Collected Poems*, New York: Macmillan, 1959.

———. 'A General Introduction for My Work', *Essays and Introductions*, London: Macmillan, 1961.

———. *Collected Letters: Volume I, 1865–1895*, ed. John Kelly, Oxford: Clarendon Press, 1986.

Index